THE LAST DAYS OF ST. PIERRE

THE LAST DAYS OF ST. PIERRE

THE VOLCANIC DISASTER
· THAT CLAIMED ·
THIRTY THOUSAND LIVES

Ernest Zebrowski, Jr.

RUTGERS UNIVERSITY PRESS
New Brunswick, New Jersey, and London

·

Library of Congress Cataloging-in-Publication Data

Zebrowski, Ernest.
The last days of St. Pierre : the volcanic disaster that claimed
thirty thousand lives / Ernest Zebrowski, Jr.
p. cm.
Includes bibliographical references and index.
ISBN 0-8135-3041-5 (alk. paper)
1. Pelée, Mount (Martinique)—Eruption, 1902.
2. Saint-Pierre (Martinique)—History. I. Title.
QE523.P26 .Z43   2002
972.98′2—dc21   2001019839

British Cataloging-in-Publication data for this book is available from the
British Library.

Manufactured in the United States of America

• CONTENTS •

CONTENTS

• PREFACE •

On May 8, 1902, a volcano on the French West Indian island of Martinique exploded and launched a pyroclastic surge down its southern flank. The deadly cloud of steam and ash churned through plantations and villages, flattened the grand city of St. Pierre, then thundered into the bay, where it sank eighteen ships and hundreds of smaller craft. Within a minute or two, nearly thirty thousand humans died. The splintered rubble of their homes and belongings burned for three days.

This book is the story of that eruption, the complex web of human commitment and folly that snared its victims, the passions and pains of those who survived, and the experiences of the contemporary scientists and journalists who sifted through the aftermath. Then, bearing gruesome testimony to the inadequacy of knowledge alone, the tragic tale of the deaths of thousands more.

A century has passed since that cluster of disasters. The population of St. Pierre has recovered from zero to around five thousand—about one-sixth of its peak in 1902. Some buildings have been completely reassembled from the ruins; others are combinations of old rubble and newer concrete and stucco. The original paved streets, many with stone gutters two feet deep, today carry modern traffic and do a great job of breaking the axles of vehicles that wander out of the thoroughfares. Yet here and there, dispersed through the town, the visitor still finds remnants of the 1902 destruction: old foundations embracing empty lots, burned gravestones and twisted iron gates in the cemetery, a truncated lighthouse, the ruins of a prison, the foundations of a once-magnificent theater. Compared to the rest of the lovely island of Martinique, modern St. Pierre has an uneasy, temporary look about it—as if its residents view themselves as just camping there until the next catastrophe.

From virtually everywhere in town, one gets a grand view of the majestic Mont Pelée. During the past ten thousand years, this mountain has exploded at least forty-seven times—an average of one major eruption every couple of centuries. Will it awake again? Almost certainly. When?

That answer is far from certain. Pelée has sometimes slept peacefully for four or five centuries; during other intervals, it has erupted every few decades. And because there has been no decipherable pattern, there exists no equation that can predict the next event. Mont Pelée's appointment schedule for its tantrums remains its deepest secret.

If we cannot see clearly into the future, perhaps we can at least be informed by the past. Reconstructing what happened on Martinique in 1902, however, presents some challenges. By the time they were reduced to writing, many eyewitness accounts were corrupted by rumor and imagination. Other documents survive today only in edited versions and in translations of unknown veracity. Scores of contemporary writers, in rushing their stories into print, managed to confuse various details of the chronology and/or the geography. Over the decades following the holocaust, new errors and unfounded speculations masquerading as fact crept into the literature of the disaster. Today, one can read about the great eruption of 1902 on various Web sites and consume a vast quantity of misinformation.

This book is a modest attempt to set the story reasonably straight.

Regarding the geophysical aspects of the event, I talked to geologists and studied scientific journals with the confidence that scientists are notably diligent about correcting one another's errors of fact. To get a sense of the geography, I tramped through the towns and villages of northern Martinique and hiked Pelée's slopes. I sweated in the sun at the lower elevations and shivered in swirling rains at the summit. I pored over old and current maps, then examined in the field how the eruptions of the last century have resculptured the terrain.

Yet on the scale of Planet Earth and the calendar of geologic time, the 1902 cataclysm was no more than a hiccup. The essence of a disaster lies not in its geographic or physical upheavals, but in its human devastation. Had those tens of thousands not died and the fruits of their labor been scoured from the face of the planet, Mont Pelée's antics of a century ago would be but one small entry in a long catalog of volcanic events of interest only to scientific specialists.

Counting both the victims and those otherwise affected (from surviving friends to devastated investors), there were at least eighty thousand human experiences of the disaster. Certainly the majority of these personal stories have since succumbed to the ravages of time. Nevertheless, to the extent possible, I have let the dead speak for themselves. I do not claim that they always spoke with accuracy or authority, and in fact part of the fascination of this story lies in this very confusion of conflicting impressions and the occasional opportunistic fabrication.

Including dialogue in a work such as this one creates a dilemma for the author. The spoken words themselves evaporated a century ago, and most were in French, not the language I am using here. At best, the dialogue in the old sources probably only approximates what was actually said, and indeed some of the published conversations appear to be completely fictitious. Nevertheless, there can be little doubt that interpersonal communication played a significant role in the events in northern Martinique in 1902, and to exclude most or all dialogue from this story would be to neglect a key element of the unfolding tragedy. My final decision was a compromise between ignoring the unsubstantiated and presenting as complete a story as can reasonably be inferred from the evidence. Accordingly, I have limited the dialogue to what I judge to be the most important conversations, and in every case possible I have drawn that dialogue directly from the sources identified in the "Notes" section. In those few instances where I felt it necessary to reconstruct a conversation, I did so based on records that the conversation indeed took place and on persuasive evidence that its content was substantially as I give it. Where the dialogue is speculative, I acknowledge so in the text. The main example of such a reconstruction is my description of the deliberations of the governor's Scientific Commission the evening before the catastrophe.

To the historical purists, I apologize up-front for whatever transgressions I may have committed. In my defense, my objective was not to create a reference encyclopedia of this century-old event, but rather to share a fascinating true story that today still offers grave lessons about the tumultuous relationship between the forces of nature and human civilization.

Numerous librarians and archivists, including the staff of the Schoelcher Library in Fort-de-France, were generous with their time in helping me track down obscure publications. My students, colleagues, and personal friends were notably tolerant of my distractions while I grappled with this project. My thanks to all of them for their patience and support. I am indebted to Jan Shoemaker and Kathleen Werner for their invaluable guidance and constructive criticism of the early manuscript; they will both notice their intellectual imprints on many of the pages that follow. And I especially acknowledge the contributions of my son, David, who accompanied me to Martinique, assisted with the field observations, and helped me judge the credibility of the eyewitness accounts that, I hope, bring this story to life.

Creating a manuscript is one thing; turning it into a book is quite another. My deep thanks to Helen Hsu, senior editor at Rutgers University Press, for her enthusiastic support of this project; to Marilyn Campbell, director of the Prepress Department, for keeping me on task when I would have preferred to take a rest; to Tricia Politi, senior production coordinator, for her artistic vision and commitment to quality; and to Vicki Haire, copyeditor, for identifying numerous inconsistencies that this bleary-eyed author had missed. If any substantive errors happen to remain, I have no doubt that I introduced them quite on my own, and I take full responsibility for them.

Ernest Zebrowski, Jr.

THE LAST DAYS OF ST. PIERRE

• CHAPTER 1 •

ASHES FROM THE SKY

•

It was the best of times to be a young seaman. Modern steamers like the *Horace* rendered to anachronism the old-timers' tales of dangling on spars to furl sails in the face of a gale, or of sitting for days in the doldrums waiting for a wind to kick up. Even the anchors on this freighter were raised by donkey engines. And what luxury when working in a ship's bowels could possibly beat electric lighting?

The year, 1902. Early May. As the *Horace* steamed from Barbados to St. Lucia, second engineer Billy Anderson scribbled an observation in his personal journal:

> On the afternoon of May 8 (Thursday) we noticed a peculiar haze in the direction of Martinique. The air seemed heavy and oppressive. The weather conditions were not at all unlike those which precede the great West Indian hurricanes, but, knowing it was not the season of the year for them, we all remarked that there must be a heavy storm approaching. So peculiar was the atmosphere that we talked of nothing else during the evening. Toward Martinique there was a very black sky, an unusual thing at this season of the year.

In those early years of steam propulsion, an acute ear for detecting expensive squeals or chatters through the usual din of noisy machinery was an essential qualification for becoming a ship's engineer. And indeed, Anderson had a knack for hearing the way a bloodhound has a knack for smelling. Tending to his duties in the engine room that night, he heard a

1

rumbling beyond the normal pounding of the engines. It seemed too deep and resonant to be metal destroying metal, yet he had to be sure. He went to the flywheel, the governor, the feedwater pumps, the bank of compound double-acting cylinders, listening, listening, until he could assure himself that the sound was coming from something other than the machinery. Yet it surely wasn't common thunder, for the *Horace* was riding smoothly on an even keel and a squall would be kicking up a sea that would certainly be felt down below. Puzzled and concerned, he sent his fireman topside to investigate.

As he made the rounds of his oil reservoirs and pressure gauges, the strange rumbling continued, sometimes as a series of short bursts, occasionally in a long roll. He had no inkling that the unfamiliar sounds might be coming through the sea itself. The fireman took longer than seemed necessary, to the point that the boiler pressure started to drop. The young engineer yanked open a firebox door and grabbed a shovel, the muffled booms persisting as he stoked. He cursed. He shoveled. The minutes ticked. And only as the head of steam stabilized did the fireman scamper back down the ladder.

In his exuberance, the stoker was oblivious to Anderson's annoyance. Everyone on deck, he blurted, was watching a rip of a lightning show on the northwest horizon. Electricity zigzagging every which way, and the thunder near continuous. Damnedest storm he had ever seen!

Yet calm air and sea? Anderson bit his tongue about the fireman's malingering and handed over the shovel. Weather being the thing that kicks up a sailor's adrenaline as much as a good fight, he could hardly wait to see this phenomenon for himself. When his replacement arrived at the end of his shift, Anderson ignored the customary exchange of small talk and dashed topside.

Greeting him in the predawn was a dramatic display of electrical activity in the north, some streaks scissoring laterally, other weird funnel-shaped flashes springing upward. Yet even after hours of this meteorological violence within visual distance of the ship, the sea remained calm. Anderson joined a handful of others napping on deck, where they could open an eye now and then to check on the spooky phenomenon.

The sun rose brightly on May 9. Yet to the north, in the direction of Martinique, the sky remained ominous and turbulent, the curtain of darkness on that horizon punctuated only by the lightning. On the decks of the *Horace,* there still was no wind other than that of the steamer's forward motion. Anderson wrote further:

About nine o'clock Friday morning I was sitting on one of the hatches aft with some of the other engineers and officers of the ship, discussing the peculiar weather phenomena. I noticed a sort of grit that got into my mouth from the end of the cigar I was smoking. I attributed it to some rather bad coal which we had shipped aboard, and, turning to Chief Engineer Evans, I remarked "that coal was mighty dirty," and he said he himself had noticed that it was covering the ship with a sort of grit. Then I saw that grit was getting on my clothes, and finally someone suggested that we go forward of the funnels, so we would not get that dirt on us. As we went forward we met one or two of the sailors from the forecastle, who wanted to know about the dust that was falling on the ship. Then we found that the grayish-looking ash was sifting all over the ship, both forward and aft.

Every moment the ashes rained down all over the ship, and at the same time grew thicker. A few moments later, the lookout called down that we were running into a fog-bank dead ahead. Fog banks in that section are unheard of at nine o'clock in the morning at this season, and we were more than a hundred miles from land, and what could fog and sand be doing there?

Before we knew it, we went into the fog, which proved to be a big dense bank of this same sand, and it rained down on us from every side. Ventilators were quickly brought to their places, and later even the hatches were battened down. The dust became suffocating, and the men at times had all they could do to keep from choking. What the stuff was we could not at first conjecture, or rather, we didn't have much time to speculate on it, for we had to get our ship in shape to withstand we hardly knew what.

At first we thought that the sand must have been blown from shore. Then we decided that if the Captain's figures were right we wouldn't be near enough to shore to have sand blow on us.

Just as the storm of sand was at its height, Fourth Engineer Wild was nearly suffocated by it, but was revived. About this time it became so dark that we found it necessary to start up the electric lights, and it was not until after we got clear from the fog that we turned the current off. In the meantime they had burned from nine o'clock in the morning until after two in the afternoon.

Third Engineer Rennie was running the donkey engine when suddenly it choked, and when he finally got it clear from the sand or ashes, he found the valves were all cut out, and then it was we discovered that it was not sand, but some sort of a composition that seemed to cut steel like emery.

That evening, its decks covered with gray volcanic ash, the *Horace* steamed into the port of Castries on the island of St. Lucia. The harbor was a mess; here the ash had gotten wet, and all the docks and equipment were blanketed in a thick dirty substance that had the consistency of newly poured cement. Ship's engineers were typically the last offboard after docking, and by the time Anderson stepped ashore, most of his crewmates had long scattered into the taverns and other establishments that catered to itinerant sailors.

In the twilight, Anderson slogged through the warm gritty slush. It looked a lot like the dirty snow that piled up in New England ports in the winter, except that here the stuff was not slippery. Lanterns began to flick on in the collection of vessels in the harbor. One particular ship, however, showed no sign of life. Anderson squinted at it, then rubbed some grit from his eye. The ashfall had not completely abated.

It was a big freighter, around one hundred yards long, but was curiously naked of most of the usual steamer's superstructure. It was taking up dock space even though there was no sign that it was being loaded or unloaded or repaired. The merriment on the waterfront failed to distract the young engineer's attention from the ghostlike hulk. He stuck the stub of his cigar between his teeth and walked out to the quay for a closer look.

The ship smelled of recently charred wood and other odors he couldn't quite identify. Masts, rigging, and tarpaulins had been destroyed. The sections of its decks that remained intact lay buried under several feet of wet gray ash—much deeper than the ash that blanketed the rest of the port. Most of the paint on the iron hull was blistered. He strained his eyes to decipher the scorched lettering on the transom. "*Roddam*," he read aloud. "London."

"Pride of the Scrutton Line," responded a voice. The ash carpet had muffled the sound of the stranger's approach. He was an older man, with weary eyes that didn't bother to acknowledge the young engineer but instead were stuck on the burned hulk. "Steamed off from this very pier yesterday," he said.

"Off to where?"

"To hell, my boy," said the old man. "Steamed off to hell. And we're lookin' at what the devil sent back."

• • •

Through the night of May 8, all undersea cables that had survived the tremors of the previous week were clogged with frantic messages. Although the first sketchy report of a disaster on neighboring St. Vincent Island had reached London a day earlier, the main flurry of telegraphic activity began when the captain of the French cruiser *Suchet* sent a terse cablegram from Fort-de-France to the minister of marine in Paris. The volcano Mont Pelée had exploded, the city of St. Pierre lay in ruins, most if not all of its inhabitants had perished, and thousands displaced from surrounding villages needed food and assistance.

On May 9 and 10, the major newspapers in Paris, New York, and London blared headlines of the deaths of tens of thousands in the Lesser Antilles. Although the initial cablegrams from the region were sketchy and inconsistent, those details that couldn't be confirmed were creatively supplied by some of the editors. Socialites who had traveled in that region years earlier were interviewed and quoted, regardless of whether they had ever strayed far from their cruise ships or city hotels. Professors who had never seen a volcano, let alone Mont Pelée or La Soufrière, were cajoled into providing learned explanations of the nature of lava flows and chlorine gas—never mind whether lava or chlorine had anything to do with these particular catastrophes. Quotations were modified to fit the stories, and when the names of the principals couldn't be found or verified in time to meet press deadlines, they were sometimes invented. Thus did the story of the demise of St. Pierre reach the public as a mixture of fact and fiction, science and speculation. Yet of one thing there could be no doubt to anyone: a disaster of stupendous proportions had struck in the Lesser Antilles.

• • •

On Monday, May 12, 1902, members of the U.S. Congress received a letter from the White House:

To the Senate and House of Representatives:

One of the greatest calamities in history has fallen upon our neighboring island of Martinique. The Consul of the United States at Guadeloupe has telegraphed from Fort-de-France, under date of yesterday, that the disaster is complete; that the city of St. Pierre has ceased to exist, and that the American Consul and his family have perished. He is informed that 30,000 people have lost their lives and that 50,000 are homeless and hungry; that there is urgent need of all kinds of provisions, and that the visit of vessels for the work of supply and rescue is imperatively required.

The government of France, while expressing thanks for the marks of sympathy which have reached them from America, informs us that Fort-de-France and the entire island of Martinique are still threatened. They, therefore, request that for the purpose of rescuing the people who are in such deadly peril and threatened with starvation the United States government may send, as soon as possible, means of transporting them from the stricken island. The island of St. Vincent and perhaps others in that region are also seriously menaced by the calamity which has taken so appalling a form in Martinique.

I have directed the Departments of the Treasury, of War and of the Navy to take such measures for the relief of these stricken people as lie within the executive discretion, and I earnestly commend this case of unexampled disaster to the generous consideration of the Congress.

For this purpose I recommend that an appropriation of $500,000 be made, to be immediately available.

Theodore Roosevelt
White House, Washington
May 12, 1902

• • •

The following day in Washington, George Kennan received a one-line telegram from the editor of the magazine the *Outlook:* "Can you go to Martinique on the *Dixie?*" The ship was to sail from New York, some 240 miles from the District of Columbia, in just thirty hours.

Kennan was then fifty-seven, a seasoned world traveler, and at the peak of his journalistic career. His father had been a man of futuristic vision, if not of sound economic judgment, and had abandoned a legal practice in 1846 to manage the newly built telegraph station in Norwalk, Ohio. On his sixth birthday (when telegraphy itself was barely seven), young Kennan had sent his first message over the wires. When he was twelve, the family's dire financial circumstances forced him to take a full-time job as a telegrapher, and over the next few years he educated himself as best he could. He soon discovered that he had a natural talent for language, and he learned to edit convoluted prose into models of clarity before (and sometimes while) dispatching it by wire. With the outbreak of the Civil War, he enlisted in the Military Telegraph Corps and did duty in Cleveland, Wheeling, Columbus, and Cincinnati. But by that time, telegraphy itself offered him no further challenges, and he longed for something more exciting.

The opportunity of a lifetime came when he learned, in 1864, of an ambitious project to construct a telegraph line from the United States through Russian America (Alaska), across the floor of the Bering Strait, then through Siberia to European Russia. He telegraphed one General Stager and requested a position with the surveying team. The general responded, "Can you get ready to go to Alaska in two weeks?" Kennan wired back, "I can get ready in two hours!"

The next two years were a period of incredible hardship. Kennan was assigned to supervise the construction of a section of the line across frozen tundra from the Bering Strait westward to the Anadyr River. Temperatures during the eight-month winters dropped as low as minus sixty-two degrees Fahrenheit, and during the short summer the tundra degenerated into an impassable marsh swarming with hungry mosquitoes. Yet incredibly, by the spring of 1867, the entire line had been surveyed, a portion of it constructed, and poles distributed along the remainder.

Then came the bad news: Cyrus Field had finally succeeded in his attempts to lay a transatlantic cable, and there would no longer be any reason for anyone to send telegraph messages across Siberia to get them to Europe. The Russian-American telegraph project was summarily abandoned.

A disappointed Kennan returned to the United States and began to lecture and write about Russia. That brought a measure of fame but not fortune. He then went into banking for a while but soon realized that was a bad idea; he preferred even the tundra to the regimentation of a daily desk job. In 1878, he accepted a position with the Washington office of the New York Associated Press, and the next year he married. His writings gained him a national reputation for journalistic integrity, and when President James Garfield was shot in 1881, he served as the official White House correspondent-telegrapher during the president's final weeks of life. Words converted into electrical signals by the writer himself, as Kennan did with both proficiency and eloquence, were viewed even then as more credible than words that may have been passed through a longer series of intermediaries. His bylines during this period made him a journalistic celebrity nationwide, and from then on, he was never at a loss for job offers and freelance assignments. He found freelancing to agree with his disposition, and he made Washington his home base.

Kennan made additional trips to Russia and wrote several controversial books about the exile system in Siberia that drew international attention. He became friends with Alexander Graham Bell, got elected to membership in the American Association for the Advancement of Science, and was one of the small group that founded the National Geographic Society in 1888. He also knew Teddy Roosevelt personally and was not too timid to confront the president on issues he disagreed with.

By 1902, Kennan knew enough French to travel on. And he had recently completed a book of Russian folktales about Napoleon, which gave him a French cultural connection of sorts. To the editors of the *Outlook*, his journalistic integrity was beyond reproach. Who better to commission to go to Martinique, and to telegraph back, with his own finger at the key, a series of factual reports to satisfy the nation's hunger for more information about the mayhem and death in that out-of-the-way place?

Kennan immediately accepted the assignment, and within a few hours a courier arrived with an order for his transportation, signed by the secretary of the navy. This in hand, he packed, kissed his wife, Lena, goodbye, and caught the midnight train to New York. He spent the morning shopping for a tropical outfit (whose quality he was later to complain about), then made his way to the Brooklyn docks. There, the cruiser *Dixie* was being loaded with relief provisions, its decks crowded with military officers, newsmen, and scientists. A total of forty-four civilian passengers were to travel to Martinique on a warship that had no passenger accommodations whatsoever. For his personal belongings, each civilian was given twelve square feet of floor space under the after-hatch; for sleeping, he got one of four dozen hammocks suspended over a hold stuffed with dried codfish. It would be an odiferous seven-day voyage.

Among the scientists on board, Kennan met the three-man investigative expedition sponsored by the National Geographic Society: Robert T. Hill, a geologist with the U.S. Geological Survey; Israel C. Russell, professor of geology at the University of Michigan; and Commander C. E. Borchgrevink, a prominent Antarctic explorer. Each day during the voyage, they and the other civilian-scientists got together on deck and took turns delivering lectures on their areas of expertise. Kennan made light of the creature discomforts and took notes on everything anyone had to offer about geology, volcanoes, and the history and politics of the Lesser Antilles. This was the kind of assignment he loved, and for those seven nights on the sea, even the smell of the codfish below his hammock could not stifle his enthusiasm.

• • •

In Philadelphia, Professor Angelo Heilprin was not upset that he hadn't been invited to join the crowd on the *Dixie*. He could tolerate physical discomfort as well as anyone, but only for a purpose. Although the American journalists and relief administrators may have had reason for impatience in getting to Martinique, the professor was confident that the geologic aftermath of the disaster would wait for him.

But Heilprin also knew that this was not an opportunity to miss, for at forty-nine he was not as young as he used to be, and here was the

possibility of conducting a study that would capstone his career as a physical geographer and ensure his place in the annals of natural science.
Having been recently appointed to the board of managers of the National Geographic Society, he knew the officers. Heilprin phoned the society's president and asked him to authorize the society to pay his passage
to Martinique. He would also need a cameraman, some rugged camera
equipment, a few basic instruments, and the other provisions one needs
before embarking for the tropics with the rainy season at hand.

The president demurred, for the society was already paying the team
it had dispatched on the *Dixie*. The officers were concerned that this
could get expensive. How much news of this disaster could there possibly
be, before it got redundant? And how much could be published in
National Geographic before readers began to lose interest? What could
Heilprin offer that Hill, Russell, and Borchgrevink couldn't do while they
were there?

But Heilprin persisted. The others were part of a relief expedition, he
explained, and they were looking primarily at the human aspects of the
disaster. Their job was to supply timely news reports. Heilprin pointed
out that he would stay longer. He would climb the volcano. He would
take a lot of photographs. He would study the geologic evidence and reconstruct what had happened from a geophysical perspective. He would
take as much time as the scientific integrity of his study would demand.
He would try to unveil the mysterious processes that were occurring deep
within the planet's crust, and which would surely generate other disasters
in the future. The editors of *National Geographic* had an obligation to
their readership, he argued, to provide an in-depth scientific follow-up to
the initial anecdotal reports of the disaster.

The president relented; he would get the society to pay Heilprin to go
to Martinique. But a photographer was another matter. There were already photographers on the *Dixie*, including some of the best. It would
be up to the professor to connect with one of them on the island.

The next passenger ship leaving the port of Philadelphia for Martinique was the *Fontabelle*, scheduled to sail on May 17. Heilprin booked
passage, then sent a cable to Fort-de-France to be delivered to the photographer A. F. Leadbeater and several other of the journalists and artists
when the *Dixie* arrived there. Then, with a few days still remaining be-

fore his departure, he scoured the Philadelphia libraries and began to devour every book and article he could find about the eastern Caribbean.

• • •

In France, the public was in a state of shock. Many had lost loved ones; others had lost major investments. According to the newspaper accounts, the Martiniquians had received no forewarning at all of the disaster. The few bureaucrats in the Ministry of Colonies who had reason to suspect otherwise were astute enough to remain silent about their conjectures, and the real reasons St. Pierre had not been evacuated would only emerge much later. For the present, the main order of business was to send aid. Then, of course, to appoint a scientific commission to study the matter and to issue a formal report.

In reviewing the list of candidates to head the commission, the prime minister wanted someone young and vigorous enough to venture into the field and not simply file a report based on interviews conducted in some café. This person also had to have an established reputation in the scientific community. One dossier stood out from the others.

At thirty-nine, Alfred Lacroix had already published two major books on mineralogy, one in 1889 and the other in 1893. The latter was a survey of the mineralogical features of mainland France and its various colonies. He had recently returned from a geologic expedition to Madagascar and had a book on that field study in press. Every colleague who had worked with him respected him highly.

This was clearly the man to lead the French scientific expedition and to conduct a formal scientific study. Lacroix eagerly accepted the assignment. And, in keeping with the efficiency of the French bureaucracy, he and his assembled scientific team would actually set foot in the devastated city just seven weeks later.

• • •

It was with the expectation that the destructive event had already been rendered to history that these various investigators converged on Martinique in May and June of 1902. But as their ships steamed toward that small island, Mont Pelée continued to rumble. The volcano, it turned out, had yet to complete its terrible agenda.

· CHAPTER 2 ·

ISLANDS IN THE SUN

·

Geography was in Professor Angelo Heilprin's blood. Born in 1853 in Satoralja-Ujhely, Hungary, he spent his early years in Philadelphia and Brooklyn, then traveled to London to study natural sciences at the Royal School of Mines. Over the next few years he studied in Paris and Geneva, hiked through the Swiss Alps to investigate their glaciers, and journeyed through Italy, Hungary, and Russian Poland to meet the prominent scientists of those countries. When he settled in Philadelphia at the age of twenty-seven, he had seen most of the nations of Europe and was competent in at least four continental languages.

Heilprin joined every scientific organization that would take him and eagerly accepted speaking engagements from any group with the slightest interest in hearing him. In 1884, he published his first book: *Contributions to the Tertiary Geology and Paleontology of the United States*. Although this work fell considerably short of making anyone's best-seller list, it did catapult Heilprin's scientific reputation beyond the Philadelphia area. In the next four years he wrote three additional books on geology and physical geography, including one devoted to the geologic evidence for biological evolution (then still a controversial topic).

Yet Heilprin was not the stereotypical bookish intellectual. Physically vigorous, he had climbed mountains on three continents and was vice president of the American Alpine Club. In 1891, Robert Peary invited him to participate in his first arctic expedition, exploring the northeast coast of Greenland. Heilprin not only endured the physical hardship of that adventure but subjected himself to another grueling excursion when he led a relief expedition in 1892. Those experiences led him to write several scientific reports and another book: *Arctic Problem and Narrative of the Peary Relief Expedition,* published in 1893.

Now, in 1902, he held a number of impressive titles, including lecturer on physical geography in the Sheffield Scientific School of Yale University, fellow of the Royal Geographical Society of London, professor of Geology at the Academy of Natural Sciences of Philadelphia, and member of the Board of Managers of the National Geographic Society. Yet he was well aware that his titles did not reflect a great deal of personal knowledge about volcanoes. Although he had seen a few Italian volcanoes smoldering, he had never witnessed one in full eruption. And Mont Pelée, where the eruption was now apparently over, would be the first volcano he would study in depth. He would need to do a considerable amount of reading in the meager few days before the *Fontabelle* sailed.

•   •   •

Stretching from Puerto Rico to Venezuela, the Lesser Antilles are a crescent of small islands that define the eastern limits of the Caribbean Sea. Even in 1902, it was common knowledge that at least a dozen of the islands along the inside of this arc are of volcanic origin: Saba, St. Kitts, Nevis, St. Eustatius, Redonda, Montserrat, Guadeloupe, Dominica, Martinique, St. Lucia, St. Vincent, and Grenada. They rise steeply from a deep ocean floor, generally a bit deeper on the Caribbean side than on the Atlantic, and although several are separated by only twenty-five miles or less, the sea floor between them often drops three thousand feet or more. More than sixty years before the theory of plate tectonics would emerge, it occurred to Heilprin that this volcanic island-arc might define a line of weakness in the crust underlying the Caribbean Sea. And indeed, geoscientists now recognize that the Caribbean Plate is locked in place while the westward-creeping floor of the Atlantic is sliding beneath it and lifting it, just outside this very "volcanic crescent."

In 1902, the historical record of the Antilles went back but four centuries, and of that ledger Heilprin found the first three centuries to be disappointingly incomplete. Only here and there, buried within accounts of the turbulent political history of the region, were there any descriptions of volcanic activity. Several stories of the British invasion of Martinique

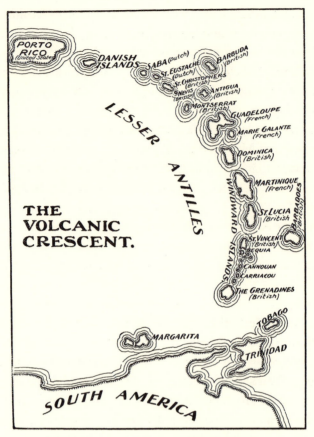

The eastern Caribbean. (Morris 1902a)

in 1762 mentioned, almost as an afterthought, that on January 22 of that year there had been earthquakes and mudflows on the slopes of the volcano. Mont Pelée had another minor eruption in August of 1851, when it expelled an ash cloud and generated a mudflow but claimed no victims. The volcano La Soufrière on St. Vincent had similar rumblings in 1718 and 1785, and in 1880 locals grew concerned when its crater lake swelled to five times its normal size and its temperature rose to near boiling. Fortunately the lake then returned to normal. Other sources made casual references to the venting of steam and sulfides, or to a minor ashfall, from one or another of the volcanoes of the crescent. While a few writers reported "lava," none described it as anything similar to the sluggish flows of incandescent molten rock from the volcanoes in Hawaii or Iceland. So, although there was indisputable evidence of extensive volcanic activity in the Lesser Antilles in the geologic past, the literature suggested that within historical times the volcanoes in that region had generally been behaving themselves.

But as he continued to read, Heilprin discovered that there had indeed been one notable eruption in the Lesser Antilles within historical times. That event happened not on Martinique but on St. Vincent Island, one hundred miles to the south. It began in mid-April of 1812 with a series of earthquakes, followed on April 27 by the explosion of a huge black cloud from the mountain La Soufrière. As the volcano churned furiously for the next three days, every part of the island was blanketed in at least a foot of ashes.

This 1812 event caught Heilprin's attention, for La Soufrière was the same volcano that had exploded just a week ago, only one day prior to the St. Pierre catastrophe. As he dug further through the newspapers and journals, he was rewarded with other intriguing snippets of information: one of the largest streams on St. Vincent Island had dried up after the eruption, never to flow again, and the ash clouds had expanded far to the east, contrary to the direction of the trade winds in the region. Then he made another literary find—Charles Kingsley, writing in 1874, described the effect of this eruption on the people of Barbados, more than one hundred miles due east of the volcano:

> The day after the explosion, "Black Sunday," gave a proof of, though no measure of, the enormous force which had been exerted. All Saturday a heavy cannonading had been heard to the eastward. The English and French fleets were surely engaged. The soldiers were called out; the batteries manned; but the cannonade died away, and all went to bed in wonder. On the first of May the clocks struck six, but the sun did not, as usual in the tropics, answer to the call. The darkness was still intense, and grew more intense as the morning wore on. A slow and silent rain of impalpable dust was falling over the whole island. People rushed shrieking into the streets. Surely the last day was come. Some began to pray who had not prayed for years. The pious and the educated (and there were plenty of both in Barbados)

were not proof against the infection. Old letters describe the scene in the churches that morning as hideous—prayers, sobs, and cries, in Stygian darkness, from trembling crowds. And still the darkness continued and the dust fell.

I have a letter written by one long since dead, who had at least powers of description of no common order, telling how, when he tried to go out of his house upon the east coast, he could not find the trees on his own lawn save by feeling for their stems. He stood amazed not only in utter darkness, but in utter silence; for the trade-wind had fallen dead, the everlasting roar of the surf was gone, and the only noise was the crashing of branches, snapped by the weight of the clammy dust.

The account set Heilprin the naturalist musing about experiencing such a phenomenon for himself. Little did he expect that in just a few weeks he would experience something much more memorable and be lucky to escape with his life.

He looked up the heights of the region's volcanoes: Saba at 2,000 feet above sea level, Mount Misery on St. Kitts at 4,300 feet, the Soufrière of Montserrat about 3,000 feet, the Soufrière of Guadeloupe at 4,070 feet, Diablotin on Dominica towering 4,740 feet, Mont Pelée on Martinique at 4,300 feet, and La Soufrière of St. Vincent at 4,050 feet. To Heilprin, these were more than mere statistics. His mind's eye could visualize these mountains from a vantage point that did not begin at sea level but rather at the sea floor 3,000 feet below; if measured from their bases, all would be around 7,000 feet tall. Only about half the height and less than 20 percent of the volume of these volcanoes poked above the sea.

Clearly, immense quantities of material had flowed from the Earth's innards to build these islands. And yet, on a human historical scale, eruptions were unusual events. In fact, on Saba, which was hardly more than a rock rising from the sea, eruptions were so rare that people had actually settled inside the crater! With eruptions so infrequent, yet their ejecta accumulating to such massive volumes, Heilprin pondered that it must be in the nature of volcanoes to remain active for an extremely long time. It seemed reasonable to expect that the lifetime of a given volcano could span tens of thousands of years, mostly spent in dormancy between eruptions. (And in fact, today's volcanologists do not consider a volcano to be extinct unless it has failed to erupt within the last ten thousand years.)

Heilprin searched further for information about the volcanoes of the Lesser Antilles, but there wasn't much more to be found. A snippet of information here, some topographical information there, a disconnected analysis of some geologic samples in another source. To some academics, this might have been discouraging, but to Heilprin it was a source of inspiration. Geology, after all, was a young science—the seismograph was developed only in 1880, and the American Geological Society dated only from 1884. Starting with a virtual blank slate like this gave Heilprin the opportunity not only to write the definitive scientific work on the 1902 eruption of Pelée but also to possibly create the seminal source for all future research on volcanoes in the West Indies, if not the world.

• • •

Science progresses largely by analogy. The ancient Greeks explained eclipses in the heavens by examining shadows cast by lamps on Earth. In 1805, Thomas Young explained the curious zebra-like bands that arise in optical systems by suggesting that light behaves like a water wave. Chemists found it useful to picture the chemical bonds between atoms as analogous to springs connecting billiard balls, and even biologists had made progress in genetics by noticing analogies between their experimental results and combinatorial mathematical principles. Although in 1902 geology was a fuzzier academic discipline than the other natural sciences, analogies might be useful here too. Earthquakes could be pictured as the failure of elasticity when a stick is broken over a knee, and volcanoes— well, volcanic eruptions had to be analogous to something, didn't they?

Heilprin was well aware that any useful scientific analogy must grow out of an extensive collection of observations of the phenomenon. Yet, as of 1902, only one major volcanic eruption had ever been studied scientifically. In 1883 in the Dutch East Indies, a volcano on the obscure uninhabited island of Krakatau (often spelled "Krakatoa") exploded and launched five cubic miles of rock and ash into the atmosphere. Where a mountain had stood, there remained only a giant gaping hole extending 950 feet below sea level. The sea rushing in to fill the void generated a series of monstrous waves, some towering as high as 135 feet and with wavelengths of hundreds of miles. These giant sea swells (today called "tsunamis") completely swept away 165 towns and villages on neighboring islands and damaged 132 others. The sound of the explosive climax was heard over one-thirteenth of the planet's surface, and barometers everywhere on the globe recorded the event. The official death toll from that disaster tallied to 36,380. Heilprin himself remembered the years 1884 and 1885, when evening after evening he, like millions of others everywhere around the globe, found himself awestruck by the incredibly colorful sunsets. The airborne dust from the cataclysmic explosion had actually spread over the entire planet!

A great deal was written about the Krakatau eruption—not only technical and scientific reports but many articles intended for a general readership. After Heilprin digested the Royal Society's scientific reports on the event, he moved on to some of the eyewitness stories. One in particular grabbed his attention.

In the district of Katimbang, separated from Krakatau by twenty-four miles of sea, the Beyerinck family had a harrowing experience. On the evening of August 26, 1883, with the offshore volcano roaring and ash clouds obliterating the sky, the sea suddenly swelled and engulfed the string of buildings along the coast. The Beyerinck family took this as a bad sign of things to come and fled inland. A four-hour trek through rice paddies and forests brought them at midnight to a cabin at an elevation of four hundred feet above the sea, and there they took shelter. On the morning of the twenty-seventh, they found a large group of natives camping outside. Although the sky was so dark and the ashfall so heavy that it was impossible to see what the volcano was doing, the Beyerinks felt secure. After all, they were dozens of miles from the eruption, far above sea level, and they had a roof over their heads.

Then something incredible happened. In Mrs. Beyerinck's words:

> Someone burst in shouting "shut the doors, shut the doors!" Suddenly it was pitch dark. The last thing I saw was the ash being pushed up through the cracks in the floorboards, like a fountain.
>
> I felt a heavy pressure, throwing me to the ground. Then it seemed as if all the air was being sucked away and I could not breathe.

Large lumps clattered down on my head, my back and my arms. Each lump was larger than the others. I could not stand.

No sound came from my husband or children. Only part of my brain could have been working for I didn't realize I had been burned and everything which came in contact with me was hot ash, mixed with moisture. . . . I noticed that the door was ajar and I forced myself through the opening. I tripped and fell. I realized the ash was hot and I tried to protect my face with my hands. The hot bite of the pumice pricked like needles.

Then something got hooked into my finger and hurt. I noticed for the first time that the skin was hanging off everywhere, thick and moist from the ash stuck to it. Thinking it must be dirty, I wanted to pull bits of skin off, but that was still more painful. My tired brain could not make out what it was. I did not know I had been burned.

Mrs. Beyerinck, her husband, and two of her three children survived their burns but were scarred for life. The hundreds of natives who had huddled in the afternoon darkness outside their cabin were killed almost instantly. In fact, of that 1883 catastrophe's 36,380 deaths, at least 3,000 were due to burns. None of those burn victims had been any closer than twenty-four miles from the volcano. None had been on the island of Krakatau itself.

Heilprin found this curious. What agent of destruction could possibly travel horizontally across twenty-four miles of sea, surge uphill, and still be hot enough to inflict fatal burns? Could an emission from a volcano actually travel fast enough to catch everyone by surprise? It would have been easy to dismiss the Beyerinck account as apocryphal, but Heilprin decided to withhold his judgment, at least for a while. He sifted through more stories about Krakatau. And then he learned the following:

On August 26, 1883, the English ship *Charles Bal* had passed just ten miles south of Krakatau while the volcano was in full eruption. Captain W. J. Watson had recorded his observations in the ship's log, portions of which found their way into the *Liverpool Daily Post*. More significantly, Heilprin found the same account in the prestigious and peer-reviewed scientific journal *Nature*.

At 2:30 p.m. we noticed some agitation about the point of Krakatoa, clouds or something being propelled from the NE point with great velocity. At 3:30 we heard above us and about the island a strange sound as of a mighty crackling fire, or the discharge of heavy artillery at one or two seconds' interval. At 4:15 p.m., Krakatoa bore N1/2E, ten miles distant. We observed a repetition of the noise noted at 3:30, only much more furious and alarming; the matter, whatever it was, being propelled with amazing velocity to the NE. To us it looked like blinding rain, and had the appearance of a furious squall, of ashen hue.

It occurred to Heilprin that if the volcano were indeed blasting material at high speed toward the northeast, this might have something to do with Mrs. Beyerinck's strange tale. The direction was approximately right. Then, on reading more carefully, Heilprin noticed that the timing was wrong by almost a day. By the time of Mrs. Beyernick's trauma, the *Charles Bal* had moved to a point thirty miles northeast of the volcano and had become so heavily engulfed in an ashfall that no one on deck could see beyond a few hundred feet. Heilprin combed the literature for other observations of Krakatau dated August 27, 1883, but either no captains had been foolhardy enough to pass close to the volcano that day, or else they didn't live to tell their tales.

But what *was* this strange agent, Heilprin wondered, that could travel so many miles even over water, yet still be hot enough to burn human flesh? And did a similar phenomenon have anything to do with the disaster at St. Pierre? Heilprin jotted these questions in his notebook, returned the stack of books and journals to the librarian, and went home to pack for his voyage.

CHAPTER 3

PUBLIC SERVANT

•

He had been in Martinique only five months—too short a time to have forged many deep and trusting friendships. At forty-four, Governor Louis Mouttet was also by some appraisals a bit young to be dealt a crisis of such magnitude. Politics he understood, power he had observed in action, but this situation went beyond anything in his experience. Nor did any of the handbooks of the French Colonial Service give any hint of guidance on how to deal with a volcano on a rampage. He was on his own.

History has not been kind to him. He has been described as arrogant, superficial, stupid, headstrong, inept, a glutton, and a racist. And indeed, hindsight tells us that his misjudgments helped seal the terrible fates of thirty thousand human beings. Yet Mouttet was more multidimensional than described later by many writers who had never met him. He was a man of global perspective—charismatic, tenacious, committed to the responsibilities of his stewardship, a devoted family man, and (as would be demonstrated by at least some of his actions during the crisis) color-blind in his sensitivity to the needs of those who had suffered tragedy. Any apologist on his behalf would also mention that during the eventful final weeks, Mouttet held no personal monopoly on ignorance or bewilderment.

Born into a family of simple means near Marseilles on October 10, 1857, Louis Mouttet was expected to follow his father into farming. Animals and farm life, however, did not capture his interest; it was people and politics that fascinated him. Who he adopted as a role model is anyone's guess, but he did take his schoolwork seriously and became an effective writer and an articulate speaker. Well liked by almost all who met him, in his early twenties he was invited into the Cercle Saint-Simon, a French variation on freemasonry. When the Cercle moved to Paris in 1883, Mouttet went with them. There he leveraged his connections to get a job as a proofreader for the weekly newspaper *La Patrie*. His editor, Emile Massard, would later remember the young Mouttet for his motivation:

> He often worked until 2 a.m., sometimes going without dinner, kept going by a single dream: that of getting a byline on the law report page. One day, by chance, his dream came true. He was asked to fill in for an absent colleague, got his fingers into the scissors, and never took them out again. From that time Mouttet was a happy man. He bought himself a top hat and started to frequent Paris café society.

Although one of the biggest international news stories of 1883 was the explosion of the volcano Krakatau in the Dutch East Indies, Mouttet took scant notice of the stream of Krakatau stories that crossed his desk. He had no interest in volcanoes and such; it was society that fascinated him, and his bylines on legal news articles were now gaining attention in Paris social circles. When he was offered the position of secretary to the Historical Society of Paris, he jumped at the opportunity to improve both his salary and his social life. Blue-eyed, with curly black hair and a trim goatee, he soon became a popular figure at the salons and attracted bevies of female admirers.

Yet the Historical Society job was clearly a dead end for a young man of ambition. Mouttet resigned in 1886 to enter the French Colonial Service, expecting to quickly climb the ladder of that bureaucracy on the strength of his charisma. But here he ran into tough competition among the many young Frenchmen of similar ambitions, and for two years he languished as a minor bureaucrat in Senegal, French West Africa. In 1889 he was transferred to the Far East, where for the next three years he would serve as the personal secretary to the governor of Indochina. Only later would this tenure prove to have been well spent, for it would allow him to make an eloquently convincing case to the Colonial

Service that he knew from firsthand experience every facet of being an effective governor.

Meanwhile, Mouttet was seduced by the colonial lifestyle in French Indochina: the spacious homes provided by the Colonial Service, the retinues of servants, the elegant social life, the salary that in the local economy permitted luxuries unheard of by government employees back in the homeland. He was granted a leave in the spring of 1890, and during the long voyage from Indochina to France, he decided that one small addition to his dossier above all others would do the most to advance his career: a wife.

Not just any wife, of course. She would need the grace, charm, and wit to engage guests at social functions. She would need to be of childbearing age. And, absolutely essential, she would need to come from a family with the proper political connections in France, to compensate for the Mouttet family having none of its own.

It is said that chance favors the prepared mind. Mouttet met the lovely niece of the deputy for Le Havre, one Maria Coppet. It was a whirlwind courtship, and they married in September of that year. Courtesy of the political connections of his new in-laws, on their wedding day the French government awarded Louis Mouttet the cross of the Legion of Honor for "political services in the name of the Republic." The specific "services" were not stated. He was then a month shy of thirty-three.

When offered the post of director of internal affairs in Guadeloupe in 1892, Mouttet accepted immediately. The couple, and soon there was an addition, spent the next two years in Guadeloupe while Mouttet campaigned relentlessly for a promotion. He and Maria found that Caribbean island to suit their temperaments, in climate, in people, in food, in ambience. This is where they would choose to stay for life, if only he could get an appointment to a more prominent position. Unfortunately, too many others shared the same positive feelings about the beautiful island, and the upper levels of that colony's government were clogged with politicos with no disposition to vacate their posts before death. Mouttet came to see no alternative to making another move, and in 1895 he accepted an appointment as interim governor of Senegal, a country he was familiar with even if he had no interest in staying there for the long term. There were high rates of turnover among officials in all of the colonies of French West Africa, and high turnovers spelled opportunity. The fact that Senegal was a big place compared to Guadeloupe, and that he would be governor (albeit an interim one), would surely enhance his dossier. Maria was not pleased by the move, but she went dutifully, in the tradition of that culture and those times.

Mouttet's opportunity came quickly. In 1896 he was appointed interim governor of Ivory Coast; a year later he was promoted to governor fourth class, and in 1898 he became governor third class. At last, his career was taking off. But his heart was never in Africa, and neither was Maria's. During their walks on the beaches near Abidjan, they would often stop, hand in hand, and in wistful silence gaze westward across the Atlantic toward the Caribbean they both loved so much.

Then, in 1899, Mouttet received a cable offering him the governorship of French Guiana. He knew that Guiana would be far from a pleasant place, with its steamy tropical forests, rampant malaria and dysentery, and virtually no infrastructure one would associate with French civilization. A significant fraction of the Frenchmen under his jurisdiction would be the convicts on Devil's Island. But it was a governorship on the right side of the Atlantic, on the northeastern shore of South America not far from the Lesser Antilles. He and Maria discussed the matter in the customary style of most marital discussions of those times, and Maria resigned herself to enduring a few more years of physical discomfort in support of their ultimate goal—an appointment somewhere in the French West Indies. Again they packed their belongings and steamed across the Atlantic. She was pregnant with another child.

Mouttet rolled up his sleeves; he was determined to minimize the length of their stay in Guiana. And indeed, within a couple of months, he gained attention in the French press as a key player in getting Captain Alfred Dreyfus, incarcerated on Devil's Island, to return to France for a second trial in the celebrated "Dreyfus Affair." Mouttet leveraged this publicity to his best advantage, stepping delicately around the numerous controversial aspects of the case, and in his frequent missives to the Colonial Service he deftly worked in mentions of all of his prior experience. The effort paid off. In October of 1901, Louis Mouttet received an ap-

pointment to the coveted position of governor of Martinique. He was to
begin in December.

Maria wept with joy. This was the ultimate reward for all their sacri-
fices, and there would never be any reason to aspire to more. Eleven years
of repeatedly uprooting their lives and of risking the health of their children were finally ended. Martinique was to become their permanent
home. They would raise their family in a paradise, secure from turmoil,
with no needs or wants denied. With the headquarters of the Colonial
Service bureaucracy thousands of miles away, there would be little interference with Louis's autonomy. The news the bureaucrats received in
France would be the news that Louis Mouttet, governor of Martinique,
would choose to send them. And that news would always be good news.

Louis embraced Maria's vision. Yet there are always deeper turmoils in
a man's mind, and Louis Mouttet apparently had several. He could never
forget that he was not part of the social elite by birth. He knew he had
succeeded largely through luck and opportunism, and had used his charisma to deflect any rude inquiries into his true qualifications and accom-
plishments. Many others in the Colonial Service had aspired to the same
governership, and they would be watching him closely, poised to seize any
opportunity to bring him down. He could not afford to be too glib about
the appointment; he would need to tread very cautiously during the next
few years.

He viewed Martinique much differently than his previous assignments
in Indochina, Africa, and Guiana: he hadn't cared deeply about those
places; he was just passing through, and it wasn't necessary to integrate
himself with the cultures there. But this Martinique appointment was
very special; if he handled it right, the island would be his home for the
rest of his career, the rest of his life, maybe the lives of his children and
their children. What higher post could he realistically aspire to? Moving
into the Paris bureaucracy was out of the question; there were few positions there equivalent to governor of Martinique, and those were already
hard-wired far into the future. Return to Marseilles? And do what? Farm?
Run for elected political office as an unknown?

No, Martinique was where he would stay, and he would commit himself to being the best governor this colony ever had. Meanwhile, he would

do nothing to endanger his position there in the eyes of the bureaucrats in Paris. Until he had a firm grasp of what was going on, and knew whom he could trust among his new coterie, he would certainly keep his cablegrams to Paris skimpy at best.

• • •

It was on June 15, 1502, that the first Europeans under Christopher Columbus set foot on the island. By then, there had been a decade of geographic discoveries in the New World, and another small island populated by ill-tempered Caribe Indians was of little interest to the four shipfuls of explorers or to their mother country of Spain. That initial expedition stayed but a day—just long enough to gather provisions before sailing on westward. Columbus recorded the discovery in his ship's log but did not bother to plant a flag or to give the place a European name.

Over the next century, European cartographers began to make sense of the piecemeal information generated by hundreds of expeditions of discovery, and a picture began to emerge of a Caribbean Sea bounded loosely on the east by a crescent-shaped string of mountainous islands. Those were times when it never occurred to European adventurers that the people found living in a newly discovered place might be considered that place's rightful owners. Soon the imperial nations of Europe— Portugal, Spain, England, France, and Holland—began fighting over their conflicting claims to the right to steal homelands around the world from their native inhabitants. Some of those conflicts took place in the Lesser Antilles.

In 1635, Belain d'Esnambuc landed on Martinique and raised the French flag at the site of the present town of Le Carbet. The first order of business in establishing a colony was always to build a fort, and d'Esnambuc named his after his patron saint: Fort St. Pierre. Set on high ground overlooking the coast a few miles north of his landing site, it attracted a cluster of settlers who built homes under the shelter of its cannons. In 1638, Lieutenant-General Jacques du Parquet decided that the island would be better defended from a site a dozen miles to the south, and there he built a stronghold named Fort Royal, around which a second community of colonists settled. Meanwhile, the larger settlement

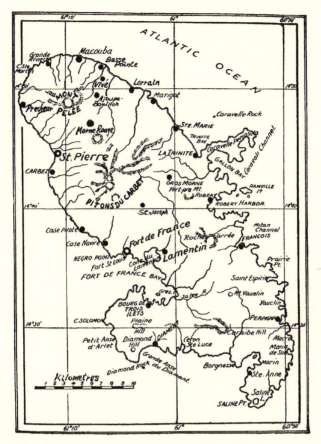

The island of Martinique. (Morris 1902a)

around the original Fort St. Pierre continued to expand, to become a town and eventually the city of St. Pierre.

In 1642, Louis XIII authorized the use of African slaves in the French Antilles. Soon after, Jacques du Parquet introduced sugarcane from South America, and Martinique began its march to prosperity on the backs of imported Africans. In 1685, France imposed the Code Noir on all its colonies, granting slaves certain rights (including limited working hours, standards for food and housing, and restrictions on punishment), while also clarifying the strict constraints on their activities. This statute at least raised African Martiniquians above the lowest rung on the social ladder. At the very bottom were the few remaining Caribe Indians, who in one slaughter after another had been mercilessly driven to the northern end of the island.

The settlement of St. Pierre continued to grow, its economy fueled by the trade in sugar and other tropical agricultural products. With its natural deepwater port and its proximity to the rich volcanic soil of nearby Mont Pelée, St. Pierre was ideally situated to prosper. And indeed, the influx of planters to the area attracted a throng of businessmen and merchants, shippers and shipwrights.

The terrain surrounding St. Pierre, however, was so rugged that it was difficult to get to the town from other parts of the island except by boat. If the entire island were ever to develop into a prosperous colony, its seat of government needed to be more centralized. On this logic, the political capital of Martinique was moved from St. Pierre to Fort Royal in 1692. Yet, for the next two centuries, the growth of St. Pierre continued to outstrip that of the colony's new capital.

The Dutch made a vain attempt to invade Martinique in 1674. In 1759, during the French and Indian War, the Martiniquians repelled an English naval attack on Fort Royal. The English, however, were persistent, and by landing on the Atlantic side and marching overland, they captured Fort Royal in 1762. The resulting English occupation lasted nine months, until the Treaty of Paris restored Martinique and several other small islands to France in exchange for France's humiliating agreement to cede Canada to England.

Those who figured that this treaty settled definitively the matter of who owned Martinique were to be proven wrong. The turmoil of the French Revolution of 1789 spilled from the European continent into the French colonies, and in Martinique, the rural planters remained loyal to the Monarchy while the merchants of St. Pierre supported the Republic. When the Republicans captured Fort Royal in 1794, their immediate concern was to establish the legitimacy of their government of the island. One way to do so was to create an expanded code of law. The most obvious candidate for a new legal statute—one that was substantive yet not controversial among the Republicans—was to abolish slavery. And so, quickly and decisively, the Republican Party officially ended slavery in Martinique in 1794.

Unfortunately, given that almost all of Martinique's Africans lived in rural areas that were under Royalist control, it was impossible for the revolutionary government to enforce an emancipation. The Royalists, however, panicked at the statutory threat to their economic vitality, and in a desperate overreaction they entered into an alliance with the heretofore-hated English. It proved to be a bargain with the devil. The English, no fools, exploited the opportunity to occupy the island once again. This time, they stayed for six years.

The year 1794 was also the height of the Reign of Terror in France. One of the victims of the guillotine was the Martinique-born Alexandre de Beauharnais, a vicomte and general, veteran of the American Revolution, and moderate member of the National Assembly, who had made the mistake of angering the wrong people. He left two children, one of whom would later become viscount to Italy, the other queen of Holland. He also left a widow—a Martiniquian Creole named Marie-Josèphe Rose Gascher de la Pagerie, more commonly known as Josephine. She remarried in a civil ceremony in 1796, taking as her second husband a man six years her junior. Eight years later, they would restate their vows in the Catholic Church as her husband was about to be coronated Emperor Napoleon I and she, Empress Josephine.

In 1802, Napoleon recovered Martinique for France through the Treaty of Amiens, and it was time to reestablish French law on the island. But what should be done about the Republicans' abolitionist statute of 1794, which the English had never enforced? Napoleon, who had never been to Martinique, conferred with his wife, who had been born and raised on the island. Josephine advised Napoleon that abolishing slavery would destroy Martinique's economy and raise the ire of not only the plantation owners on the island but the investors living in France as well. Deferring to her judgment, the emperor invalidated the 1794 law and kept the institution of slavery alive. In the same edict, he changed the name of Martinique's capital from Fort Royal to Fort-de-France.

An apocryphal story tells of a British cannonball impacting at Josephine's feet in 1790, and the trauma of this near miss establishing her lifelong hatred of the English. A statue of the empress marks the supposed site in today's Fort-de-France. It is a controversial monument that has often been defaced, and as of this writing stands headless and splattered with red paint. For good reason. Because of Josephine, slavery continued for forty-six years after it would have been abolished.

The English had one final hurrah in Martinique. They conquered again in 1809, the same year that Napoleon annulled his marriage to Josephine. This time they occupied the island until Napoleon abdicated his emperorship in 1814, when by treaty France recovered Guadeloupe and Martinique but gave up St. Lucia and Tobago. Since then, the island of Martinique has been continuously a French possession.

In 1834, England abolished slavery in all its colonies. This triggered a mass exodus of Africans from Martinique and Guadeloupe to the nearby English Caribbean islands. Slave revolts became increasingly common, and it was clear that the inhumane institution could not survive for long. With the February Revolution of 1848 in France, the Second Republic immediately abolished slavery in all French colonies. Victor Schoelcher, who as undersecretary of the colonies was the driving force behind this reform, signed the official emancipation decree on April 27, 1848. Although the law was not intended to be enforced for another two months, a general revolt in St. Pierre forced the governor of Martinique to announce the abolition of slavery on May 22, 1848.

The French government gave generous compensation to former slaveowners, and with this infusion of capital many of the plantation owners reorganized their production and pooled their resources to build mechanized sugar refineries. Within the next few decades, the island had at least twenty-five large sugar factories and 112 rum distilleries.

Although Martinique was officially termed a "colony" of France, it was not a colony in the American sense of the word. Americans usually thought of colonies in the English tradition, implying dependencies without participation or representation in the legislature of the mother country. In the colonial system of Great Britain, subjects did not possess citizenship or much voice in self-government. Martinique, on the other hand, was essentially part of France itself, with elected representatives in the French Senate and Chamber of Deputies. Its people were free citizens of a republic that took responsibility for their welfare and prosperity and left them to exercise their personal rights. The only thing obviously colonial about Martinique was that its governor was appointed rather than elected; even here, however, there was a difference between the French and English systems in that the French colonial governors had relatively limited powers. Compared to the blighted and exploited British West Indian islands, Martinique and the other French West Indian islands were better off in every way: in education, infrastructure, health, welfare, economic opportunity, culture, and the participation of natives in the government of the mother country.

At the dawn of the twentieth century, Martinique's population stood at 187,692. Fort-de-France, the political capital, had 17,274 permanent residents. St. Pierre, some eleven miles to the north by boat, had a population of 26,501—a number that did not include temporary workers from out of town and the sailors one always finds in a busy port. In December of 1901, when Louis Mouttet arrived to take the reins of government, the grand city of St. Pierre was effectively the social and economic capital of the colony.

All contemporary accounts describe St. Pierre as the gem of the French West Indies. Its picturesque two- and three-story masonry homes were roofed in red tile, its gardens and courts landscaped with lush tropical plants, its paved streets displaying a level of craftsmanship that astounded visiting Americans of those times. The theater rivaled in elegance the best that could be found in other world cities of many times the size. The city had electricity, a local telephone service, intercontinental telegraph access, two banks, and the offices and presses of the colony's main daily newspaper, *Les Colonies*. It also had a streetcar line, with women conductors. Writers waxed eloquent about the place; even in France, the city was often referred to as "the little Paris" and "the Paris of the Antilles." And although the surrounding mountains and ravines made it difficult to travel overland to the capital, ferries plied the sea regularly between St. Pierre and Fort-de-France, a trip that took but an hour.

The city was far from level; steps had been built into many of its streets, and it was bordered at the northeast by a steep precipice. There was no harbor in the conventional sense, just a wide bay with an open roadstead. The sea bottom dropped so steeply from the shore that large steamships could anchor within a stone's throw of land, where their cargoes were easily transferred to and from shore on lighters. On any given day, the roadstead held at least a dozen visiting ships in

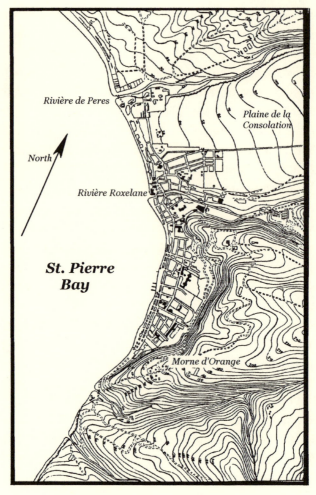

Contour map of St. Pierre.
(Adapted from Hovey 1902)

addition to the hundreds of smaller boats and work vessels owned by the locals.

Running along the seafront, and following the curve of the coast for a mile and a half, was the Rue Bouille. On this street stood the fruit houses, the headquarters of the sugar companies, the customhouse, the rum warehouses, and various other commercial operations. Behind and parallel was the Rue Victor Hugo, the principal shopping street, lined with showy French shops filled with goods from Paris. It was said that Americans either owned or had financial interests in as many as half of these commercial operations in St. Pierre. And indeed there was a significant American presence in the city, including the U.S. consul Thomas Prentiss and his wife, Clara.

One-fourth of St. Pierre's population was of white French origin, the remainder of mixed ethnicity. One Lafcadio Hearn, after spending two years here a decade earlier, had nothing but praise for the city:

A quaint, whimsical, wonderfully colored little town . . . the sweetest, darlingest little city in the Antilles. Palm trees rise from courts and gardens into a warm blue sky,—indescribably blue,—that appears to touch their feathery heads. And all things, within and without the yellow vista, are steeped in a sunshine electrically white,—in a radiance so powerful that it lends even to the pavements of basalt the glitter of silver ore.

Men wearing only white canvas trousers, and immense hats of bamboo grass,—men naked to the waist and muscled like sculptures. Some are very black; others are of strange and beautiful colors: there are skins of gold, of brown bronze, and of ruddy bronze. Women pass in robes of brilliant hues,—women of the color of fruit, orange-color, banana-color,—women wearing turbans with such burning yellow as bars the belly of a wasp. . . . The warm air is thick with the scents of sugar and cinnamon,—with odors of mangoes and custard-apples, of guava-jelly and of fresh coconut milk,—a grand tepid wind enveloping the city in one perpetual perfumed caress.

Straight as palms and supple and tall, these colored women and men impress one wonderfully by their dignified carriage and easy elegance of movement. They walk without swinging of the shoulders— the perfectly set torso seems to remain rigid; yet the step is a long, full stride, and the whole weight is springingly poised on the very tip of the bare foot. All, or nearly all, are without shoes, and the treading of many feet over the heated pavement makes a continuous, whispering sound.

The greater number of the women carrying burdens on their heads—peddling vegetables, cakes, fruit, ready-cooked food from door to door—are very simply dressed in a single plain robe of vivid colors reaching from neck to feet. These women can walk all day long up and down hill in the hot sun, without shoes, carrying heavy loads on their heads. And the creole street cries, uttered in a sonorous, far-reaching high key, interblend and produce random harmonies very pleasing to hear.

• • •

As his family's trunks and furniture were being carried into the governor's mansion in Fort-de-France, Louis Mouttet was already making arrangements to meet the colony's most prominent citizens. Among them: Amédee Knight, Martinique's elected senator to the French Parliament and the first black man to hold that office; Fernand Clerc, one of the island's most successful planters and a major employer; and Andréus Hurard, publisher and editor of *Les Colonies*, the leading newspaper, published daily in St. Pierre.

Two of these three overtures did not get off to a good start.

Senator Knight promptly snubbed the new governor. Knight was well educated, having studied at the École Centrale in Paris. He owned his own plantation. He had been an assistant mayor of Fort-de-France, secretary of the chamber of commerce, and had served as president of the town council. In 1899, he ran for the Senate as the candidate of the Radical Party, a new and loosely organized voice of Martinique's heretofore politically silent black and mulatto majority. His spectacular victory in that election had stunned many whites, and for the first time ever it gave the black population a voice in Paris. In the French Senate, Knight aggressively pushed for reforms in education, housing, and employment.

Coming up in May was another election, not for Knight's Senate seat but for Martinique's two members of the lower house, the Chamber of Deputies. Knight had been working feverishly to transform Martinique's Radical Party into a philosophically and politically coherent organization that could carry the election and amplify Knight's voice in Paris. He had little interest in talking to a white Frenchman who had just arrived from another colony, whose motives were automatically suspect, and who in any case (as an appointed rather than an elected official) was supposed to remain politically neutral. In fact, the Radical Party had been busy establishing a position that the governor should be *elected locally* rather than appointed. Amédee Knight felt that to accept Mouttet's invitation would be to acknowledge the legitimacy of an inherently illegitimate office, and this he would not do.

Mouttet's meeting with Fernand Clerc was awkward at best. Clerc traced his ancestry to the first shipload of colonists that had settled in Martinique in 1635, and he expected that his own descendants would continue to live in the colony forever. He had an elegant home in St. Pierre, a large plantation on the northeast shore of the island, other landholdings near the town of Trinité, where he was mayor, and a country retreat at Parnasse, two miles outside St. Pierre. He had chosen the site of his country home to give him a view of St. Pierre below and Mont Pelée above, and his workers frequently saw him on his balcony with a telescope watching the activities on the shoreline with an almost paternal interest. He was a man of strong religious conviction, generous to the church, fair to all who worked for him, and deeply concerned about education and the plight of the poor as the colony entered the twentieth century. The presence of bordellos and other seamy activities in St. Pierre troubled him. And, he was thinking of running in the legislative election as a Progressive Republican. If he did, he would be opposing two other candidates: Louis Percin, a Radical, and Joseph Lagrosillière, a Socialist. Meanwhile, Fernand Clerc and Senator Amédee Knight knew each other well, and they conducted their political rivalry in an atmosphere of mutual respect. On issues of better education and working hours for the nonwhite laboring class, Clerc's position was close enough to that of the Radical Party that Knight had once remarked publicly, "If only he were black he might be a Radical!"

Mouttet's meeting with Clerc had barely passed the initial pleasantries when the planter asked the new governor about his heritage and education. Mouttet quickly shifted the subject back to Clerc's plantation and his business activities—an avoidance that Clerc didn't fail to notice. The planter then pointed out that "vice" was becoming a problem in St. Pierre, and said he hoped that Mouttet was the kind of leader who would take some strong corrective actions. Accustomed to letting everyone know where he stood, Clerc was not one to consider that this might not be the most appropriate topic for a first meeting with the new governor.

Meanwhile, it was by no means clear to Mouttet that prostitution was even a problem; indeed, in his travels around the globe he had seen many port cities much more decadent than St. Pierre. Where there were sailors, there was bound to be some sin. He was also well aware that taking any rash action to clamp down on "vice" before first learning who of importance he might offend would not be a wise way to begin his new position. Mouttet promised Clerc that he would take the suggestion under advisement.

To Fernand Clerc, the new governor came across as an opportunist with no convictions of his own. To Louis Mouttet, the planter seemed provincial and naive. Their short meeting ended awkwardly, both men realizing that their worldviews did not mesh very well. Had their relationship started out better, some terrible mistakes might have been avoided five months later.

Compared to his first two overtures, Mouttet found Andréus Hurard to be a breath of fresh air. Given how important it was for a new governor to have a sympathetic press, and with Hurard's *Les Colonies* the island's leading newspaper, Mouttet had wondered whether Hurard might expect special favors. Or worse, whether (like Senator Knight) the publisher might be too ethical to entertain a friendship with an appointed governor. But when Hurard walked in, Mouttet immediately knew that he liked the man's style. He was carrying a bottle of cognac and had already asked the housemaid to bring in a couple of glasses. After shaking hands, Hurard promptly poured the drinks and raised a toast to Mouttet's success and the happiness of his family. Mouttet lifted his glass and smiled.

Over the brandy, Hurard explained how *Les Colonies* had for many years supported Martinique's past governors on every issue. He assured Mouttet that he had every intention of continuing that practice, and that in return he asked nothing. Yet, of course, his newspaper did depend on advertising revenue, and the previous governors had always "encouraged" the island's businessmen to place ads with him. But he was asking no special favor; he was confident Mouttet would do what was best for Martinique.

Point made. Mouttet grinned and assured Hurard that they would be mutually supportive. This was a fellow he might get to like. And given the level of understanding that had so quickly developed, and possibly aided by the cognac, Mouttet brought up another matter: Fernand Clerc's concern about prostitution in St. Pierre.

Hurard stumbled only momentarily. Yes, there were a few bawdy houses on Rue St. Jean-de-Dieu, he admitted, but the women generally behaved themselves during the day and were pretty inconspicuous to polite society. And besides, wasn't it good for the economy if the sailors were happy?

Mouttet laughed at the rhetorical question. Hurard laughed back. And that was the end of the prostitution issue.

The conversation moved to Mouttet's experiences in Africa and Guiana, his family, the social scene in Martinique, France's subsidy of the island's sugarcane industry, and a few jokes about the weird Americans. The meeting would have lasted longer if it weren't for the ferry schedule. As he left, Andréus Hurard planted a parting thought: he told Mouttet that he personally found Fernand Clerc boring, his self-righteousness abominable, and that it was a damn shame that they were going to have to support the man's candidacy for the North Martinique seat in the French Chamber of Deputies.

• • •

Maria Mouttet settled into the governor's mansion with grace and dignity. It was indeed a beautiful colony, and Fort-de-France was a wonderful place to raise her family. She was elated that the children agreed; they had never before displayed such exuberant happiness. The social events, though loosely patterned after the traditions of France, were never high-pressure affairs here. And it was a simple matter for Maria and Louis to leave the children with the nannies for a day or two and take the ferry to St. Pierre, which always bustled with excitement and glamour. If there was prostitution in that city, she remained blissfully unaware of it. For Maria, life was perfect. For a few months, anyway.

And then, in the spring of 1902, Mont Pelée began to stir.

• CHAPTER 4 •

TARNISHED SILVER

•

For two generations, the mountain had been peace itself. Families picnicked on its slopes, children played on its paths and trails, and leeward residents viewed it as a benevolent protector against the fury of hurricanes. The first settlers had named it Bald Mountain in reference to the barren strip of rock that circled its broad summit. Later, whimsical locals began calling it Pelé, or French for "peeled" (curiously similar to but having no connection with Pele, the Hawaiian goddess of volcanoes). When an unknown mapmaker added a second "e" to the name in the mid-1700s, the mountain became Montagne Pelée.

Below an altitude of about 2,500 feet, Pelée's slopes were a picturesque rolling patchwork of forest, cane fields, and banana plantations, punctuated here and there with clusters of brightly painted homes. Above the tree line, and sustained by the cooler temperatures and substantial rainfall at the higher elevations, a thick growth of thigh-high ferns blanketed most of the mountain. Yet even through its vegetation, Pelée had a distinctly corrugated appearance, its flanks cleft with gorges and ravines that carried some twenty-five streams radially from the summit toward the coasts. At least ten of these streams flowed even during the dry season, supplying the villages as well as the city of St. Pierre with a continuous source of fresh water. This plentiful resource was used to keep everything from streets to laundry sparkling clean, to supply the local sugar and rum industries, and to provision the ships making port. No one considered that the gurgling rivulets could ever be harbingers of a catastrophe.

Eight miles to Pelée's southeast and reaching to an altitude of 3,963 feet (just a few hundred feet short of Pelée's own summit) stand the weathered cones of a cluster of older volcanoes, the Pitons du Carbet. The terrain here is even more rugged and gouged by ravines than Mont Pelée. In 1902, these mountains and their many dozens of gorges and arêtes presented insurmountable practical difficulties to building roads through the northern third of the island. Even today there are but a small number of roads through this region, and the ones that do exist often get washed out or buried under rockslides during the rainy season.

Around 1900, an English correspondent, commenting on the scarcity of roads and the impossibility of escape from St. Pierre should a calamity occur, described the city as shaped "like a dilemma, with a volcano on one horn and a tropical jungle on the other." Although a road did run along the coast from Fort-de-France through Carbet to St. Pierre, it was a maintenance nightmare and frequently impassable. This was also a tortuous path for both man and beast, for it snaked crazily while climbing from sea level to an altitude of a thousand feet or more, only to return again to sea level, then to climb and descend again. The most practical way, and sometimes the only way, to travel between St. Pierre and Fort-de-France was by ferry.

There were, however, two other land routes out of St. Pierre. Both took the traveler closer to Mont Pelée rather than away from it. One followed the coast north to the town of Precheur and a few small coastal villages beyond. The other was a picturesque, windy road that paralleled the Rivière Roxelane for a few miles, then, in a long switchback, climbed steeply to an arête where it continued on to the town of Morne Rouge. Here, about five miles into the interior and some 1,600 feet above sea level, many of St. Pierre's merchants maintained summer villas and retreats—places where they and their families could escape the coastal summer heat. The town itself, with a permanent population of about four thousand, straddled the saddle-shaped ridge that connected Mont Pelée and the Pitons du Carbet. From this vantage point, one got a grand view of the Atlantic Ocean to the northeast and of St. Pierre and the Caribbean Sea in the opposite direction. And to the northwest, just three miles from Morne Rouge, towered Mont Pelée.

Despite its proximity, getting to Pelée's summit took more than a casual stroll. The mountain's slopes grew steeper with altitude, and the last quarter mile or so of each of the alternative trails required hand-over-hand climbing on exposed rock. During the dry season, the sun could beat down mercilessly. During the rainy season—roughly May through November—the trails got muddy and slippery, and during a cloudburst they became torrents. Off the beaten paths, one was thigh-deep in ferns that were home to the potentially lethal pit viper, the *trigonocéphale*. And, during the rainy season, it was not uncommon for clouds to drift in and reduce visibility to a dozen feet or less.

But when conditions were right, the view from the top was spectacular. One could gaze in wonder at all the villages and towns below, the courses of the streams to the sea, the pitons and mornes and their wrinkled green blankets, the bustle of ships entering and leaving the roadstead at St. Pierre, the tip of the island of Dominica on the northern horizon, and overhead, a sky more beautifully blue than any Parisian baby's eyes.

The summit was not as flat as it appeared from below. It was a bowl-shaped crater, a hundred feet deep, that cradled a small crystal-clear lake. L'Etang de Palmistes, about three hundred feet across and averaging four feet deep, was lifeless and had a high mineral content, yet its water was potable. After the trek up the mountain, few could resist taking an invigorating swim here.

The rim of this summit crater was a circle of rocky humps, the tallest rising another two hundred feet. This highest point in all of Martinique gained the name Morne LaCroix after Morne Rouge's parish priest, Father J. Mary, engaged some of his parishioners to erect a twelve-foot crucifix here. On clearer days, his cross could be seen in silhouette against the sky from as far as St. Pierre.

But there was also a second larger crater, obscure to most of the area's inhabitants because it was surrounded by precipitous cliffs that all the beaten footpaths avoided. This crater, called L'Etang Sec (the dry lake) because it so rarely contained any water, lay at a lower elevation and closer to St. Pierre than the main crater. On the St. Pierre side, its rim had a great gash that dropped nearly a thousand feet into a rugged canyon. Spring water pouring into this gorge became the Rivière Blanche, which emptied into the sea between St. Pierre and the town of Precheur. Although there were occasional reports of a fumarole ejecting steam from the floor of L'Etang Sec after the eruption of 1851, for the most part this crater offered little of interest to justify the difficult hike to reach it. Many locals didn't even know it was there.

• • •

There is never a clear point in time when a volcanic eruption begins. Some would claim that Pelée's devastating explosion of 1902 was programmed by Mother Nature a billion years earlier, when she initiated the shifting motions of our planet's crustal plates. Others would cite the minor eruption of 1851 as the disaster's beginning, noting that volcanoes live on geologic rather than human timescales, and that to a volcano a fifty-year silence is like a human taking a moment to swallow in mid-sentence. Others would pick May of 1901.

It was then that a young couple strayed from a picnic party at L'Etang de Palmistes and ventured to the edge of the precipice bordering L'Etang Sec. Peering down into the dry crater, they noticed fumes rising from a small opening at the base of a dead tree. The air smelled of sulphur. They shared their observation with the rest of their group, everyone took a look, all shrugged, and no one thought much about it again for nearly a year.

At the Lycée Colonial in St. Pierre, Professor Gaston Landes had a habit of training the school's telescope on pretty much everything within view, including Mont Pelée. A few times in late 1901 he thought he had noticed wisps of vapor rising from the Etang Sec crater, and after some faint ground tremors in February of 1902 he began to watch more diligently. Some days the wisps seemed to be there, some days they weren't, and some days he couldn't tell, because the mountain was shrouded in clouds. But as a man of science, Landes continued his observations after many others would have gotten bored. And on April 2, 1902, there could be no doubt: clouds of steam and smoke were indeed rising from the upper valley of the Rivière Blanche.

During the following week, snakes, rodents, and beetles began abandoning the flanks of the mountain and creating a general nuisance in the villages below. On the plantations, cattle became skittish, and dogs barked through the night. In the cane fields, a change in wind direction sometimes delivered a blossom of sulphur oxides that could knock over a strong man. On Sunday, April 20, Professor Landes hiked close enough to see that fumes were pouring from at least two separate vents. And in St. Pierre, Clara Prentiss, the fastidious wife of the American consul, discovered to her displeasure that her silverware had tarnished again only a day after her servants had polished it.

Although Gaston Landes had more scientific training than anyone else on the island, he readily admitted that he knew little about volcanoes. The collections in the library at the Lycée, and even at the Bibliothèque Schoelcher in Fort-de-France, were not much help; the small amount of literature they had on the subject was fairly general. A few of those books did, however, include illustrated accounts of some dramatic flows of molten lava from Icelandic and Hawaiian volcanoes. Landes noted that such lava flows seldom killed anyone unless they weren't paying attention. Lava apparently does not move all that fast (its viscosity is usually similar to that of molasses), and of course it obeys the law of gravity and follows the contours of the land. When a lava flow threatens, Icelanders and Hawaiians know enough to get away from the lowest ground until the event is over. Here on Martinique, it would seem that Pelée's numerous gorges and ravines would channel any imaginable lava flow directly to the sea without threatening St. Pierre or its neighboring towns and villages. If that assessment were correct, then in the event of a major eruption people would simply need to stay out of the ravines.

Books, however, are written by humans, and Landes realized that no human can ever be the final authority on the mind of Mother Nature. He would need to continue making regular observations, decide what further questions needed to be explored, and then, if it seemed warranted, send a cablegram to the experts in Paris to seek their opinions on what he might do next.

On April 22, the seismoscope at the Lycée registered a small earthquake. Although Landes hadn't felt it himself, and neither had anyone else he talked to, he recorded the observation in his notebook. Meanwhile, the telegraph operators in St. Pierre discovered that they could not raise a response from Guadeloupe. Just north of Martinique, a cable lay severed on the sea floor. Dispatches, most of them describing commercial transactions, began to pile up.

On April 23, no one could deny that the volcano was indeed in eruption. Everyone on the northern third of the island heard the rumbling and felt the ground tremble. The wisps of steam of the previous weeks escalated to a column of dark ash billowing from the lower crater. The mountain seemed to have opened. A heavy smell of sulphur drifted into St. Pierre.

On April 24, early risers at the north end of town were greeted to a weird scene in the predawn shadows: a dusting of fine white ash covered everything in sight, as if there had been a frost or a snowfall. Throughout the rest of the day, Pelée monopolized everyone's attention with bursts of steam and ash. Some began to worry.

With daybreak on Friday, April 25, many breathed more easily on seeing only a benign-looking white plume rising from the mountain. Gaston Landes set up his telescope at the chamber of commerce so that a group of curious local businessmen could take turns inspecting the volcano. Then suddenly, around 8 a.m., the atmosphere reverberated with a series of detonations, and a cloud of smoke exploded from the mountain. Landes dashed to the telescope, peered through the eyepiece, then gasped at the sight of small rocks being tossed as high as one thousand feet above the Etang Sec. For the next two hours, a huge gray cloud poured from the volcano. The prevailing winds swept it over the coastal town of Precheur some three miles west of the crater, raining dust all along the way.

Duno-Émile Josse, a resident of Precheur, described the event in a letter that Andréus Hurard would publish in *Les Colonies* the following day:

GRAND-FONDS (PRECHEUR)
April 25, 1902

To the Editor of *Les Colonies*,

Permit me to ask a column of your esteemed journal in which to recite to the public a curious phenomenon that has surprised the inhabitants of our quarter of Mont Pelée.

Since more than three months ago we have sensed the odor of sulphur which has caused considerable disquietude with the inhabitants, and finally led to the recognition that it comes from the volcano. It increased steadily in intensity and quantity, and threw us into great fear, as the older inhabitants well recalled the eruption of 1851. In fact, at about eight o'clock on Wednesday morning, April 23, the earth trembled with a quite severe shock. Today, the 25th, at about the same time, it was noted that the atmosphere was darkening, and almost immediately it turned as if into an eclipse of the sun, accompanied by a deep growling. Suddenly a loud detonation, like the firing of a cannon, was heard; the sky appeared to be in places on fire, and there was a continuous fall of fine white ashes which the volcano was vomiting out. . . . These ashes were so abundant that at two meters distance people were unable to distinguish one another.

The frightened inhabitants, snatching with them their children and valuables, ran bewildered, as if stricken with blindness, to the right and to the left, returning to their houses, crying, praying, and at the same time asking assistance from near neighbors, who, themselves paralyzed by fear, were unable to respond to the appeals of their co-citizens. This condition continued for over an hour before a calm again settled. The rain of ashes lasted for about two hours.

Unfortunately, [in an effort to reach the source of the eruption] as we came within a certain distance of it, we were obliged to return. We were in the face of a steam-cloud that could be likened to that of several high-pressure boilers united, and which was in part white, in other parts black.

On the east side of St. Pierre, Julien Romaine stared in fascination at the billowing eruption cloud, but without a telescope he couldn't visually pinpoint the vent or see the flying rocks. Like many others, he assumed that the activity was taking place at the summit, the upper crater. When the incident subsided, he saddled his horse and rode to Morne Rouge to investigate more closely. There, he found the people surprisingly calm; apparently none of the episode had taken place on their flank of the mountain. Given that there seemed to be no danger, he continued up the slope as far as possible, then dismounted and climbed the rugged last two miles to the crater rim. And there he was greeted by a strange sight: where he expected to see the crystal-clear water of L'Etang de Palmistes, he instead found a pool of dark liquid bubbling like a witches' boiling brew. Puffs of vapor and jets of boiling water gurgled from it surface. Although visually it was a weird spectacle, intellectually he found it reassuring, for what harm could a big puddle of dirty boiling water possibly do? Particularly given that it was ringed by a high crater rim? He was too tired to carry on and check the lower crater (if he had done so, he might have become a bit more concerned). Riding back to St. Pierre, Romaine decided that the worst of the matter was that it would be a long time before the next mountaintop picnic or swim party.

The volcano remained calm into Sunday, April 27, emitting nothing more than a few intermittent puffs of vapor. After church services that morning, Eugène Berté led a group of five friends on an ascent to the summit. There they tramped around L'Etang de Palmistes and confirmed Romaine's observation of two days earlier: yes, it would certainly be quite a while before anyone would swim again in the crater lake. But the investigators were also interested in the lower crater, which several had viewed through Landes's telescope. They made their way around Morne LaCroix and descended the steep slope to the rim of L'Etang Sec. There, they discovered to their astonishment that the "dry lake" was now a frothing brew of silvery-gray liquid some six hundred feet in diameter and to all appearances quite deep. A new cinder-cone, around thirty feet tall, had formed at one side of the crater and boiling water was gushing from it. Ashes were everywhere. All the plant life was dead. And during the short time they took in this surreal scene, every piece of silver on their persons—from watch chains to vest buttons to the coins in their pockets—immediately tarnished. The next day, Berté reported the group's observations to Andréus Hurard at *Les Colonies*. Inexplicably, ten days would pass before Hurard published the account.

• • •

It was customary in Martinique to schedule elections for Sundays, when the balloting would not compete with commercial activities. On April 27, as Eugène Berté and his friends were hiking the mountain, voters throughout Martinique went to the polls in the first round of elections for the French Chamber of Deputies. The turnout was fairly typical, with 46.4 percent of the eligible voters casting ballots. For the constituency of North Martinique, Fernand Clerc topped the poll with 4,495 votes;

Louis Percin, the Radical Socialist, came in second with 4,167 votes; and the Socialist Workers' candidate, Joseph Lagrosillère, drew 753 votes. Because no one had gained a majority, the statutes called for a runoff election between the two top candidates. The date of the final balloting would be Sunday, May 11.

Although Andréus Hurard would not get these exact figures for another couple of days, it was pretty clear to him where matters were headed. He thought about the implications. It seemed likely that Lagrosillère's supporters would transfer their votes to Percin rather than Clerc, and if that happened, Clerc could lose the final election by a few hundred votes. Although Hurard personally had no great love for Fernand Clerc, a Radical Socialist like Percin in the Chamber of Deputies allied with Knight in the Senate would be a political disaster for the businessmen of the colony. At least Clerc was a businessman, and as such he wouldn't try to completely upset the island's economy.

With the outcome teetering on a few hundred ballots, Hurard knew that voter turnout would be a major factor. And the damned volcano could mess everything up.

• • •

On Monday, April 28, Mont Pelée growled a little but emitted almost no smoke or steam. The next day, an ash cloud again puffed from the summit and fine dust fell on St. Pierre, but the episode was benign compared to the startling ejections of the previous Friday. Then, despite the fact that it hadn't rained recently, several of the mountain streams began to swell, and the water of the Rivière Blanche took on a dark hue unbefitting its name. This curious phenomenon should have caused considerable concern, and even alarm, had it been interpreted properly. Instead, given that the activity at the summit hadn't escalated, many residents began to breathe a sigh of relief that the current eruption would be no more than a repetition of the 1851 event—when a bit of ash fell and smothered some vegetation; then after a few days the volcano returned to dormancy and slept quietly for fifty years.

When Professor Landes arrived at the Lycée on the morning of April 30, he noticed more wild scribbles on the seismoscope. He took the paper strip off the recording drum and unrolled it on his desk. No mistaking—there had been three small earthquakes during the wee hours that morning: at 3:40, 5:10, and 6:10 a.m. The vibrations had not been severe enough for most people to notice them, but they were earthquakes nonetheless. Landes added the observations to his notebook, then refilled the instrument's ink cartridge and clipped a fresh strip of paper around the recorder.

Only a few hours later, without any obvious collateral activity by the volcano or the weather, the usually benign Roxelane and Des Peres rivers swelled into raging torrents. The monstrous flash floods carried boulders and tree trunks into the city, striking so suddenly that they swept away several women who had been washing laundry in the streams. Dozens of others on the banks barely escaped with their lives. Until now, the only times these rivulets had ever been known to flood were during the heaviest of rains, and in fact the Rivière Des Peres often went completely dry.

Then, to further compound everyone's bewilderment, a hard rain fell that night, *after* the rivers had gone on a rampage. And during this downpour, contrary to all common sense, the water levels actually *receded*. Clearly, this was evidence that the flash floods had nothing to do with rain and surface runoff. Gaston Landes wrote the question in his notebook: "Where did all that floodwater come from?"

The morning of May 1 broke in splendor. The rain had washed most of the volcanic dust from the foliage, and the city sparkled in the sunshine. Although Pelée's summit was hidden in a white mist, such clouds at the mountaintop were a common enough sight. The commonplace can be reassuring, and it was; St. Pierre's marketplace quickly filled with the normal throng of vendors and customers.

Suddenly, a deep growl came from the mountain, as if some spirit from the underworld were warning people not to get too smug. The cloud at the summit darkened and expanded. All eyes went to the mountain. The anxiety, however, lasted only a few minutes. As abruptly as it started, the rumbling ceased, and the black cloud silently mushroomed upward and outward. The market went back about its business. An hour later, a sifting of fine ashes fell through the air and caused some sneezing, but to most it was only a minor annoyance. That night, the municipal band played in St. Pierre's plaza, just as it did every other Thursday night, weather permitting, and adolescents had their usual weekly supervised occasion to mingle.

Meanwhile, the people of Precheur did not fare as well, for through the entire afternoon the winds blew frightening amounts of ashes and fumes down the western slopes of the mountain and into that coastal town.

Friday, May 2, began with a violent, driving thunderstorm and ended with a heavy mist settling over St. Pierre. This was not a cleansing rain like that of the night of April 30 but rather a deluge of wet ashes. Had the volcano been visible that day, everyone would surely have grown alarmed at the size of the towering eruption column. In fact, throughout the day the giant ash cloud dumped tons of volcanic dust into the rain clouds below. Several inches of wet cementlike paste accumulated at the northern end of St. Pierre, and in Precheur the ash fell so thickly that lamps had to be lit. Those few children who showed up at the schools were sent back home. Meanwhile, in that day's issue of *Les Colonies,* Andréus Hurard announced that an expedition would climb to the summit that Sunday to again investigate the volcano's activities. Although the editor might be just as annoyed as anyone by the volcano, it was clear to his readers that he was not at all frightened by it.

When the rain lifted around sundown, Mont Pelée reverted to its quiet mood. Then just before midnight, as if the volcano had been merely resting up for its next tantrum, a violent series of ground tremors and brilliant flashes of lightning jolted everyone awake in the entire northern half of the island. At Morne Rouge, just three miles from the summit, the villagers rushed into the streets in pandemonium. Father J. Mary opened the doors of his church and herded his flock inside. As volcanic detonations rattled the windows of the sanctuary, the priest lit candles and led his parishioners in praying the rosary to their patron saint, Notre Dame de Délivrande.

This time, the volcano did not quiet down as quickly as in its earlier outbursts. Instead, it raged through the night, and by the morning of Saturday May 3, a monstrous black cloud enveloped the entire northern half of the island. Morne Rouge was now ankle-deep in ash, and Father

Mary sighed at the sight of the long line of parishioners waiting for him at the confessional. This would not be an easy day for him.

In St. Pierre, Clara Prentiss, wife of the American consul, sat and wrote a letter to her sister, Miss Alice Fry of Melrose, Massachusetts. This letter—an odd mixture of truth, imagination, and the unsubstantiated rumor of dying horses—would later contribute to a considerable amount of misunderstanding about the disaster:

My Dear Sister,

This morning the whole population of the city is on the alert, and every eye is directed toward Mount Pelée, an extinct volcano. Everybody is afraid that the volcano has taken into its heart to burst forth and destroy the whole island.

Fifty years ago Mount Pelée burst forth with terrific force and destroyed everything for a radius of several miles. For several days the mountain has been bursting forth, and immense quantities of lava are flowing down the side of the mountain.

All the inhabitants are going up to see it. There is not a horse to be had on the island. Those belonging to the natives are kept in readiness to leave at a moment's notice.

Last Wednesday, which was April 23, I was in my room with little Christine, and we heard three distinct shocks. They were so great that we supposed at first that there was someone at the door, and Christine went and found no one there. The first report was very loud, but the second and third were so great that dishes were thrown from the shelves and the house was completely rocked.

We can see Mount Pelée from the rear windows in our house, and although it is fully four miles away, we can hear the roar and see the fire and lava issuing from it with terrific force.

The city is covered with ashes, and clouds of smoke have been over our heads for the past five days. The smell of suphur is so strong that horses on the street stop and snort, and some of them are obliged to give up, drop in their harness, and die from suffocation. Many of the people are obliged to wear wet handkerchiefs over their faces to protect them from the strong fumes of sulphur.

My husband assures me that there is no immediate danger, and when there is the least particle of danger we will leave the place. There is an American schooner, the E. J. Morse, in the harbor, and it will remain here for at least two weeks. If the volcano becomes very bad we shall embark at once and go out to sea. The papers in this city are asking if we are going to experience another earthquake and volcano similar to that which struck here some fifty years ago.

. . .

That same morning, May 3, Pelée belched a thunderous cloud of dense yellow-brown smoke and vapor that expanded as far as Fort-de-France. When volcanic dust began to fall on the capital, Governor Mouttet could not avoid the fact that he had a problem.

He took the regular Girard Company steamer, *Rubis*, from Fort-de-France to St. Pierre, then he chartered a small launch to take him on to Precheur. There, just a few miles northwest of St. Pierre, he found that the eruption cloud had cast a deep shadow on that whole quarter of the mountain, flimsier roofs were collapsing under the weight of the ash accumulations, and people were on the verge of panic. Mouttet tried to offer assurances. If the situation were to warrant it, he promised, he would provide refuge for everyone in the barracks in St. Pierre and Fort-de-France. For now, however, no one's life was in danger, and there was no need for alarm.

In fact, Mouttet did not have the unilateral authority to quarter civilians in military barracks, and he well knew this. He could request such authority through channels, but that would be laborious: first the Ministry of Colonies in Paris, which would probably send the proposal through a labyrinth of other functionaries and offices to the upper military command, which might then (and who could say when?) filter it down to the officers in Martinique. That approach was clearly too risky to Mouttet's effectiveness, if not to his career. It would be better to approach the problem by discussing it directly with the local military command, which had certain discretionary powers in cases of emergency. But then, of course, *those* fellows would be taking a chance with their careers. Clearly, the whole matter hinged on whether the volcanic eruption was indeed an emergency. This was not a time for anyone to make a knee-jerk decision. Mouttet decided to think more about it.

At 1:05 p.m., as Mouttet was returning to his boat, a weird mudflow cascaded down the Rivière Blanche. Dr. Auguste Guérin, a wealthy industrialist whose sprawling sugar factory stood at the mouth of the river, began to worry. No one had the foggiest notion of what was causing all of these floods, nor of what strange thing might happen next. And, he noted cynically, volcanoes certainly don't obey dictums of assurance pronounced by a governor.

CHAPTER 5

AN OMINOUS WEEKEND

•

Andréus Hurard was no fool. He lived in St. Pierre himself, and he certainly knew that if the volcano should claim lives in the city, one of those lives could be his. On the other hand, he was far from convinced that the threat was that serious, and if other people's fear of the eruption should become a factor in the upcoming election, he did not want that development to favor Percin and the Radical Socialists. Percin was more popular with the simple folk in the country, while Fernand Clerc had a stronger constituency in St. Pierre and Morne Rouge. It surely wouldn't hurt Clerc's chances if the country people failed to get to the polls, but if throngs of St. Pierre's voters were to evacuate their city, that could spell political disaster for Clerc and the Progressive Republicans.

It would make no sense to try to have the election postponed. The governor had no authority to take such an action without the approval of the Parisian bureaucrats, and even if Mouttet were to go that route, what would a postponement accomplish? Nothing more than assuring that the election would be fair, in which case Clerc could easily lose!

Hurard's course of action was clear: encourage the rural folk to get off the mountain, prepare the people of St. Pierre for the influx, and try to keep St. Pierre's own voters in the city as long as possible. Hurard went to his print shop, fired up the burner under the melt pot, sent for his pressman, and sat at his linotype machine. Several hours later, thousands of copies of his broadsheet were distributed throughout the city:

St. Pierre Bay in 1766. (Heilprin 1903)

St. Pierre Bay circa 1900. (Morris 1902a)

St. Pierre Bay circa 1900. (Royce 1902)

The Rivière Roxelane in St. Pierre. (Heilprin 1903)

St. Pierre's theater. (Royce 1902)

Interior of St. Pierre's cathedral. (Heilprin 1903)

A street scene in St. Pierre. (Morris 1902a)

A street at the north end of town. (Morris 1902a)

Carrying goods to market. (Royce 1902)

A cane field on a lower slope of Mont Pelée.
(Royce 1902)

The steamship Roraima. *(Royce 1902)*

The Guérin sugar refinery. (Garesché 1902)

A cottage in the foothills. (Royce 1902)

Morne LaCroix, highest point in Martinique, circa 1900. (Kennan 1902)

The main street of Morne Rouge. (Royce 1902)

Front page of the last edition of St. Pierre's daily newspaper.

The only known photograph of Mont Pelée on the morning of the disaster. St. Pierre is off the photograph to the right, Precheur is to the left. (Heilprin 1903)

Les Colonies

EXTRAORDINARY EDITION

May 3

Mont Pelée and St. Pierre. Yesterday the people of St. Pierre were treated to a grand spectacle from our majestic smoking volcano. While lovers of beauty could not take their eyes from the volcano's ash cloud and the ensuing falls of cinder, more timid people in St. Pierre were committing their souls to God.

It would seem that many signs have warned us that Mont Pelée was in a state of serious eruption. There were slight earthquake shocks this noon. The rivers are in overflow. The need now is for the people outside St. Pierre to seek the shelter of the town. Citizens of St. Pierre! It is your duty to give these people succor and comfort.

Because of the situation in the interior, the excursion to Mont Pelée which had been organized for tomorrow morning will not leave St. Pierre, the crater being absolutely inaccessible. Those who were to have joined the party will be notified later when it will be found practical to carry out the original plan.

• • •

That afternoon, a primary teacher in St. Pierre, Roger Portel, wrote to his brother in France of the "flight of the frightened folk" from the slopes of Mont Pelée to the haven of St. Pierre. Women and children covered in gray ash carried all they could, and "great black lads strode along, bent double under the mattresses needed for the coming nights." Meanwhile, "old women at their windows mumbled their interminable prayers—for protection either from Montagne Pelée, or from the refugees or, perhaps, from both." Factories, shops, and businesses closed. The mayor sent out the fire department to hose ashes from the streets. Some onlookers joked that they should be hosing down the volcano instead.

Meanwhile, a second undersea cable snapped and cut off St. Pierre from Dominica. The local cable-repair ship *Grappler* was already occupied trying to repair the earlier failure of the cable to Guadeloupe. Martinique officials sent a frantic message to St. Lucia for assistance, and Admiral

Pierre Gourdon, commandant of the French naval force of the Atlantic, ordered the cable steamer *Pouyer-Quertier* under Captain Jules Thirion to leave Castries to assist with the repairs. Thirion's task would be to survey a corridor extending from just south of Dominica to St. Pierre, laboriously taking soundings and logging them before deciding where it might be most productive to begin dragging the bottom for the second broken cable. Meanwhile, the telegraphers in Martinique struggled with the complications of rerouting the increasing burden of dispatches over the six cables that remained intact.

In St. Pierre, that dismal Saturday, May 3, was a good day for writing to loved ones in France. Of the many letters that would later appear in the Paris newspapers, one that would be particularly widely quoted was mailed that day by a young lady to her sister in Paris:

> My calmness astonishes me. I am awaiting the event tranquilly. My only suffering is from the dust which penetrates everywhere, even through closed windows and doors. We are all calm. Mama is not a bit anxious. Edith alone is frightened. If death awaits us there will be a numerous company to leave the world. Will it be by fire or asphyxia? It will be what God wills. You will have our last thought. Tell brother Robert that we are still alive. This will, perhaps, be no longer true when this letter reaches you.

In the envelope, she included a sample of bluish gray powder that smelled slightly of sulphur. Her letter with its volcanic dust would arrive in Paris on May 18, 1902, ten days after the catastrophe that ended her life.

• • •

When Louis Mouttet returned to Fort-de-France that afternoon, he arranged for relief provisions to be loaded on the steam ferry *Topaz* for immediate distribution to the people of Precheur. The boat chugged off early that evening and would have docked at its destination around 7 p.m. if Precheur's shoreline had been visible. Unfortunately, the relief team found the town completely engulfed in another ash storm. When cinders began raining down on the *Topaz* itself, the captain retreated back to Fort-de-France, his cargo undelivered.

But even before Mouttet got this disappointing news, his concerns had been mounting. He foresaw that the eruption could grow into a serious threat to public safety, and if it did, he would need to be on record that he had not been ignoring it. He sat down that afternoon and wrote an official telegram on the matter to the Ministry of Colonies in Paris.

And here the story gets muddy, for there is a discrepancy about what he actually wrote. The version in the archives in Fort-de-France reads as follows:

FORT-DE-FRANCE, 3 MAY
Last night Montagne Pelée's volcanic eruption reached major proportions. The city of St. Pierre and the surrounding regions were covered by a thick layer of gray ashes, many detonations were heard, and there is a report that the summit of the mountain was surrounded by flashes of lightning. For around 2 hours in the morning, the crater emitted flames and projected a great volume of stones, some of which fell on the district of Montagne D'Irlande and Precheur, which is located more than 2 km east of the crater.
LOUIS MOUTTET
GOVERNOR

Although this document contains an error of geography (Precheur is actually west, not east, of the crater), its substance is generally consistent with the other published reports of the volcano's antics on the night of May 2 and the following morning. What is curious, however, is that the leading sentence of this telegram does not read at all like the first news that a volcano erupted, but rather like a follow-up report that the volcanic activity had escalated. Yet, based on the archives in Fort-de-France, this would seem to be the earliest communication Mouttet sent to Paris about the eruption.

There are, however, reports of another telegram. Some writers claim that on May 3 (or possibly May 4; the date is fuzzy), Mouttet sent the following cablegram to the Ministry of Colonies:

An eruption of Mont Pelée has taken place. Large quantities of ash were showered on the neighboring countryside. The inhabitants have had to abandon their dwellings hastily and seek refuge in St. Pierre. The eruption appears to be on the wane.

Much has been made of this latter message, whose original seems to have disappeared. Its language certainly reads like a *first* report of volcanic activity. If in fact this communication was cabled on May 3 or 4 and its wording is authentic, it suggests that Mouttet was being criminally irresponsible with the lives of his constituents. By no means, as Mouttet definitely knew, was the eruption *on the wane* at that time. Moreover, how could anyone defend his having waited so long—more than ten days—to inform the colonial ministry that there was an eruption in progress?

The writers who cite this second version of the telegram use it to support their arguments that Mouttet was culpable for thirty thousand deaths. His alleged motive was to keep people in St. Pierre at least through the election. Unfortunately, such writers conveniently ignore the other version of Mouttet's May 3 cablegram—the one that is actually on record. Compounding the confusion, the colonial ministry never did go out of its way to circulate the text of any "official" document. Apparently, some of the French bureaucrats were content to see blame for the disaster heaped on a dead governor whose family name was far from prominent.

The issue of what Mouttet did or didn't write on May 3 can be evaluated (if not perfectly resolved) without attacking the authenticity of either cablegram. If both messages are assumed genuine, then one was obviously written before the other, and the content of the one with the missing date clearly puts it first ("An eruption . . . has taken place . . . " versus "Last night . . . [the] eruption reached major proportions"). And when might that initial message have been sent? The numerous eyewitness accounts tell us that the volcano awoke gradually, then erupted briefly on April 23 and 24, again briefly but more violently on the twenty-fifth, then did little more than vent steam on the twenty-sixth, twenty-seventh, and twenty-eighth. On the twenty-ninth, it again ejected ash, and several streams swelled. There were serious floods on the thirtieth. On May 1, a large burst led to a heavy ashfall in Precheur. And on May 2, the volcano threw a violent fit. Any governor would surely have cabled a message to the colonial ministry early in this sequence, and indeed the wording of the "An eruption . . . on the wane" telegram suggests that it was probably sent on April 26, 27, or 28, when the eruption indeed seemed to be on the wane. Given that in 1902 April 26 and 27 fell on a Saturday and Sunday, it seems most likely that Mouttet cabled the first news of the eruption to Paris on or about Monday, April 28.

One other titbit suggests that the "An eruption . . . " telegram, if authentic, had to have been dispatched prior to May 3. On that date, Louis Mouttet witnessed firsthand the effects of the ashfall in Precheur. It seems unlikely that he would omit mention of this town in a message he would write that same day; indeed, his later actions would demonstrate a considerable concern for the safety of Precheur's residents. But a few days prior, he would have had no reason to mention Precheur in an initial cable to Paris, simply because nothing serious had yet happened there. The archived telegram, dated May 3, indeed mentions Precheur; the undated dispatch does not.

It seems, then, that Mouttet did responsibly inform the colonial ministry of the initial eruption on or about April 28, then followed up on May 3 with a second cable reporting the escalation (". . . eruption reached major proportions"). Yet in neither instance did Paris reply.

Why not? Probably because the Paris offices of the colonial bureaucracy were so routinely swamped with trivial cablegrams from distant governors attempting to go on record only to cover their behinds. For a bureaucrat to acknowledge one of these messages meant to enter a bond of shared responsibility for its consequences. Mouttet had made no specific requests, and the system provided no incentive for anyone in Paris to answer. "No action requested, no response expected" was the modus operandi of the colonial ministry.

Under these circumstances, it is hardly surprising that Mouttet's initial cablegram would disappear after the disaster. Nor is it surprising that when a version of it eventually did surface, its missing date would be represented as some five to seven days later than its actual transmission. Who would want to admit that official news of the eruption had reached Paris a full ten days before the disaster yet was never acknowledged? Better to let Louis Mouttet become a convenient and silent scapegoat for the sea of blood that was shed through the ineptitude of the colonial bureaucracy.

And so, as the calendar ticked toward doomsday, Mouttet's cablegrams languished in a pile of inconsequential papers on the desk of an obscure bureaucrat in the Ministry of Colonies in Paris.

• • •

Rural families living on Pelée's slopes watched their crops being smothered, outbuildings collapsing under the weight of the ash, and livestock and poultry dying. The usually pure water from the streams had become murky and foul-tasting. Overhead, the ash cloud showed no sign of shrinking. From time to time the volcano made ominous rumbling noises, and sometimes the rumbles could even be felt through the ground. Then came the word that everyone living in the hills would be welcome in St. Pierre; the newspaper had just said so. Hundreds of families picked up what they could carry and began the trek to the city.

Even before the extra edition of *Les Colonies* hit the streets, Philomène Gerbault, a forty-seven-year-old widow and cousin to the deputy governor, had already made up her mind. She told her stable man to hitch up her carriage while she helped her maid pack her trunks for the tortuous journey over the coastal road to her second home in Fort-de-France. A few weeks later, she would describe her experience to Professor Angelo Heilprin:

> The passing of the carriage made no noise. The wheels were well muffled by the ash. The horses, removed from the shelter of their stable, snorted from the effects of the sulphur fumes. The streets were hard to negotiate. People would not give way, and it demanded a lot of patience and firmness to force a passage.
>
> One can hardly imagine a more hopeless scene of impending ruin; for what the volcano had thus far spared, or seemed disposed to spare, the torrential waters of the descending streams threatened to claim. Birds lay asphyxiated by the ash. The cattle suffered greatly. Children wandered aimlessly about the streets with their little donkeys, like little human wrecks. We passed a group of children going hesitantly down the Rue Victor Hugo. They looked as if they were covered with hoar frost. In the countryside, desolation prevailed. Little birds lay dead under the bushes, and in the meadows the few living animals were restless—bleating, neighing, and bellowing in despair. But as we travelled deeper into the countryside, an eternal silence seemed to envelop everything. It was all the eerier when viewed by the light of the glowing cone of Pelée.

Madame Gerbault's carriage was but a quarter of the way to Fort-de-France that evening of May 3 when the silence was broken by a series of explosions.

They were frightful detonations. And then we observed one of the most extraordinary sights in nature—Mont Pelée awake at night. The glowing cone was soon hidden by an enormous column of black smoke traversed by flashes of lightning. The rumbling grew deeper. A few moments later a rain of ashes fell upon the countryside.

Through that night, the lightning and explosions continued. The rural folk huddling in mountainside cabins deliberated their options for the next day. In most cases, they decided to move into St. Pierre as soon as possible. St. Pierre's population began to swell.

• • •

On Sunday, May 4, early risers found thousands of dead birds littering St. Pierre's streets and floating in the bay. An inch of new ash had accumulated overnight, and more was falling. Most of the mountain lay invisible behind swirling clouds of volcanic dust and fog.

In Fort-de-France, Louis Mouttet had spent a sleepless night. Although the volcano lay thirteen miles from the Governor's Mansion, the sounds of the distant eruption had kept his mind churning. He knew he had been indecisive the past few days, and that he would not get away with such behavior for long. In earlier years in the Paris salons, he had heard the aphorism "to not decide is to decide," at that time jokingly applied to the wide choice of available women. Now the cliché took on a whole new and more serious meaning: any decision without a full understanding of the risks was a sure program for disaster. He thought about the issues. His personal career and reputation. Families who might lose everything they owned. Possibly lives. But those were general risks; could he get more specific? Was there a danger from earthquakes? Noxious gases? Floods? And what perils might result from an unnecessary evacuation? As these loosely related thoughts raced through his mind, it occurred to him that his quandary arose from the fact that he was totally ignorant about volcanoes: what they were capable of doing to humans and the things humans value.

He decided to assemble a commission of experts to advise him. He rolled out of bed, sent for his secretary, and went to his office. To chair the commission, he appointed Lieutenant Colonel Jules Gerbault, the chief artillery officer on the island. The other four members would be: Paul Alphonse Mirville, head chemist of the colonial troops; William Léonce, a civil engineer; and Eugène Jean Doze and Gaston Jean-Marie Theodore Landes, both professors of natural science at the Lycée of St. Pierre. Appointment letters were to be dispatched immediately, and notifications sent to a list of officials and diplomats that this commission would begin its work as soon as possible. Not in the capital, but in St. Pierre, where everyone could actually see the volcano.

Many writers have since criticized this commission as a farce, suggesting that it was handpicked to rubber-stamp the governor's preconceived intent to keep people from evacuating St. Pierre. But was its composition really that inappropriate? Although Gaston Landes was no expert on volcanoes, he did know more about them than anyone else on the island, and not a whole lot less than anyone else in the world knew in 1902. Landes and Doze worked together, so Doze was a natural choice to give Landes someone to bounce his ideas off without violating the confidentiality of the commission's deliberations. Léonce did not know much about geology, but he did know about structures like bridges, roads, and buildings, and the forces they could withstand. Mirville, as a chemist, could assess the risk from the sulfurous gases and ash. As for Gerbault—if the situation should require an evacuation or a declaration of martial law, a military participation in that decision would be essential.

Mouttet charged this commission with advising him on how long St. Pierre could "scientifically" withstand the strain of the ash and the sulfur. The group's objective was to establish the safety of St. Pierre, and not to waste time talking about the phenomenology of the eruption. Mouttet has been criticized for this restricted agenda as well, as if this seals the verdict that he had preordained conclusions and wanted his handpicked commission to simply act as window dressing. But this is not likely. This was, after all, 1902—long before anyone would see the dramatic videotapes of the 1980 explosion of Mount St. Helens or the frightening re-creations of pyroclastic events in later Hollywood productions. Pelée's eruption was a full four miles from St. Pierre, and in 1902 the only imaginable hazards at that distance were tainted air, falling ash, and molasses-like flows of molten lava. Mouttet was interested in having his commission stay on-task, so they could quickly advise him on a course of action. To demand any less under the circumstances would have been irresponsible.

. . .

Sunday, May 4. St. Pierre's bishop was on a three-month retreat in France, and the vicar-general of Martinique, Monseigneur Gabriel Parel, drove in from Fort-de-France to offer Sunday mass at St. Pierre's cathedral. That morning, he made an announcement from the pulpit: He was bringing word that the governor had established a scientific commission to determine whether the volcano posed any risks to the city. With that, he began his homily with a reading from Psalm 46: "Therefore we shall not fear, though the earth be moved, and though the mountains be carried into the midst of the sea. Though the waters thereof roar and be troubled, though the mountains shake with the swelling thereof."

Fernand Clerc fidgeted in his pew and pulled at his collar. The previous day, he had pleaded with a group of prominent townspeople, including Mayor Rodolphe Fouché, to take the volcano seriously and petition the governor to evacuate St. Pierre. Already, some twenty people and scores of animals had been swept out to sea by the misbehaving Rivière Roxelane, and now other rivers were also flooding. Birds and small animals were dropping dead, and the smell of sulfur hung everywhere. Yet Clerc had garnered no cooperation or support.

Part of Clerc's problem was that he wasn't much of a rhetorician. Even when he gave campaign speeches to his supporters, they often yawned. Meanwhile, Senator Amédee Knight was playing upon the superstitions of the electorate, telling his constituents, "The mountain will only sleep when the whites are out of office!" To many of the illiterate Martiniquians whose culture was rooted in an amalgam of animism and Catholicism, Knight's antics found fertile ground. And Knight, in supporting Clerc's opponent in the upcoming election, did not consider this the best time to agree with Clerc on *anything*.

But that disappointment had come yesterday. Today, Clerc found it especially aggravating that even the vicar-general was denying the danger from the pulpit and actually lulling the parishioners into an unwarranted sense of security. Clerc dutifully discharged his Sunday obligation by staying through communion, then hustled his wife and three children back toward their city home. The streets were clogged with refugees. Four miles away, the mountain continued to rumble. Clerc was convinced that the city needed to be evacuated. But instead, more people were actually moving in!

Clerc would later explain that the only reason he himself had stayed in St. Pierre the previous day was to try to persuade the local leaders to take action. During the ride home from church, he reflected that he was probably not cut out to be a legislator. He didn't have much patience with other politicians' personal agendas; all he wanted was the best for the colony and its citizenry. Perhaps he shouldn't bother to campaign anymore for the legislative office. And if by some chance he were actually to be elected in the May 11 runoff, maybe even then he should just resign and go about his own business, which was much more personally rewarding.

It was time, he decided, to leave St. Pierre and go to his country home in Parnasse. If it seemed that his family might not be safe there, they would move on to their plantation at Vivé, on the northeast coast. And if Vivé appeared threatened, they could go to Trinité, where he and his brother had properties and Clerc himself was titular mayor.

In front of his city home, an elegant place with a dozen bedrooms, he climbed out of his carriage with the intention of telling his servants to begin packing. Before he could get that far, two families he knew socially pulled up in wagons heaped with personal belongings. They had left their hillside plantations to seek the safety of St. Pierre until the danger passed. Would the Clercs take them in?

Fernand Clerc looked at the volcano, said a quick prayer, then opened his doors to his unexpected guests. This coming Thursday was the Feast of the Assumption, a holy day of obligation; he and his family would stay in St. Pierre at least until then.

• • •

On the remote northeast slope of Pelée, connected to Morne Rouge by a winding five-mile road, lay the village of Ajoupa-Bouillon. Its most significant structure was its small baroque church, built in 1846 and enlarged over the following decades, which had survived the great hurricane of 1891 essentially unharmed. Flowing east through the lower part of the village was the Rivière Falaise, usually a tiny brook at this time of the year. On the evening of Sunday May 4, news began to trickle into St. Pierre that there had been horrible flash floods in Ajoupa-Bouillon and several other villages on the eastern flanks of the volcano. The rumor was that hundreds of people had died. It proved to be only a slight exaggeration.

• • •

In St. Pierre, Clara Prentiss couldn't sleep. She arose, went to her desk, and wrote another letter to her sister Alice in Massachusetts:

I write under the gloomiest of impressions, although I hope I exaggerate the situation. Thomas laughs, but I sense that he is full of anxiety. He has stopped telling me to leave, knowing that I cannot go alone. The heat today is suffocating. When we came out of Mass, I saw that many of the people were obliged to wear wet handkerchiefs to ward off the sulphur fumes. Even though there have been no fresh ashfalls for some hours, the air is oppressive. Your nose burns. I ask myself if we are all going to die asphyxiated. I wonder what tomorrow will bring.

There are rumors everywhere of impending disaster. People talk of a flow of lava, a rain of stones, or even a cataclysm from the sea. Who can tell? Though for myself I do not believe all I hear. The volcano continues to surpass itself. After producing a great black cloud, evil yet impressive, it disgorged huge shapes of cloud which were lost in a storm. But in the last hour it is calm. My thoughts now turn to other things. Food is scarce. This lunchtime the cook could only offer chicken, beans, and potatoes. It was poor fare for a Sunday, but probably better than most could expect. . . .

The atmosphere in town is strained. There are outbreaks of stealing and fighting. Troops are on hand to keep order, and Thomas says they are succeeding. Yet most people, in spite of it all, are content to stay in the town. This morning there was a small exodus from here, but now it has stopped. People sleep where they can, in the streets, even against the walls of our home. They wait, as we all do, for the arrival of the Governor's Commission. It is a curious thing, but I cannot share their relief at the coming of the Commission. How will the Commission end the dust that enters everywhere, burning our faces and eyes?

At least one member of the commission, Gaston Landes, would find himself wondering the same thing.

• CHAPTER 6 •

LAHAR

•

Thousands of feet beneath the Lesser Antilles, the slow but relentless westward creep of the Atlantic floor was driving a wedge under the Caribbean plate and squeezing a huge bulge of hot magma toward the surface. The planetary crust here is pockmarked with old and not-so-old volcanoes—sites that have vented geothermal pressures in the past, then were plugged when the upward-swelling molten rock cooled and solidified. In the spring of 1902, on the islands of both Martinique and St. Vincent, a great unplugging had begun.

Earth's "crust" is just that: a thin flaky layer of rock that floats on a hot, viscous mantle. This solid portion of our planet extends down only fifteen to thirty-five miles below the continental masses, and as little as three miles beneath the oceans—not very thick at all for a globe whose radius measures 3,964 miles. The terra firma we take for granted is but a thin and fragile shell separating us and our human artifacts from the searing heat of the viscous mantle beneath. And this thin crust is everywhere moving: whole continents drifting, sea floors disappearing into the subduction zones of the great oceanic trenches, and new sea floors emerging from midoceanic rifts. Meanwhile, the underlying mantle is not static either; it also moves in slow but huge swirls and eddies, differentially heating the crust above and causing it to expand and contract unpredictably. The thinner the section of overlying crust, the more volatile this interaction. Too thin, and the combination of magma pressure and thermal stresses can trigger earthquakes and crustal fractures. And volcanic eruptions.

But such ideas about geological processes were still in their scientific infancy in 1902. Although seismology had demonstrated its potential as a scientific tool with the terrible Japanese earthquake of November 3, 1880, its full credibility would not be established until after April 18, 1906, when it would be used to locate the epicenter of the great San Francisco earthquake. After that success, twentieth-century scientists analyzing seismographic data would begin to unlock the puzzles of the planet's interior structures and their dynamics: learning of the existence of Earth's mantle and core, measuring the thickness of the crust, and exploring the correlations between earthquakes and volcanic activity. But in 1902 all of these discoveries were yet to come, and the paper recordings from Professor Landes's crude seismoscope still lacked a theoretical framework to interpret them. The scribbles on those charts at the Lycée remained cryptic messages from the depths of the planet with no guide to their translation.

The higher elevations of Martinique get a lot of rain, sometimes as much as two hundred inches in a year. Before it can reach the sea, much of this precipitation seeps into the underground streams and reservoirs inside the island's ancient volcanoes. As Louis Mouttet grappled with his responsibilities as governor and tens of thousands of his constituents worried about their personal priorities, the magma swelling beneath everyone's feet was heating those underground lakes and streams to a boil.

More than a century earlier, James Watt had noticed that boiling away just a quart of water will produce 1,700 quarts of steam, and he used this expansion principle to build the steam engine that would drive the Industrial Revolution. Mother Nature, however, was way ahead of Watt, for she had been using the expansion of steam to power her earth-moving equipment since the first mists of dawn on the planet. In early May of 1902, expanding steam was forcing hot subterranean water toward the surface of northern Martinique, in a precursor of the terrible events to come.

• • •

Monday, May 5. At daybreak, ash was raining over the entire northern half of the island. The Rivière Blanche was acting strangely—oscillating between ebbing and swelling, with an occasional surge that swept boulders along its bed. A few miles upstream of Precheur and three thousand feet higher in elevation, the normally dry crater lake of L'Etang Sec was growing wider and deeper, its surface licking at the base of the crater's great southwestward-facing gash.

By 8 a.m., the misbehaving Rivière Blanche had attracted hundreds of spectators on both of its banks. The flow was no longer oscillating but had stabilized at a high level of continuous fury. A few brave souls watched from the wooden bridge, which shuddered visibly as the furious stream pummeled its piers. Gaston Landes was not about to take a chance crossing that bridge; he climbed off his horse and walked to the south bank, where he scooped out a handful of water. He was tempted to taste it, but its murky grayish brown color discouraged him. It was also uncharacteristically warm—not that there could be any doubt about the source of that heat. But what mainly piqued his curiosity about this water was that there was *so much of it* when the rainy season had yet to begin. He held his pocket notebook at arm's length, using it as a gauge to estimate the stream's width, then he tossed a series of sticks into the river and timed their motion. He surmised the torrent's depth from the observation that it was now teasing at the bridge's deck. Then he did some arithmetic and rechecked his figures in amazement.

Landes's activity attracted the attention of Dr. Auguste Guérin, whose sprawling sugar and rum factory at the river's mouth employed more than two hundred men and women. The economic ripple effect of the Usine Guérin supported at least ten times that employment figure; in fact, the town of Precheur would never have grown beyond a collection of a few fishermen's huts if Guérin's factory were not located so close by. The distillery's eighty-foot chimney was a colony landmark visible from most of St. Pierre and had become a nautical bearing point for vessels approaching Martinique from the northwest. But Guérin's well-developed operation had been plagued in the past week by a weird problem: hordes of ants and centipedes, apparently displaced from the upper slopes by the eruption, were invading his warehouses. And they loved sugar. A conversation took place whose exact words have long been lost, but whose general substance seems to have been as follows:

Guérin asked Landes if he could estimate when all this nonsense was likely to end. Landes shrugged and held out his page of calculations. The Rivière Blanche, he explained, was now flowing at a volume five times greater than ever before recorded.

"And does that explain the centipedes and ants?" asked Guerin.

"No," said Landes, "but it does suggest that the problem may be more serious than centipedes and ants."

Guérin and Landes stood gazing up the valley at the weird sight. Pelée's summit was engulfed in a swirling black cloud that seemed to be belching in two directions at once: from its top, a turbulent eruption column rising high into the sky; from its bottom, this angry runaway river. Maybe it was a similar event, Landes may have mused, that had led the ancient Greeks to postulate the four "essences" of earth, air, fire, and water. Certainly those four ancient elements seemed to be intimately intertwined here this morning. As for more modern scientific ideas, Landes grappled with how they might apply to this strange event.

"So what's going to happen next, Professor?" the industrialist asked.

Landes shrugged. "I wish I knew."

"But don't you scientists know everything?"

"Hardly, Dr. Guérin. If we did, we wouldn't be scientists. We'd be encyclopedias."

"I'm a man who likes answers."

"Sorry, Doctor, but I'm a man who doesn't have them. Right now, all I have is questions."

With that, Gaston Landes mounted his horse, wished Dr. Guérin good luck, and rode back toward St. Pierre, brushing ash off himself the entire way. One thought was apparently on his mind: Nothing he had ever read in any book had mentioned flooding streams as a collateral effect of volcanic activity.

Although Auguste Guérin usually projected the air of a tough businessman, in fact he was growing more deeply concerned about his family than he was about his factory. A few days earlier, he had booked passage for his wife, children, daughter-in-law, and household staff to sail to Paris on the Quebec liner *Roraima* on May 9. Until now he hadn't considered that any of them were in any mortal danger; he had made the travel arrangements independent of the volcano, to attend a long-planned family reunion. Today, for the first time, he began to think about the proximity of his mansion to the rampant river. He returned home, directed a servant to check whether a close friend's yacht, the *Carbet*, was getting ready for departure to St. Pierre, and advised his son Eugène and his daughter-in-law to get ready in case they needed to evacuate.

That much preparation, he figured, was certainly prudent. But to actually shut down the factory would be a serious decision: the boilers and furnaces ran continuously through night and day, and if they cooled off it would take many days to restart the operation. Moreover, he could not simply walk away from a warehouse full of rum and expect it to still be intact on his return. He would make all possible contingency preparations, keep a close watch on the raging river and the volcano, then plan his actions that afternoon. As he sat at his dining room table for lunch, he briefly felt the floor tremble.

• • •

In St. Pierre, it was 12:45 p.m. when the sea abruptly receded. Detritus of the harbor bottom lay exposed out to fifty yards from shore: old rusted machinery, the hulks of fishing boats sunk in the hurricane of 1891, items of cargo that had fallen overboard during loading or unloading. In coastal towns in other places at other times, such incidents had been known to attract throngs of the curious, who then perished in the return wave. In St. Pierre, the residents somehow knew better. Rather than descend to the uncovered harbor bottom to root for items to salvage, most ran immediately in the opposite direction to higher ground. And indeed, within a few minutes, the sea returned in a huge swell that inundated the entire waterfront area to a depth of five feet.

The damage in St. Pierre was minimal: one yacht sunk and some cargo on the docks lost. Although thousands of barrels of rum were swept into the harbor, they floated fairly well, and all were quickly recovered. The main unfortunate effect of this tsunami would be to convince many people that the threat was from the sea rather than from the volcano.

Then, within a few hours, terrible news began to trickle in from Precheur. Some stories reported dozens of victims; other accounts said up to 150. Whatever the number of dead, there clearly had been a disaster close to home. And a truly weird one.

• • •

The Usine Guérin was more than an industrial operation; it was a complex that sprawled over hundreds of acres in the style of the island's plantations, with a mansion, gardens, dependencies, cottages for the house servants, and then the factory itself. At age seventy-two, Dr. Auguste Guérin had spent most of a lifetime building the place, and even the visual appearance of his mill and warehouses reflected his loving attention. The distillery part of the operation was close to the river, where it could draw fresh water, with the mansion standing on only slightly higher ground.

Shortly after noon on May 5, one of the foremen, Joseph Du Quesne, burst into Guérin's dining room screaming. "Hurry! Hurry! It's an avalanche! Run!" Guérin, already on edge, bolted out the door and looked up the valley toward the volcano. Du Quesne was already running toward higher ground. A monstrous steaming mass was speeding in their direction, riding on the floodwaters of the Rivière Blanche. For everyone else in the household, there was no hesitation in running toward the yacht. But Guérin stopped and went back to the house—to get his hat, he would later explain—and this saved his life. In Guérin's words:

Then I heard a noise I can't compare with anything else—an immense noise—like the devil on Earth! A black avalanche, beneath white smoke, an enormous mass more than ten meters high and at least 159 meters wide, full of huge boulders, was coming down the mountain with a great din.

My unfortunate son and his wife ran away from it toward the shore. All at once, the mud arrived. It passed ten meters in front of me. I felt its deadly breath. There was a great crashing sound. Everything was crushed, drowned, and submerged. My son, his wife, thirty people, and huge buildings were all swept away.

Three of those black waves came down . . . making a noise like thunder, and made the sea retreat. Under the impact of the third wave, a boat moored in the factory harbor was thrown over a wall, killing one of my foremen who was standing near me. I went down to the shore. The desolation was indescribable. Where a prosperous factory—the work of a lifetime—had stood a moment before, there was now nothing left but an expanse of mud forming a black shroud for my son, his wife, and my workmen.

All remaining visible of the factory was the top half of its eighty-foot chimney, still smoking. Guérin lost his wife, Josephine, his youngest son Joseph and Joseph's wife, his daughter, Sarah, and five of his household staff, all of whom were to have sailed for Paris on the *Roraima* on May 9. The destiny of this particular set of victims was doubly cursed, for on May 9 the *Roraima* itself would be in flames and sinking.

Meanwhile, Father Alte Roche was on a mountain footpath south of St. Pierre, on a trek to Morne Verte to administer to the pastoral needs of some rural families. At an altitude of about 2,200 feet, he sat to rest and looked out on the volcano and the coast below. He could see Precheur and had a good view of the lower end of the Rivière Blanche. His own words describe what he saw next:

> Hardly had the midday hour passed on this Monday when the gates of the volcano were parted and a flood of boiling mud was sent hurling down the mountainside to be flung from it into the sea. In three minutes, it had covered its last three miles to the ocean, and within that time it had left nothing visible of the Guérin refinery but the chimney—a post projecting from a desert of black boiling and seething mud. The factory had stood as a symbol for what it represented through long years of toil and conquest. Now it had disappeared as if the hand of the Devil had smothered it.

Another witness, Louis Labatut, watched in horror from a spot just outside the zone of destruction. That evening, he would tell his story to Andréus Hurard:

> At the outer edges of the mud flow, I could see people struggling to free themselves. One of them was Julie Gabou, the coalwoman. Then moments after the factory had been drowned, which was a little after twelve o'clock, a boiling waterspout burst from the mountain, leaping all obstacles in gigantic bounds, flowing over the already vanished works and killing all those still struggling in the mud. Then I

saw that the mud and the waterspout were no more than a terrible prologue. Behind them a torrent of water laden with rocks and earth came pouring down the side of Pelée to raze the whole region and to form a mud plain that extends from the sea to the *grand-bois*. The mud destroyed the yacht of the Moregut family as it rode at anchor, waiting in vain for the household of Dr. Guérin to appear. Where there had been sea, there was now nothing but mud.

The "mud" was saturated volcanic ash. One theory suggested that under the combined stresses of the earthquakes and the increasing hydrostatic pressure of the growing crater lake, a natural dike separating L'Etang Sec from the upper gorge of the Rivière Blanche had ruptured. The waters of the unleashed lake, which was probably close to one thousand feet deep at that time, then swept a gargantuan mass of accumulated ash and loose boulders from the upper valley while it plummeted its remaining two thousand feet to the sea. Another theory, however, proposed much later, was that the crater lake had little or nothing to do with the disaster. Instead, the floor of the upper valley may have fractured along a rift running radially from the volcanic vent, allowing a massive underground reservoir to be forced out by the swelling subterranean pressure. No one, of course, can run an experiment to find the actual answer. Quite possibly, both answers are correct.

Regardless of the mechanism, however, the terrible effects were well documented. At the river's mouth, the avalanche of mud was traveling at nearly ninety feet per second, or sixty miles per hour. No one had a chance of outrunning it without a considerable head start and higher ground in sight. And, of course, downstream was exactly the wrong direction to run. It is likely that Dr. Guérin knew this instinctively, and that his hat had nothing to do with his survival. But how could one ever explain in words that moment of despair on seeing one's loved ones about to be engulfed and having no way to draw them back? Claiming to have forgotten a hat is a good excuse for not having to share one's pain with a journalist.

Today the phenomenon is referred to as a "lahar," from the Javanese word for "lava." Lahars have nothing to do with molten rock, nor is a boiling crater lake a necessary precondition. Any place that gets as much rainfall as Mont Pelée is bound to be riddled with underground streams and lakes, and if magma begins to rise from below, such reservoirs of groundwater must go somewhere. In 1902, this phenomenon was not well documented, let alone understood. Today it is recognized as one of the two most serious hazards to populations that live near dormant volcanoes. In fact, as recently as 1985, during a relatively mild eruption of Nevado del Ruiz in Colombia, a lahar surged down a river valley and killed 22,940 people, some in towns as far as thirty-five miles from the source.

• • •

On the afternoon of May 5, a courier delivered a telegram to Louis Mouttet from the garrison commander in St. Pierre. It was a convoluted and internally contradictory message, describing a general panic from a tidal wave that did little damage, yet telling of the total destruction of the Usine Guérin by a flow of muddy lava. As for the town of Precheur, it made no mention whatsoever.

In the harbor at Fort-de-France, the French naval cruiser *Suchet* had just docked and still had a full head of steam. Although Mouttet had no formal authority to commandeer a naval vessel, he sent his deputy governor, Edouard L'Heurre, to deliver a message to Captain Pierre Le Bris: an urgent situation had developed on the northwest coast, he explained, and the governor would arrive shortly in the hope that the *Suchet* would escort him to Precheur. It might be necessary to evacuate that town, and the cruiser was the only sizable ship available to undertake such an effort.

Captain Le Bris was not pleased. He took orders from the naval ministry in Paris, and this was a highly unusual request. If every colonial governor on a whim was able to commandeer a naval vessel that happened to be docked within his jurisdiction, the French navy would be thrown into chaos. Besides, the *Suchet*'s men had been promised shore leave, and they would not be happy at the news that their liberty would be delayed.

On the other hand, knowing that he couldn't afford to ignore a volcano in eruption, the captain kept the fireboxes stoked. When Mouttet arrived, Le Bris explained that their departure would need to wait until he exchanged telegrams with Paris. Mouttet responded that several of the cables were broken, and that numerous lives might hang in the balance while they waited for a reply that might not come. Le Bris gave the order to cast off.

Mouttet stood at the starboard bow, grasped the rail with both hands, and studied the passing shore as he collected his thoughts. He knew full well that evacuating Precheur would lead to terrible upheavals in human lives and equally difficult political problems. Of course he would have to do it if necessary. But only as a last resort.

Although from Fort-de-France the volcano lay hidden behind the Pitons du Carbet, the grim swirling ash clouds could leave no islander ignorant of the ongoing eruption. In stark visual contrast, the late afternoon sun bathed the near shoreline in a beautiful golden glow. North of the capital, the coast alternated between rugged cliffs and narrow valleys, two with villages harboring small fishing fleets — Case-Pilote, then Bellefontaine. Protected by the terrain, these hamlets did not seem to be at any risk from the eruption. The first coastal settlement of any size was Le Carbet, where a high ridge again blocked sight of the volcano from most vantage points in town. As the *Suchet* steamed past the north end of Carbet, a spectacular sight came into view: Mont Pelée in its fury, belching smoke and ash, its summit invisible in the swirling plumes of dust, while below, the grand city of St. Pierre and its roadstead of ships and smaller boats lay bathed in a wide horizontal swatch of golden sunlight.

Mouttet picked out the city landmarks that he had come to know so well in his five months on the island. Pointe St. Marthe and the tunnel excavated back in the 1840s. The rum warehouses on the waterfront, the Cathedral of Notre-Dame de L'Assomption, the rooftops of the Lycée Colonial where Gaston Landes taught, the theater, the prison, the road snaking up the hillside to Morne Rouge. Toward the north end of town, the Rivière Roxelane with its stout stone bridge, its banks lined with stately homes, including that of Andréus Hurard. A bit farther to the north, the smaller Rivière des Pères, which had been dry every time Mouttet had seen it but was now flowing with gusto. Then the rock-strewn stream known as the Rivière Sèche, which was also discharging an uncharacteristically sizable flow at its mouth. And then . . .

Mouttet squinted. Something had changed drastically since a couple of days ago: the Rivière Blanche had disappeared! Where it had emptied into the sea, there was now only a broad expanse of gray. Where yesterday the Usine Guérin had bustled with activity on its bank, there now stood only a single naked chimneytop jutting from the gray muck. He visually followed the course of the mud back up the mountainside. Although the drifting steam and smoke alternately hid one then another part of the view, it seemed that the mudflow had begun in the vicinity of L'Etang Sec. Indeed, the valley below that crater was completely clogged with the stuff. Was this what the geography books referred to as a lava flow?

Despite the scene of destruction before him and the volcano thundering above, Mouttet found something to reassure himself. Even if one hundred or more people had indeed been killed, the only affected area seemed to be in the valley of a river that had already shown signs of misbehaving. The townspeople of Precheur had been badly frightened, but were they really in any danger? Clearly, the gorge of the Rivière Blanche had done an effective job of directing the lava, or whatever it was, toward the sea, and at a point nearly a mile from the main part of town.

The *Suchet* dropped anchor, and Mouttet and several of his aides took a boat to shore. Precheur's Mayor Grelet and Father Desprez met them at the dock and immediately asked the governor to evacuate the town. An apprehensive crowd watched from the beach.

Mouttet advised the entourage not to be rash. If some roofs in Precheur had already collapsed, he pointed out, then surely even more would collapse if no one stayed to shovel them off. There would also be a security problem if the town were left empty. Meanwhile, the displaced population would need to be crowded into uncomfortable public buildings in St. Pierre or Fort-de-France. Would the townspeople be happy to endure weeks of discomfort as evacuees, only to return to the prospect of finding their homes collapsed or ransacked?

The priest and the mayor, priding themselves on being reasonable men, agreed that the issue was not an easy one and should not be decided before evaluating all the ramifications. But they also insisted that one matter above all must be addressed immediately: the food shortage. Yes, some provisions had arrived yesterday by boat, but not nearly enough. The ashfall had made local fishing all but impossible, and with the road destroyed by the mudlow, food could no longer be brought overland from the south. The markets were bare, and people were hungry. Mouttet quickly agreed to send a shipment of relief rations the following morning. Then before leaving, he assured everyone within earshot that he would arrange a rapid evacuation by sea should the village become seriously threatened.

The *Suchet* steamed back to Fort-de-France. Mouttet was relieved that the Precheur problem was still under control. Captain Le Bris, however, was annoyed that he had allowed himself to be talked into taking a French naval cruiser on a fruitless mission, without orders and at considerable inconvenience and cost. It was a mistake, he assured himself, that he would not allow to happen again.

•   •   •

That night back in Fort-de-France, Mouttet ordered that six metric tons of cod, salted pork, and beans be shipped by boat to the people of Precheur. That same night, a bank of electric generators at the power station on the Rivière Roxelane failed when they clogged with volcanic ash. Half of St. Pierre joined all of Precheur in plunging into darkness.

• CHAPTER 7 •

KETTLE OF FROGS

•

D rop a live frog into a pot of boiling water, and the creature will instantly hop out. But gently place a frog in a pot of cold water, then light a fire beneath, and it will stay put until it has been cooked. If the people of St. Pierre had been strangers dropped into that city in the first week of May, 1902, there can be little doubt that most would have sprung out without hesitation like frogs from a hot cauldron. Yet many of those who had been there all along somehow managed to accommodate themselves to the increasingly uncomfortable situation: sulfur fumes, detonations, ashfalls, earthquakes, lahars, and even deaths. Many indeed complained, but few were hopping out.

On the morning of May 6, no one in St. Pierre could miss the posters, prominently displayed all over town and carrying the signature of Mayor Rodolphe Fouché, assuring everyone that they were in no immediate danger. Citizens were advised to continue about their normal activities and not succumb to groundless panic. The posters promised that no lava flow would reach the city, and that future events "would be localized in those places that had already suffered." Meaning, apparently, Precheur.

Some people did leave. A few families headed overland to Carbet or to other points south on the rugged Trace Road, while others took the ferries to Fort-de-France. But exceptions prove the rule; in fact, the number of refugees entering town from the hills more than compensated for the relatively few that were evacuating the city. And although some writers have pointed out that there was standing-room-only on the steam ferries to Fort-de-France that Tuesday, this is hardly surprising. That day, one of the Girard Ferry Line's boats was chartered by the governor and another by the Plissonneau family, leaving the remaining shuttles operating on a reduced schedule. The ferries in service were indeed more crowded than usual, but not because particularly large numbers of people were leaving St. Pierre. There were simply fewer boats left available to carry paid passengers.

As for the family that chartered one of the ferries, the following article would appear in the May 8 edition of *The Voice of St. Lucia,* published at Castries:

At about nine o'clock on the morning of the 6th a private telegram came from Martinique, stating that the Plissonneau family had chartered the steamer Topaze, one of the boats of the Compagnie Girard, and had started for St. Lucia. At about eleven o'clock the Topaze arrived with Mrs. Plissonneau, Mr. and Mrs. Joseph Plissonneau and three children, Mrs. Pierre Plissonneau and child, and others. [Apparently, a total of about thirty-five people.]

They report that at noon on Monday a stream of burning lava suddenly rushed down the southwestern slope of the mountain, and, following the course of the Rivière Blanche, the bed of which is dry at this season of the year, overwhelmed everything which obstructed its rush to the sea. Estates and buildings were covered up by the fiery wave. When the torrent had poured itself into the sea, it was found that the Guérin sugar factory, on the beach, three miles from the mountain and two from St. Pierre, was embedded in lava. The burning mass of liquid had taken only three minutes from the time it was first perceived to reach the sea, three miles away.

Then a remarkable phenomenon occurred. The sea receded all along the western coast for about a hundred yards and returned with gentle strength, covering the whole of the sea front of St. Pierre and reaching the first houses on the Place Bertin. This created a general panic, and the people made for the hills. Though the sea retired again, without great damage being done ashore or afloat, the panic continued, intensified by terrible detonations, which broke from the mountain at short intervals, accompanied with dense emissions of smoke and lurid flashes of flame.

This was awful in daylight, but, when darkness fell, it was more terrible still, and, at each manifestation of the volcano's anger, people, in their nightclothes, carrying children, and lighted by any sort of lamp or candle they had caught up in their haste, ran out into the dark streets, wailing and screaming, and running aimlessly about the town.

The mental strain becoming unendurable, the Topaze was got ready, and the refugees hurriedly went on board and started for St. Lucia. In the afternoon the gentlemen of the party, having placed their families in safety, returned by the Topaze to Martinique.

The men actually returned not just to the island of Martinique but to their family homes in St. Pierre.

• • •

In Precheur, the situation that morning was more intense than in St. Pierre. Here, at least, the frogs were ready to jump—if there were just someplace to hop to. The community was trapped between a thundering volcano and the sea, with the only possible overland evacuation route to the south blocked by an expanse of volcanic mud some 1,500 feet wide and up to 40 feet deep.

Governor Mouttet's six metric tons of relief provisions arrived just after daybreak on May 6—a significant accomplishment for such a short time. Yet despite Mayor Grelet's best efforts, this aid did little to raise morale in Precheur. At the food distribution stations that morning, several of the more vociferous residents shouted to their fellow citizens that a flotilla of ships anchored in the harbor would be a lot more reassuring than the free breakfasts and a mere promise that ships would arrive if necessary. A naval cruiser had been there the day before, but no one had been evacuated. What would it take to convince Mouttet that the people of Precheur were at risk? How many more would need to die to motivate him?

Mouttet misjudged. Expecting to arrive on a tide of goodwill after the provisions he had sent, he chartered the *Rubis* for a follow-up visit to Precheur later that morning. As the boat approached the dock, he stood at the bow and waved to the townspeople, fully expecting to be greeted with appreciation and applause. Instead of welcoming him, however, the crowd at the pier swarmed over the small boat before it was even moored. The commotion attracted a throng from shore, and a human mass surged onto the dock toward the *Rubis*. To keep his vessel from being swamped, the captain quickly reversed the engine. Dozens of people fell into the ash-covered water as the *Rubis* backed away. Mouttet realized immediately that this would not be recorded as one of his shining moments.

The fiasco angered the crowd even more. As some of the men pulled their fellow citizens from the water, others stood shaking their fists and swearing at the governor. Meanwhile, women stood forlorn on shore with groups of small children huddled around their skirts. Throughout the debacle, the ash had continued to fall, and everyone both on deck and shore looked like ghosts. Most devastating to Mouttet, he now realized he couldn't land in Precheur after all; the ferryboat was already packed with humanity, and there was no way of controlling the crowd on shore. Mouttet ordered the captain to head back to St. Pierre.

Something had to be done with the refugees who had jumped aboard, none of whom had any provisions other than the clothes on their backs. Rather than carry them to Fort-de-France and alarm people there, Mouttet decided to drop them off in St. Pierre, where they could be sheltered temporarily in the police barracks. In one of the many ironies of the next few days, this group of refugees would die, while the friends and relatives they had so hastily abandoned in Precheur would live.

• • •

Mouttet returned to his office in Fort-de-France and checked his messages. To his disappointment, there was still no response to the cablegram he had sent to the Ministry of Colonies back on May 3. Surely, he figured, he should have gotten a reply by now. He called for his carriage and rode to the city telegraph office. There, he found the manager gone but the operators diligently keying dispatches into the overland lines and trying to funnel a backlog of messages into the two undersea cables that were still alive.

All keying stopped, and all eyes went to him. It was unusual, to say the least, for a governor to walk into a telegraph dispatch room. Mouttet asked if any cables had arrived for him from Paris. None had. But one

nervous operator handed the governor several messages with the explanation that they had just arrived from St. Pierre.

Mouttet read. They did not bring good news. Several officials in
St. Pierre were requesting either leaves of duty or immediate transfers to
posts farther from the volcano. And Mayor Fouché and the St. Pierre garrison commander were both asking that the governor dispatch more gendarmes to St. Pierre to help keep the peace in the increasingly crowded
streets. Mouttet responded decisively to both sets of requests: Yes, he
would immediately send additional gendarmes from the Fort-de-France
garrison to St. Pierre. And no, under no circumstances would he approve
leaves or transfers in this time of emergency. Moreover, any official who
left his post in St. Pierre would be summarily fired from his job and black-
balled from ever again holding a government position.

As the operator sent those responses, Mouttet picked up one of the
messages from the backlogged outgoing stack. It was from Thomas
Prentiss to Washington. The U.S. consul at St. Pierre was informing the
U.S. State Department of the dangerous state of Pelée's eruption and requesting permission for the Americans, himself included, to vacate their
posts in St. Pierre and move to Fort-de-France until the danger passed.

This was not good, thought Mouttet. Officials, even American officials, must be among the *last* to leave town, not the first. He would take
the matter up with Prentiss tomorrow. "Don't send this one," he said,
waving the page at the operator, "until I tell you to."

"While I'm here," he continued, "notify St. Pierre that I'm here in
your office and ask if they have anything else for me."

The operator tapped the key. The response came back:

Governor may wish to review, authorize, Senator Knight's message to
Paris as follows:

Volcanic eruption has destroyed livelihood of population of Precheur.
Exclusively composed of smallholders. Crops, livestock destroyed
along with factory. Overseas act of humanitarian help would produce
beneficial results for entire population. May I request you mention
my intervention in cable reply.
AMEDEE KNIGHT

"What the hell is this?" Mouttet muttered. "Has this gone to Paris?"

The operator shook his head. "No, sir, they just wired it here. We can send it on to Paris if you like."

"No, don't do that," Mouttet said. "Just confirm to St. Pierre that I got it and that it will be handled from this end." With that, the governor folded the message and stuffed it in his pocket.

The operator keyed back, "Received and cleared."

"Is there anything else, sir?"

"Yes," said Mouttet. "I need to send a cable to the Ministry of Colonies."

The operator held the line open and waited for the governor to compose his message. Mouttet began by jotting down a series of details of the events of the last few days, then crossed everything out. His past reports of details hadn't generated any responses from Paris. Better to keep this dispatch short and to the point. He scribbled, then the operator keyed:

FORT-DE-FRANCE, 6 MAY
Request you put Suchet at my immediate disposal.
MOUTTET

And with that taken care of, he left the telegraph office and rode back to the Governor's Mansion. The day wasn't over, and he still had a great deal to consider.

This cable of May 6 to the Ministry of Colonies would later be used to raise questions about Mouttet's mental competence. Why would a governor want to command the *Suchet*, a naval cruiser? This was no war; it was a volcano. Did he plan to shell the mountain?

In the context of his actions of the previous few days, however, it is clear that Mouttet was teetering on the brink of evacuating the town of Precheur and its surrounding villages—a possible total of as many as five or six thousand people. And just that morning, he had had a painful experience that convinced him he couldn't possibly conduct an orderly evacuation by using the Girard Line's small ferryboats. He would obviously need one or more large ships and a military or police presence to keep order. And at that time, most of the gendarmes under his own authority were already committed to maintaining peace in the streets of St. Pierre. The *Suchet*, however, happened to be in port in Fort-de-France. What would be more reasonable than requesting that this naval cruiser and its men be put at his disposal?

Meanwhile, in the St. Pierre telegraph office, Fort-de-France's response "Received and cleared" was misinterpreted to mean that the governor wanted St. Pierre to send Senator Knight's message to Paris. With the broken cables, this presented a bit of a logistical challenge, involving four links and some non–French-speaking stations. But after all, a governor was a governor. St. Pierre immediately dispatched Knight's message to St. Vincent Island on the first leg of its four-thousand-mile journey to Paris, carrying the heading "URGENT PRIORITY."

• • •

Meanwhile, a great column of dust and vapor continued to blossom from the volcano. Beginning late that morning, the ash clouds took on an ominous new feature: their undersides were illuminated by a reddish orange glow from below. At this point, a modern volcanologist would recognize that an open conduit extended from the volcano's vent all the way through the continental crust and into the planet's mantle. And that when this happens, worse is almost certain to follow.

Several times that Tuesday, Professor Landes trained his telescope on the crater of L'Etang Sec and noticed that it was tossing large boulders high in the air. After sunset he peered through his lens again and found himself marveling at the sight: large glowing projectiles tracing out one bright parabolic streak after another against the background darkness. Until now, Mont Pelée had ejected mainly gas, ash, and water. Now, on the evening of May 6, it was also upchucking great gobs of molten rock.

• • •

The morning of May 7 began with heavy explosions and intense bolts of lightning. The ground trembled, and the air resonated. Hundreds of new refugees funneled down the mountain roads and trails into the city. The ferries resumed their regular schedules and were packed in both directions. Meanwhile, St. Pierre's telegraph operators were horrified to find that the last of the undersea cables into the city had gone dead. Any further international dispatches would have to begin as overland telegrams to Fort-de-France.

On the waterfront, Captain Marino Leboffe watched the volcano with increasing apprehension while his Italian bark *Orsolina,* anchored in the roadstead, was being loaded with sugar for Le Havre. Leboffe didn't like what he saw. The loading was proceeding much slower than usual as the stevedores repeatedly stopped to wipe the grit from their faces or to rinse their mouths. The lighters and the cargo were covered with ash. The volcano, just four miles distant, was thundering with unabating intensity.

Leboffe made an unheard-of decision. He told the shipper's agent that he didn't regard St. Pierre as a safe place, and that he was suspending the loading and setting sail. Immediately.

The agent objected. Less than half the cargo had been loaded, and the rest could not just be left sitting on the dock. A captain cannot simply ignore a contract, he reminded Leboffe.

Leboffe shot back (according to more than one source): "I'd rather sail with half a cargo than run such a risk as a man must run here. I don't know anything about Mont Pelée, but if Vesuvius were looking as your volcano looks this morning, I'd get out of Naples! And I'm going to get out of here!" He stepped into his launch.

"If the *Orsolina* sails without permission," the agent threatened, "you will get no clearance papers and I will make sure that you're arrested as soon as you reach Havre!"

The captain was not intimidated. "I'll take my chances of arrest," he shouted, "but I won't take any more chances on that volcano. I'm going to get up my anchor and make sail just as soon as I get onboard my ship." And with that, he and his shore crew pushed off into the bay.

The agent dashed to the customhouse and hurriedly explained the problem. Two customs officers had themselves rowed out to the *Orsolina,* climbed onboard, and announced to the captain that they had instructions to remain on deck until the ship was fully loaded. Leboffe went about his business ordering the trimming of the rigging. Then he turned to the officers and said, "Gentlemen, I'm going to sail from this port in a few minutes. If you want to go ashore, now is your time to do it. If you stay here, I assure you I shall take you to France."

"That would be kidnapping!" shouted one of the customs agents. "That would only compound your crime!"

Leboffe shrugged and ordered the anchor raised. The two customs officials scampered down the ladder to their launch just as the wind began to fill the *Orsolina*'s sails.

The *Orsolina*'s owners, the brothers Pollio of Meta, near Naples, had a second bark anchored in St. Pierre that day. As the *Orsolina* sailed, the *Nord America* remained at St. Pierre. Within twenty-four hours, her splintered remains would be under 165 feet of water.

• • •

When Senator Knight's URGENT PRIORITY cable arrived at the offices of the colonial ministry in Paris, it drew immediate attention and jogged someone's memory that another message about a volcano had arrived a few days earlier. After a bit of searching for the first cablegram, the two communications were delivered together to the minister of colonies, Pierre Louis Albert Decrais. The most recent message, Mouttet's request for the use of the *Suchet,* had yet to arrive.

Decrais did not like the smell of Knight's request. With the runoff election coming up in just a couple of days, it seemed altogether too coincidental that a senator and party leader was asking for emergency aid for his constituents and for recognition of his personal intervention. Mouttet, on the other hand, had not expressed any sense of urgency; apparently he had the matter under control and was simply informing Decrais in case Knight tried to exploit the matter politically, as in fact he seemed to be attempting to do. With the French Parliament currently on vacation, nothing could be done anyway unless Decrais were to bring the matter to the attention of the Cabinet. And given the opportunistic tone of Knight's cable, this certainly did not sound like a Cabinet-level issue. Decrais did not respond to Knight but cabled back to Mouttet:

PARIS, 7 MAY

Kindly keep me informed of eruption and particularly let me know names of victims having relatives in France. Will send help as soon as resolution carried. Still on subject, request you and Senator Knight convey to population sympathy of government. Not having any credit for aid purposes at my disposal I have, in view of the parlia-

mentary vacation, had to seek intervention through interior and agriculture for the refugees of the eruption of Mont Pelée, and I have particularly pressed my colleagues for allocation funds. Will cable when action taken.
DECRAIS.

Months later, Albert Decrais would explain: "With an election pending, the situation was delicate. To intervene at the behest of a party leader would have slighted the governor's authority and could have been interpreted as action for political gain."

In the aftermath, Amédee Knight would defend his attempt at intervention: "The governor's cable [of May 3] gave no real picture of the situation as it was, or as it was likely to develop. It bore all the signs of the ineptness that the island's colonial administration was famed for." Yet never did anyone ask Knight to explain how, at the time, he could possibly have known of the contents of the governor's cable that he was so critical of.

And by then, Louis Mouttet would say nothing.

CHAPTER 8

LA SOUFRIÈRE

•

O n St. Vincent Island, it was late April when sailors making port at Kingstown started circulating tales of a volcanic eruption on nearby Martinique. Although welcome for their entertainment value, everyone knew that stories told by rowdy seamen on shore leave were not the most reliable sources of information. It was through telegraph transmissions between the colonial offices that island dwellers expected important news to arrive from the rest of the world. And no official report had arrived in Kingstown about a volcano erupting anywhere in the Antilles.

But between Martinique and St. Vincent, there had never been much traffic in cablegrams. Few Martiniquians had economic or social interests in the impoverished British colony one hundred miles to their south, nor were the French colonial officers on Martinique particularly fond of the British. The language barrier, of course, didn't help matters. And so, as Mont Pelée thundered and rained ashes on Precheur and St. Pierre at the beginning of May 1902, few on St. Vincent Island heard anything about these events. Certainly, no one on St. Vincent learned about the flooding of Martinique's streams and the disastrous mudflows—news that might have saved many lives. And then, around 5 p.m. on May 6, the cable snapped between St. Vincent and Martinique, and no longer was it possible to send direct transmissions between those two islands.

Averaging just eleven miles wide and eighteen miles in length, St. Vincent Island was essentially a single volcano poking above the sea. La Soufrière (so named by the French during one of their occupations and translating roughly as "sulfur place") towered to an elevation of

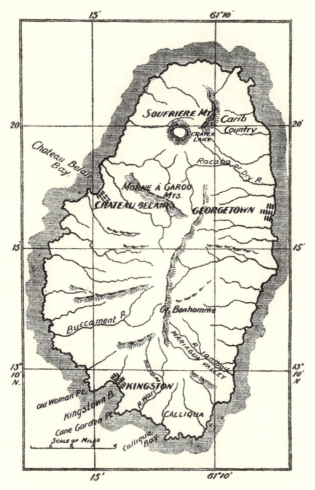

St. Vincent Island, 1902. (Miller 1902)

4,050 feet. If one drew an east-west line connecting the town of Chateau-belair on the west coast with Georgetown on the Atlantic shore, it would separate the steepest volcanic terrain at the north from the more populated regions to the south. The capital of Kingstown, with its population of about six thousand, sat on the southern coast fifteen miles from the summit.

The British had never done much to develop the colony's infrastructure. There were few schools, and these were poorly equipped. Telegraph and telephone lines linked only a few towns to the capital. The coastal roads were rugged at best, and there were no roads at all through the interior of the island or north of the volcano.

None of St. Vincent's forty-two thousand residents had ever seen a volcano in eruption. Only once in living memory had La Soufrière misbehaved even a little, and that was back in 1880 when its two crater lakes swelled and got hot. The volcano's only victims in that event were the fish it cooked. Yet every schoolchild learned, as part of the local lore, that La Soufrière had not always been so quiet. It had rumbled and ejected ash at least three times: in 1718, 1785, and 1812. During the latter eruption, the Rabacca River just north of Georgetown had curiously dried up, never to flow again. The coastal road now ran down into its dry gorge and across its bed.

The slopes of the volcano were not unoccupied; they supported hundreds of workers on a dozen plantations, and several thousand more on numerous small farms and in a few villages. And in La Soufrière's most remote northern foothills lived the last few tribes of the native Caribe Indians. Embedded in their oral traditions were tales of violent volcanic eruptions of past centuries, along with the prediction that one day the mountain would again belch smoke and fire. And when that happened, the tribe elders assured, the world would end.

As early as April of 1901, colonial officials in Kingstown reported a series of mild earthquakes. Minor tremors continued intermittently over the next twelve months, but none caused any damage and no one imagined that they had anything to do with the volcano. In the last week of April 1902, plantation workers on the volcano's slopes noticed wisps of vapor rising from the summit and the unmistakable odor of sulfur oxides. Still, no one perceived these curious sights and smells as harbingers of danger. Then on Monday, May 5, at about the same time that a lahar was destroying the Usine Guérin in Martinique, La Soufrière's crater lakes began to boil. Steam billowed into the sky, and by that afternoon the mountain was rumbling and ejecting ash along with the steam.

There were two lakes on the mountaintop, separated by a knife-edge of rock some seven hundred feet in height. The older lake, which existed prior to the 1812 eruption, was a much larger body of water than Mont Pelée's shallow L'Etang de Palmistes; it had a diameter of three-quarters of a mile and a whopping depth of 575 feet, as determined by actual soundings. The second and younger lake had appeared after the 1812 eruption when the newly formed crater filled with water; it had about the same surface area as the older lake and also had a considerable though undetermined depth. Both lakes could be viewed from a trail on the crater rim. Observing these bodies of water, however, was much easier than getting to them, for their surfaces were 1,100 feet below the crater trail. Few had ever ventured into the crater to sample their waters.

On the evening of May 5, a series of earthquakes jarred all of St. Vincent Island. The volcano immediately redoubled its activity, and huge masses of steam and ash thundered into the sky. The prevailing winds swept most of the ashfall to the west, and here some of the simpler folk heeded the warning and began packing to evacuate south. Many of the more prosperous, nervously balancing the risk to their lives against concerns about the security of their property and the survival of their livestock, subscribed to a wait-and-see posture. This eruption, however, was not destined to be an on-and-off again event; from its initial belches that morning until after the terrible climax two days later, La Soufrière never showed the slightest sign of slackening off. As it continued to roar through the night of May 5, bolts of lightning began shooting through its ash clouds.

By Tuesday morning, all of the volcano's western slopes lay buried in at least six inches of ash. Everything was gray: sky, trees, horses, and humans, and the ash was still falling. Hundreds of people, balancing baskets of belongings on their heads, crowded onto the narrow dirt road to shuffle south toward the town of Chateaubelair, holding handkerchiefs to their faces and listening to the thunder of the volcano over their shoulders. A few led heavily laden horses or donkeys; the majority did not. The Wallibou River, which was normally but a few inches deep this time of the year, was now a foot deep and rising. Ash stuck to the hundreds of bare shins and feet as they emerged from the stream. The air was oppressive, the visibility limited, the dismal sky growing darker. The grit got into everyone's eyes and mouths, with no sources of clean water for relief. Few had any idea of how far they were going, and none had any notion of how long they would be away from home or whether they would ever be able to return.

Meanwhile, residents on the east side of the island watched the eruption in relative comfort as most of the ashes continued to blow to the west. The dramatic electrical activity was several miles away, and the entire spectacle entrancing. Few in the vicinity of Georgetown saw any immediate need to evacuate; by all indications they were going to be spared any serious effects. That afternoon, La Soufrière's vent began to glow incandescently, and the ash cloud continued to swell. That evening, the eruption was visible from St. Lucia, a distance of about fifty miles.

· · ·

In Kingstown, the telegraph line to Chateaubelair went dead, and reports began arriving by courier that the people in the western region of greatest ashfall were in a state of confusion. Sir Robert Llewelyn, governor of the Windward Islands, was in Trinidad and could not be reached for instructions. At about 8:30 p.m., Captain W. Jameson Calder, the island's chief of police, set off to investigate in his eight-oared police boat. It was a distance of over ten miles to Chateaubelair. In Calder's words:

> As we approached the wharf, about midnight, the whole top of the mountain burst into flame, the long flashes of deep-red fire traveling from the top downward in a circular track, just like fire bursting from a heap of smithy coal when fanned by a strong draft from the bellows. This was immediately followed by an explosion as if of much heavy ordnance, dying away in a long-drawn angry grumble. The top of the mountain emitted a dense volume of very dark, heavy smoke, rising in an angry manner straight up. The village streets and the wharf were crowded with people in a great state of excitement, most of them having run from their homes on the mountain-sides a few hours before.

Calder was an imposing figure, a muscular six-foot five-inch Scot who had served in the British Colonial Service for twelve years and had just been transferred to St. Vincent from Jamaica in April. As he led his crew and constables ashore, several of them pleaded that they all return to the boat and leave immediately. Two of them did not wait for Calder's answer but immediately ran back toward the wharf. Calder caught up to the pair, and by using what he styled "a little Scotch persuasion," he induced them to return to duty. Dr. Hughes, the Leeward medical officer, would later explain that the captain had actually grabbed both constables by the hair and knocked their heads together.

Calder considered it his duty to prevent panic among the hundreds of refugees that were pouring into town. The volcano was about five miles away, and at that distance, he did not believe they were in any real danger. Still, it was clear why many of the natives found the circumstances terrifying: the ashfalls, explosions, lightning, and perhaps most of all, the uncertainty.

By Wednesday morning, May 7, the thunder and lightning were continuous. A dark cauliflower-shaped cloud billowed to an altitude of thirty thousand feet. "As daylight dawned," Calder would later write, "the ordinarily quiet little country village had the appearance of a huge hive of bees, disturbed and angry. On all sides one heard of the short but ominous warning that had been given the poor settlers, and their hurried flight with only the clothes in which they stood." By 10 a.m., the captain had more than 450 refugees huddled around him, with more arriving by the minute. Then the ground trembled, and there was a vertical blast that quadrupled the size of the eruption column.

• • •

Within minutes, a huge ashfall swelled to the eastern side of the island. Alexander McKenzie, estate manager of the Orange Hill plantation two and a half miles north of Georgetown, opened an underground rum cellar, where 132 people quickly took shelter. Whether he and his family planned to join them later is not clear; they were to die in their manor house. Others crowded into the stoutest available buildings: schoolhouses, warehouses, and churches. But quality structures were few; most buildings on St. Vincent had thatched roofs and walls of wattle and daub or unconsolidated masonry—not the kind of shelter that instills a sense of security with a rampant volcano thundering above. And so the miserable scene of evacuation that had begun a day earlier on the west side of the island, and was still in progress there, now was repeated on the eastern coastal road as villagers and plantation workers fled south toward Georgetown.

And then came a horrifying surprise.

Around noon, a turbulent cascade of steaming silvery mud burst down each of La Soufrière's six mountain streams. Through the Rabacca ravine, which had been totally dry since the eruption of 1812, an impassable river now roared to the coast north of Georgetown. The would-be evacuees on the north bank could only stand in bewilderment, their numbers swelling by the minute. Across the raging river, they saw through the clouds of steam that people in Georgetown were scampering south. But for those still north of the Rabacca, there was no place to go.

Meanwhile, a nearly identical scene unfolded on the western side of the island, where the normally benign Wallibou River grew to a raging flood. The influx of refugees into Chateaubelair stopped. Rampaging lahars eliminated all prospects of escape for anyone remaining anywhere north of the Rabacca and the Wallibou. Nearly two thousand people were now trapped in the shadow of the volcano.

Around 1 p.m., a series of violent detonations shook the mountain, and a fusillade of glowing rocks burst from the vent. Softball-sized volcanic bombs struck and killed people and animals as far as five miles away, and boulders up to two feet in diameter were later found a full four miles from the vent. Meanwhile, those who hoped the mudflows would subside wished in vain; the furious Rabacca was now more than fifty feet deep.

In Chateaubelair, Captain Calder announced that it was time for everyone to evacuate to the south. It was beyond his power to do anything for those unfortunates trapped north of the raging Wallibou; in fact, he realized it might now be beyond his power to do much of anything for anybody. He relieved his men of their duties and gave them permission to escape in the police boat. None took him up on the offer; all decided instead to assist with the evacuation. Days later, the boat would be found sunk in Chateaubelair's harbor. Calder would report:

> I ordered everyone in the streets to leave the town at once, and, to prevent injury by falling stones, I directed them to take old boards and shingles from the dilapidated houses and cover their heads. Stones up to half a pound in weight were now falling, while the sulphurous fumes and fine dust rendered breathing difficult.
>
> Men, women, and children of all ages scurried up the steep hill as fast as possible, mothers urging on their young children hardly able

to crawl, old men imploring the assistance of the younger and stronger, each helping and encouraging the other, clearly showing the brotherhood a common danger engenders. One poor woman, with a brood of at least eight, was kept behind by the inability of the youngest two to keep up the pace. Her agonized cry for help I can never forget, nor the thankful smile I got when I picked them up, one in each arm.

By this time the dense suphuretted cloud, which had chased us like a death-pall, began to overtake us, and it was hard indeed to get the people to continue struggling on. As the darkness settled over us, a storm of lightning and thunder broke over our heads, and so near were the flashes that one thought that each surely must strike the people on the road, especially as the dry grass on the hillsides was ignited. It would indeed be difficult to be more uncertain of another minute's life than on that hillside that afternoon.

In a later conversation, Calder would admit that he had even had an impulse to pray, but decided it would be cowardly and hypocritical to yield to it. The closest he came, by his account, was: "Lord, you will have to take me as I am. I have never been a begging man, and damned if I'll be one now!" Minutes later, a volcanic rock hit him in the head. To free his hands to scoop up the two children, he had discarded the board he was using for head protection. Calder recovered from the mild concussion, and everyone he helped evacuate survived.

•   •   •

The terrible climax came around 2:30 p.m. La Soufrière's summit burst apart with a thunderous roar, and an immense mass of turbulent vapor and ash exploded radially down all of its slopes. This ground-hugging cloud was hot—at least 750°F and as high as 1,100°F in places, and it was fast—roaring down the volcano's flanks at a speed of around 150 feet per second. Lightning zigzagged across its dirty face. Its impact flattened every tree and uprooted smaller shrubs. It scooped up flocks of chickens and churned them into an airborne mass of burning feathers. It indiscriminately destroyed every building and beast in its path. Even the masonry plantation buildings were no match for its onslaught; they collapsed immediately, and everything combustible in their rubble burst into flame.

From a distance, it first appeared as a huge gray doughnut ringing the mountain, the volcanic vent momentarily poking through its center. But it was a hellish doughnut. As it rolled down the slopes it expanded, leaving behind a dust trail that billowed four thousand feet upward. Its rumble was deafening. The crowds trapped on the banks of the Rabacca and the Wallibou couldn't help seeing it coming, for even at a speed of one hundred miles per hour, it took more than two minutes to reach them. Some ran toward the sea; others fell to the ground and buried their faces in the grass. A few scampered behind boulders. No matter, for a single breath of the fiery vapor was to bring certain death.

As the lethal cloud reached the sea, its forward motion stalled. Its heavier components began sifting to the ground, while the lighter dust and gases billowed upward in the atmosphere. On the eastern side of the volcano, however, the cloud actually reversed direction and surged back uphill as if there were a huge vacuum to be filled.

One eyewitness was the Reverend J. H. Darrell, rector of a little church in Georgetown, who later gave the following account:

In company with several gentlemen, on Wednesday at noon I left in a small boat to go to Chateau Belaire, where we hoped to get a better view of the eruption. As we passed Layou, the first town on the leeward coast, the smell of sulphuretted hydrogen was very perceptible. Before we got half way on our journey a vast column of steam, smoke and ashes ascended to a prodigious elevation, falling apparently in the vicinity of Georgetown. The majestic body of curling vapor was sublime beyond imagination. We were about eight miles from the crater, as the crow flies, and the top of the enourmous column eight miles off reached higher than one-fourth of the segment of the circle. I judge that the awful pillar was fully eight miles in height.

We were rapidly proceeding to our point of observation, when an immense cloud, dark, dense and apparently thick with volcanic material, descended over our pathway, impeding our progress and warning us to proceed no farther. This mighty bank of sulphurous vapor and smoke assumed at one time the shape of a gigantic promontory, then appeared as a collection of twirling, revolving cloud whorls, turning with rapid velocity; now assuming the shape of gigantic cauliflowers, then efflorescing into beautiful flower shapes, some dark, some effulgent, some bronze, others pearly white and all brilliantly illuminated by electric flashes.

Darkness, however, soon fell upon us. The sulphurous air was laden with fine dust, that fell thickly upon and around us, discoloring the sea. A black rain began to fall, followed by another rain of favilla, lapilli, and scoriae. The electric flashes were marvelously rapid in their motions, and numerous beyond all computation. These, with the thundering noise of the mountain, mingled with the dismal roar of the lava, the shocks of earthquakes, the falling stones, the enormous quantity of material ejected from the belching craters, producing a darkness as dense as a starless midnight, together with the plutonic energy of the mountain, growing greater and greater every moment, combined to make up a scene of horror.

Had Reverend Darrell and his friends ventured just a few miles farther to the north, they would have been engulfed by the explosion. Meanwhile, on the other side of the island in Georgetown, the wife of another minister, Mrs. A. H. Leslie, was also lucky to have been just outside the area of devastation. She described her experience:

On Wednesday morning, between nine and ten o'clock, the lightning and thunder began. Such lightning and thunder! Oh, it is terrible to remember, and thrice terrible was it to behold! Blinding flashes that zigzagged with hissing fury and a lurid light ominous of destruction.

Mr. Leslie said he had never before heard thunder in May, and declared the occurrence was most unusual. He left the house with the object of making some observations, and on his return he said that the Soufrière was active.

In the meantime some fisher girls, who came down from the mountain, said they had observed the water in the mountain lake to be boiling rapidly and the grass in the vicinity to be torn up. Then, you will understand, I got anxious. The storm grew in fury. The thunder became louder and louder. Nature's forces were cannonading with a fierceness of detonation that would have awed the bravest of human hearts.

Amid the crashing thunder peals and the dreadful lightning there began to fall a shower of small pebbles, and later on there fell stones as big as your fist. Meanwhile dismal rumblings were heard, as though the mountain groaned under the weight of accumulated fury, and the earth swayed in deep sympathy.

At half-past two o'clock the explosion occurred and darkness fell upon the land. What words can depict the sound or tell of the sensation it caused those who heard it? Language is inadequate to the task. Vain would it be to ransack the vocabularies of dead or living languages in the hope of finding adequate terms. The sounds were weird and abysmal, and caused our hearts to quiver with fear.

The rain of big stones continued up to about eleven o'clock at night, when sand began to fall. From where we were, we could see the reflection of the fire in the sky, but could not see the blaze. So terrible were the earthquake shocks as to give the impression that the end of the world had come. The hours of the night—that night of horrors!—crept slowly along with leaden feet, and morning was so long in coming that it seemed as though daylight had been extinguished for all time. But at last morning broke. Not a morning like the rosy-fingered mornings of tropical brightness and sunshiny beauty that we had been accustomed to, but a dull, dismal, dreary day came, not much distinguishable from the preceding night of Egyptian darkness. But it was day, and that fact afforded some measure of relief. We could see and hear others in the town.

Numbers of persons now began to flock into Georgetown from the adjoining country, and to bring accounts of the death of this person and that person, of the extinction of this family and that family. This continued all day. The tale of death and calamity was one long, unbroken, sad, sad one. Among those who came into the town or were brought in were many who had been stricken by lightning and were paralyzed, or who had been scorched by the burning hot sand and were blistered and sore.

The sound of the explosion was heard at least as far as Barbados, one hundred miles to the east. The vast release of energy, however, did little to defuse the volcano. La Soufrière continued to thunder and belch a monstrous ash column into the atmosphere, and ten minutes later, scoriae fell like hail over the entire island. That night, the glow from the volcano could be seen from forty miles at sea. By the morning of May 8, the ash cloud towered forty thousand feet upward to the stratosphere. Large stones pummeled Georgetown on Friday morning, May 9, and two major detonations took place the following day.

With the volcano still in continuous eruption, several days would pass before relief crews could venture even close to the stricken area. Only on May 12, six days after the explosion, did the volcano calm down sufficiently for the first terrible assessments to be made. It was to be a few more days before anyone reached the most remote northern villages.

• • •

It was said that not a human or beast north of Georgetown and Chateaubelair survived the death cloud of May 7. This was almost true; certainly everyone outside and most of those in aboveground buildings were killed almost instantly. On La Soufrière's northern slopes, all of the last native Caribes were annihilated, just as their legends had told them they would be.

There were, however, a few survivors. One man, a Samuel Brown, was watching from a sugar factory three and a half miles from the volcano when he saw the blast surging toward him and ran into a rum cellar. He emerged unscathed to later tell his story. The 132 refugees in Orange Hill plantation's rum cellar also survived, to emerge stupefied into a scene of utter devastation. And there are always those on the perimeter of a disaster that have the horrible experience of being left only half-dead. One such account was given by a man who had survived with four others of a group of ten, with no water or medical attention for four days.

> We heard the mountain roaring the whole morning, but we thought it would pass off, and we did not like to abandon our homes, so we chanced it. About half-past one it began to rain pebbles and stones, some of which were alight; but then, although we were afraid, we could not leave. The big explosion must have taken place at about half-past two o'clock. There was fire all around me and I could not breathe. My hands and feet got burned, but I managed to reach the house where the others were.
>
> In two hours everything was over, although pebbles and dust fell for a long time after. My burns got so painful and stiff that I could

not move. We remained until Sunday morning without food or water. Five persons died, and as none of us could throw the bodies out, or even move, we had to lie alongside the bodies until we were rescued.

• • •

Governor Llewelyn arrived in Kingstown on May 13, and the following day he cabled his first official report to the Colonial Office in London, advising that the state of affairs was much worse than anticipated. The next day, May 15, he sent a follow-up cable:

The total number of bodies found and buried so far is 1,300. One hundred and thirty persons are in the hospitals. All of the immediate wants of the survivors have now been supplied through the aid rendered by the neighbouring colonies. Two thousand animals have been lost. Nine of the best sugar estates have been seriously damaged. The outlook is most serious. Three thousand persons are on the relief list. It is expected that the number of lives lost will reach 2,000.

The whole of the Carib country, over eleven miles in length, from shore to mountainside, is covered with volcanic earth, and only the burned tops of trees are to be seen. In some small huts, about twenty-two feet square, over thirty bodies have been dug out. The whole of the country to windward, from Georgetown to the last northern settlement, is reeking with the stench of the rotting corpses of unburied victims and dead cattle. The survivors are being collected in the southern towns, where the government is feeding and clothing them. The crater is still rumbling, and a renewed outbreak is feared.

When the newspaper correspondents eventually arrived and rode from Kingstown to La Soufrière, they reported seeing little else but graves, graves, graves. Where people had fallen, they had been buried. Twenty-four dead had been found in the ruins of a small school building; in an overseer's house in Langley Park there were thirty-seven bodies. Everywhere there were mounds with temporary markers, some graves holding a dozen or more bodies. The village of Richmond was obliterated, Wallibou had slipped into the sea, and Georgetown was badly damaged.

Burial parties working for the government were paid at four times the usual wage rate, and an additional premium of forty cents for each dead body they found. Many of the corpses were so covered with dust that they were discovered only when someone stepped on them. The procedure was for one man to tie a handkerchief saturated with carbolic acid over his face and slip a noose over the ankle of a corpse; others in the burial party would then drag the body by a long rope to a trench in which it was rapidly covered over. No effort was made to record the names of the victims or where each was buried.

· · ·

The deadly phenomenon—the ground-hugging cloud of superheated gas and ash—had no name at the time. It was not mentioned in any book, for no writers, scientific or otherwise, realized in those days that a volcano could behave in such a way. A few months later, after witnessing such an event firsthand, the French geoscientist Alfred Lacroix would christen the phenomenon a *"nuée ardente"* (translation: "glowing cloud"). The current scientific literature still uses that term, or the alternative term "pyroclastic surge."

When a major disaster claims lives, one can usually point to human error and/or misjudgment as an aggravating factor. The St. Vincent disaster of 1902 seems to be an exception. One cannot plan for disaster without first understanding the phenomenological basis of the risks. Without a knowledge of pyroclastic surges or lahars, who would have considered developing contingency plans for evacuating the poor souls from the northern half of the island? And who would have even thought of building a bridge across a dry streambed? Compounding matters, St. Vincent's infrastructure in 1902 was in no way conducive to a mass evacuation: the roads were terrible and the communication system virtually nonexistent. Furthermore, there was a problem of time.

One of the most unusual aspects of the St. Vincent disaster is that La Soufrière was much less generous than most dormant volcanoes about giving notice that it was about to erupt. The first earthquakes and signs of volcanic activity occurred on the morning of May 5. Less than sixty hours later, La Soufrière exploded catastrophically. The time lapse between the precursors and the devastating explosion was no more than a split second in geologic time. It would have been difficult to conduct a complete evacuation even with the best infrastructure and today's scientific knowledge of volcanoes.

• • •

On May 7, a few sketchy reports of the volcanic eruption on St. Vincent Island reached Martinique via St. Lucia. These were not reports of the actual disaster, for even the St. Vincent islanders still didn't know much about that. The news was merely that another major volcanic eruption was taking place just one hundred miles to the south.

In St. Pierre, many found this information reassuring. Obviously, whatever material was being expelled from La Soufrière would not flow out of Mont Pelée. And just as an overheated steam boiler's pressure is released more effectively through two safety valves rather than one, the mysterious forces boiling up under Martinique were bound to settle down quickly now that this second vent on St. Vincent had opened up. Surely the more volcanoes in simultaneous eruption the better, for this could only mean that the venting would fizzle out that much sooner.

Nature, however, is under no obligation to adhere to human logic. Two volcanoes, it turns out, are not necessarily more benign than one. La Soufrière's eruption was actually an indication that the magma bulge was extraordinarily large—no less than one hundred miles long—and therefore that it was attempting to release an incredible amount of pent-up geothermal energy through just a couple of tiny orifices. Much worse, in fact, was yet to come.

Curiously, anecdotal evidence suggests that there may even have been a third eruption taking place simultaneously in the same region. At least a century earlier, sailors had noted strange phenomena in the Grenadines south of St. Vincent—a region where the sea sometimes bubbled and ejected clouds of steam. Navigational charts, for reasons now obscure, began to label that landless spot Kick 'em Jenny. Today it is recognized as the site of an active underwater volcano.

On May 7, 1902, the Danish steamship *Nordby* was sailing through this area. Captain Eric Lillienskjold logged the following account of the events of that day:

We were plodding along slowly that day. About noon I took the bridge to make an observation. It seemed to be hotter than ordinary. I shed my coat and vest and got into what little shade there was. As I worked it grew hotter and hotter. I didn't know what to make of it. Along about 2 o'clock in the afternoon it was so hot that all hands got to talking about it. We reckoned that something queer was coming off, but none of us could explain what it was. You could almost see the pitch softening in the seams.

Then, as quickly as you could toss a biscuit over its rail, the *Nordby* dropped three or four feet down into the sea. No sooner did it do this than big waves, that looked like they were coming from all directions at once, began to smash against our sides. This was queerer yet, because the water a minute before was as smooth as I ever saw it. I had all hands piped on deck, and we battened down everything loose to make ready for a storm. And we got it all right—the strangest storm you ever heard tell of.

There was something wrong with the sun that afternoon. It grew red and then dark red and then, about a quarter after 2, it went out of sight altogether. The day got so dark that you couldn't see half a ship's length ahead of you. We got our lamps going, and put on our oilskins, ready for a hurricane. All of a sudden there came a sheet of lightning that showed up the whole tumbling sea for miles and miles. We sort of ducked, expecting an awful crash of thunder, but it didn't come. There was no sound except the big waves pounding against our sides. There wasn't a breath of wind.

Well, sir, at that minute there began the most exciting time I've ever been through, and I've been on every sea on the map for twenty-five years. Every second there'd be waves 15 or 20 feet high, belting us head-on, stern-on and broadside, all at once. We could see them coming, for without any stop at all flash after flash of lightning was blazing all about us.

Something else we could see, too. Sharks! There were hundreds of them on all sides, jumping up and down in the water. Some of them jumped clear out of it. And sea birds! A flock of them squawking and crying, made for our rigging and perched there. They seemed like they were scared to death. But the queerest part of it all was the water itself. It was hot—not so hot that our feet could not stand it when it washed over the deck, but hot enough to make us think that it had been heated by some sort of fire.

Well that sort of thing went on hour after hour. The waves, the lightning, the hot water and the sharks, and all the rest of the odd things happening, frightened the crew out of their wits. Some of them prayed out loud—I guess the first time they ever did in their lives. Some Frenchmen aboard kept running around and yelling, 'C'est le dernier jour!' (This is the last day.)

May 7 was not the last day for the crew of the *Nordby*. Although Kick 'em Jenny's vent was more than 3,800 feet above the sea floor in 1902, it was still nearly 1,000 feet below the *Nordby*. The volcano has grown considerably since then, and eruption columns broke the surface in 1939 and 1974. Yet, as of this writing, the volcano's summit remains under about 400 feet of water. At the present rate of growth, a new island will emerge from the sea sometime this century.

CHAPTER 9

FINAL EDITION

•

Wednesday, May 7. Tomorrow, the presses at 177 Rue Victor Hugo would be idle in observance of Ascension Thursday, a holy day of obligation for Catholics. Friday, the presses would still be quiet, this time not for religious reasons but because they would lie buried under tons of smoldering debris. But Andréus Hurard was not thinking in terms of a natural disaster (in which he and everyone else in St. Pierre would perish); this morning he was thinking about the possibility of a political calamity. With the election only a few days away and the volcano making the electorate jittery, the content of today's paper could have long-term political implications. After all, people who were considering evacuating were unlikely to place voting at the top of their list of priorities. And further, if there *were* to be a wholesale evacuation, the huge masses of refugees would certainly overwhelm all the public resources that could possibly be provided, and the governor and everyone else in authority would end up looking inept at best. Such chaos would surely lay the groundwork for a Radical victory, if not in this election, then certainly in the next.

The layout of *Les Colonies* usually struck visiting Americans as a bit old-fashioned. Its front page carried no banner headlines or illustrations, just four columns of crowded print with a few column-width headings here and there. The inside pages were equally crowded. The insightful traveler would fairly conclude that newsprint stock was at a premium in Martinique (as indeed it was).

Andréus Hurard began the first column of the front page not with the latest news on the volcano but with an endorsement of the Progressive Party's candidates for the legislature. It was essential that the announcement be large enough that even those with weak eyesight would have no trouble reading it. It also had to be uncluttered enough that an illiterate voter could carry the page to the polls and easily match Hurard's endorsed candidates with the names on the ballot. He would need to set the type by hand rather than on the linotype, whose fonts and sizes were limited. He pulled out his cases of block letters and experimented with the spacing, the sizes, the styles. Although the type had to be arranged in reverse to the final printed page, Hurard did this quite automatically; he had been in the business long enough that the mental gymnastics of reading text in mirror image was second nature. He locked the type together, carried the assembled plate to a small hand press, and printed a proof. It read:

ELECTIONS LEGISLATIVES
2 tour de scrutin, Dimanche 11 Mai

Alliance rèpublicaine démocratique
Parti rèpublicaine progressiste martiniquaise

ARRONDISSEMENT DU NORD
FERNAND CLERC
CANDIDAT

ARRONDISSEMENT DU SUD
O. DUQUESNAY
CANDIDAT

Yes, that would do. And so much for treating the reader's eyes to the extravagance of white space; after this, *Les Colonies*'s customary fine print would begin.

The first article would need to deal with the volcano; after all, that certainly was the big news. But the tone had to be reassuring. Hurard flipped through an old French geology book he had borrowed from Professor Landes, marked off some passages he really didn't understand, and handed it to his linotype compositor. The heading would read "LES VOLCANS." The result: a curiously technical explanation of the contemporary geologic theory of volcanic eruptions, the source of this information unclear (and much of it misinformed, even by the scientific standards of 1902), running on for a column and a half.

Hurard moved on with the layout. The next article, he decided, would be based on a conversation he had had yesterday with Gaston Landes. He sifted through his notes and wrote the following:

AN INTERVIEW WITH M. LANDES

M. Landes, the distinguished professor of the Lycée, was pleased to grant us an interview yesterday, regarding the volcanic eruption of the Montagne Pelée and the phenomena which preceded the catastrophe of the Usine Guérin.

The following is the result of our conversation.

On the morning of the 5th (May), M. Landes observed torrents of smoke escaping from the summit portion of the mountain, from the locality known as the *Terre Fendue*. He observed that the Rivière Blanche was periodically swelling, and that it was running with five times the volume of water that the high floods normally furnish. It was hurling along blocks of rock some of which must have weighed fifty tons.

M. Landes was stationed at the habitation of Perrinelle and searched at twelve-fifty for the Etang Sec; he noted a whitish mass descend the slope of the mountain with the swiftness of an express train, and enter below the valley of the river, where it marked its course with a thick cloud of white smoke. It was this mass of mud, and not lava, which submerged the Usine.

M. Landes holds that the phenomenon of Monday is unique in the history of volcanoes. It is true, he tells us, that the mud lavas develop with very great rapidity, but this catastrophe was determined rather by an avalanche than by a flow of mud lava. The valley has received the contents of L'Etang Sec, whose dike having broken, permitted the fall of the muddy waters from an altitude of seven hundred meters. If, as a surprising fact, there is no trembling of the surface under the influence of this enormous fall, it is simply because the sea has acted as a buffer.

It follows from the observations of M. Landes that yesterday morning [May 6] the central mouth of the volcano, situated over the higher fissures, vomited out more actively than ever pulvurulent yellow and black matter. It would be advisable to leave the neighboring valleys and to locate rather on the elevations in order to escape submergence by the mud lava, as was the fate of Herculaneum and Pompeii. Vesuvius, adds M. Landes, has made but few victims. Pompeii was vacated in time, and there have been but few bodies found in the engulfed cities.

Conclusion: Montagne Pelée presents no more danger to the inhabitants of St. Pierre than does Vesuvius to those of Naples.

Gaston Landes would not live long enough to confirm or correct these words that Andréus Hurard attributed to him. Given the chance, he surely would have objected that Hurard's last sentence was purely editorial in origin and illogical in substance. The only reason Landes had mentioned Vesuvius at all was to point out the historical precedent for a prudent evacuation from the lower elevations! Given that most of Pompeii was vacated in time, it was by no means clear to Landes that St. Pierre shouldn't currently be evacuating under this comparable threat.

But to Monsieur Hurard as he picked and chose his words, political logic was more relevant than scientific logic. A mass evacuation would throw the city's economic activity into chaos, raise the problem of security of the empty homes and businesses, turn the election of May 11 topsy-turvy, and overwhelm Fort-de-France with an influx of no less than thirty thousand people with no way to house or feed them. That scenario would be a certain disaster, from which no one would emerge looking good. Against this prospect, Hurard weighed the possibility that additional lives might be lost to Mont Pelée. Looking at a map, anyone could see that the tragedy of the Usine Guérin was due to its unfortunate location at the mouth of the Rivière Blanche and its valley, and that a similar devastating mudflow into St. Pierre was a total impossibility. The prospect of a sociopolitical disaster was much more real than the chance of a serious natural disaster. The governor had apparently arrived at the same conclusion, and in fact Mouttet was already preparing to come to St. Pierre to lend his personal presence to calming the masses.

Yet people were panicking, and that was real. Hurard felt responsible for keeping the civil chaos from escalating further. He was not one to flagrantly falsify the news, but neither was he above embellishing it with his own interpretations in the service of the public welfare. Nor, for that matter, trying to nudge future developments in the right direction. As the thunder of the volcano rattled the windows of his office, Hurard considered what additional events might loom on the horizon to further terrorize the citizens of St. Pierre. He could think of one, and only one—there might be an earthquake.

Andréus Hurard understood as little about earthquakes as he did of other things geologic or scientific. But he did know of the 1839 earthquake that had rocked Fort-de-France, destroyed many buildings, and claimed five hundred lives. Although St. Pierre had never in its history suffered any serious tremors, how would the people around him react if the current rumblings of Pelée should start shaking the ground? Hurard quickly answered his own question: if even a minor earthquake were to occur when no one was mentally prepared for that possibility, the current panic would surely escalate (regardless of the historical fact that it was Fort-de-France, and not St. Pierre, that was prone to earthquakes). Clearly, Hurard needed to seed his readers' minds with the possibility of a ground tremor, yet in as innocuous and reassuring a manner as possible.

His mind growing weary, he added a comment after the interview with Landes:

> Nevertheless, this morning, the mountain being uncovered, the Morne LaCroix shows in its lower part, on the side of L'Etang Plein, a gash one hundred meters in length and forty meters in height, making possible the fall of this prominence, and with it the production of an earth tremor.

Ergo, if the ground should shake today, his faithful readers were to conclude only that some rock had fallen.

The next front-page article was a piece he had written the day before. It included some dramatic phrases—language most readers would consider appropriate (and expected) in reporting an event that was the major news of the decade. But now as he copyedited, he reconsidered the wisdom of conveying a sense of drama to his readers. The hand typesetting required for the header had already been done, and that he left intact. But the last few paragraphs he revised to blandness and had his compositor reset them on the linotype. The published version would read as follows:

AUTOUR
D'UNE
CATASTROPHE

THE PRECHEUR

The Precheur River overflowed its banks yesterday and the day before, and has carried with it enormous masses of rock. A very curious phenomenon was noted to take place at its mouth. Soundings made at this point yesterday indicate that a large excavation has been formed. The water which had hitherto at that point a depth of one meter has now eight meters. The cause of this excavation has not been ascertained.

THE RIVIÈRE DES PÈRES

A similar condition, the result of a terrible overflow, is found at the mouth of the Rivière des Pères. Yesterday evening, at about seven o'clock, the flood increased and was flowing with dark water, which was thought to be a simple rise brought on by the rains. Presently there came a torrent which swept with it great quantities of bamboo, and later, trees and giant blocks of rocks, which are still to be seen in the bed of the stream. The bridge of the estate of Perrinelle has disappeared, buried, as it were, beneath the boulders of rock. If the walls of the property had not fortunately been strong enough to resist the pressure, the stables would have been carried away by the torrent. This first overflow lasted until about ten o'clock, when it began to diminish, only to commence again at two o'clock in the morning.

It is to be reported that at its discharge the water of the river is engulfed in the enormous cavity which has been cut at this point, and that it carries down with it all the vegetable and mineral debris which it has swept up in its course. A little beyond, the current reappears at the surface of the sea, still laden with debris.

THE OVERFLOW OF THE ROXELANE

The Roxelane overflowed in its turn at about seven o'clock yesterday evening. This sudden rise was due to the heavy fall of rain on the surrounding heights. The river holds in suspension all the ash that it has caught up, and is consequently of a dark color. Great quantities of dead fish have been observed at its mouth.

AT BASSE-POINTE

The river of Basse-Pointe has overflowed since yesterday and flows with black water. It is reported—but we have no means of confirming the report, as the telegraph wires are everywhere broken—that several houses have been carried away by the waters.

AT LORRAIN

The Capot, whose waters have been slightly discolored, is now flowing so muddy that the mouth of the river is full of dead fish. About one hundred and fifty kilos of dead and torpid fish have been taken from the irrigating canal of Vivé.

MUDDY RAINS

Yesterday, throughout most of the day, there fell in the north a fine blackish rain, which was so charged with ash as to make the carrying of an umbrella a matter of discomfort.

A RESCUE

A fisherman named Thomas assisted M. Rénus in the rescue which we reported yesterday, and which was of a particularly perilous nature. The boat, which contained MM. Dupuis-Nouillé the younger, Louis Claude, Elysée Fleurisson and three other passengers, and was manned by M. Stephane Larade, was upset and broken by the muddy torrent and the numerous tree-trunks that were swept along with it.

THE DEAD

Contrary to reports that had been circulated, the body of Mlle. Pauline Fleurisson has not yet been recovered. We have to report among the dead two children of M. St.-Just Prosper, one still at the breast and the other sick, who were in a boat near to that of M. Rénus.

Following this article, and completing the front page, Hurard ran a list of the subscribers to a general relief fund for the victims of the mudflow of May 5 on the Rivière Blanche. The balance reported was 966.25 francs.

Yet if the edition didn't include something about the general state of confusion in the city, such a report would certainly be conspicuous in its absence. But how to describe a panic without escalating the hysteria? Hurard drew upon his rhetorical skills and wrote the following, stuffing it in an unfinished column on an inside page:

THE PANIC AT SAINT PIERRE

The exodus from Saint Pierre is steadily increasing. From morning to evening and through the whole night one sees only hurrying people, carrying packages, trunks, and children, and directing their course to Fonds-Saint-Denis, Morne-d'Orange, Carbet, and elsewhere. The steamers of the Compagnie Girard are no longer empty. To give an idea of this mad flight, we give the following figures. The number of passengers which on the line of Fort-de-France was ordinarily eighty a day, has risen since three days to three hundred.

We confess that we cannot understand this panic. Where better could one be than in Saint Pierre? Do those who invade Fort-de-France believe that they will be better off there than here should the earth begin to quake? This is a foolish error against which the populace should be warned.

We hope that the opinion expressed by M. Landes in the interview which we published will reassure the most timid.

Hurard saw to the loading of the last bundles of papers into the wagons, checked that the type had been sorted back into the linotype magazines, confirmed that the burners were extinguished under the melt pots and the presses wiped down, and sent off his staff with wishes for a good holiday. Then he locked up his shop and made his way home through the afternoon volcanic gloom and the turmoil in the streets, content with himself that he done his civic duty for the day.

His words *"Where better could one be than in Saint Pierre?"* would reverberate for the next century.

• • •

That afternoon, the stream of refugees pouring into St. Pierre from the outlying villages swelled to a small flood of humanity. There were no facilities to house them, and they camped wherever they could: in the parks, the streets, the churches, the two cemeteries. Relief provisions had been arriving on every ferry, but their distribution had become a problem and fights were breaking out. Around 2 p.m., Mayor Fouché telephoned the governor in Fort-de-France and explained that people were getting unruly and additional gendarmes were desperately needed to keep the peace and supervise the distribution of food. Mouttet promised to send a detachment of thirty colonial infantry under the command of a lieutenant. They would arrive the next morning. Mouttet himself would arrive in a few hours.

In the confusion that would follow during the next few days, this action would be misinterpreted, and the rumor would circulate that Mouttet was sending increasing numbers of police and militia to prevent St. Pierre's evacuation. Some versions of the story would be even further corrupted, to the claim that the militia actually *did* block the roads to evacuation. By that time, Mouttet would have no advocates still alive to defend his deteriorated reputation. A case of the French wisdom, "Les absents ont toujours tort" (The absent are always in the wrong).

Later that afternoon, an unannounced sea swell swept into the waterfronts at St. Pierre and Fort-de-France. In both places, the high water remained for several minutes before it ebbed. The damage was insignificant, but the attention it drew was not. Newly arrived refugees were bewildered; had they left the slopes for the presumed safety of the city only to look forward to being swept away by the sea? With the volcano threatening above and the ashes still falling, were they now trapped between the terrible prospects of burning, smothering, or drowning?

But some took a more thoughtful approach, for the wave had curiously arrived from the *south*. This observation, coupled with the first piecemeal stories of the eruption on St. Vincent, gave cause for optimism. If indeed this strange wave originated at St. Vincent and traveled more than one hundred miles so quickly, then the event on that British island must have been incredibly violent. And with a big volcanic eruption in progress elsewhere, surely that would help deflate Mont Pelée. With little doubt, the volcano looming above St. Pierre would settle down soon and enter another half century of slumber.

• • •

For the few days he expected to be out of town, Mouttet delegated his authority to the colony's secretary-general, Georges L'Heurre. Around 4 p.m, he and Maria kissed their three children good-bye, gave the nannies their last instructions, and boarded the *Topaze* for St. Pierre. The governor had been talking with Hurard by telephone, and that rational newsman did not view the volcano as a serious threat. Mayor Fouché had expressed concerns about the public safety, but only because of the possibility of mass panic and not because of any fears about the volcano itself. Most of the businessmen and foreign consuls in St. Pierre were going about their regular activities, and most of their families were still in town. Although the U.S. consul, Thomas Prentiss, was apparently thinking about leaving, that was probably only under the pressure of his high-strung wife; in any case, even Prentiss had not suggested that Mouttet order a mass evacuation. Only one person had been pestering Mouttet to evacuate the city: Fernand Clerc. And Mouttet had little confidence in *that* man's sense of good judgment.

As they docked at St. Pierre, Maria was struck speechless at the sight of the volcano's thundering eruption column. As she stepped ashore, she could feel the ground trembling beneath her. And then, as if the mountain was greeting their arrival with a bad joke, Pelée detonated a series of explosions that ejected boulders large enough to be seen with the naked eye. Maria stood paralyzed by the spectacle. Louis put his hand on her back, and when the last of the salvo had dissipated, he gently reassured her. "Don't worry," he said. "It's a full seven kilometers away."

• • •

As Maria settled into the suite at the Hotel Intendance, Louis went to the dining room, which had been closed to the public pending his arrival. It was a bit after 5 p.m. Waiting for him were four members of his Scientific Commission: Professors Gaston Landes and Eugène Doze of the Lycée, Lieutenant-Colonel Jules Gerbault of the artillery, and the civil engineer William Léonce. Conspicuously absent was Paul Mirville, head chemist and pharmacist for the colonial troops in Fort-de-France.

Mouttet's question was apparent in his eyes, and Gerbault responded by motioning toward a telegram lying on the table. It was from Mirville, apologizing that he had been unavoidably detained by his duties in Fort-de-France and would like to be advised of the time and place of the committee's next meeting. Mouttet did not hide his displeasure.

News of the meeting had spread quickly through the streets, and a crowd was already gathering outside the hotel, eager to hear the first news of the commission's findings. The men at the table all knew it was time for business and nothing else. Although Mouttet had appointed Gerbault as chair of the commission, no one challenged the governor when he began presiding himself. Mouttet looked around the table and asked if everyone present had been thinking about the situation from the perspective of their individual areas of expertise. They all assured him they had. The governor turned to Gerbault and asked him to begin by sharing his own expert appraisal.

Although there is no way today to know the actual words exchanged during that consequential meeting, the dossiers of the participants and the meeting's outcome suggest that the deliberations probably went something like what follows.

From an artillery perspective, Gerbault would have begun, he had observed that Pelée was occasionally ejecting bursts of large projectiles. The largest of these boulders were many times heavier than any cannonball, and no doubt were capable of destroying buildings or ships. There was, however, no risk to St. Pierre. The boulders were being ejected vertically, or nearly so, and were therefore falling back on the upper slopes of the mountain. So far, these projectiles had been observed to attain altitudes no higher than about one thousand meters (3,300 feet) above the vent, which, according to his artillery tables, gave them a maximum initial velocity of about 140 meters per second (310 miles per hour). A good French cannon does much better than that. Even if Pelée did begin to eject its bombs with more horizontal trajectories, Gerbault explained, the tables made it clear that none could possibly travel as far as St. Pierre.

"Do I understand you correctly, colonel," the governor asked, "that the risk from volcanic bombs is not a sufficient reason to evacuate the city?"

"Yes, sir," the colonel assured. "There is absolutely no danger from volcanic bombs."

"And what about the loud explosions? Do we know what is causing them?"

"Only one explanation is possible, sir: combustible fumes are being ignited in the volcano's chimney. But although these explosions may sound dangerous, I can assure you they are not. The volcano is not a cannon barrel, which is designed to direct a detonation fully against the backside of a cannonball. The volcano's chimney is very wide and irregular, and it opens vertically upward. The explosions everyone hears are no more than harmless dissipations of energy into the atmosphere. The worst they can do is to toss a few rocks into the air."

Mouttet turned to the other three members of the commission. "Do you gentlemen have anything to add on the issue of volcanic bombs?"

Doze and Léonce were silent. Gaston Landes replied, "Your Excellency, I have observed the bombs myself through the telescope. I fully concur with Colonel Gerbault's assessment on this particular aspect of the matter."

"Then," said the governor, "let's move on. May we hear from you, Monsieur Léonce?"

William Léonce took a breath and looked at his notes. "Your Excellency," he began, "the engineering issues are as follows: First, will the structures withstand the weight of the ash accumulations? Second, will they withstand an earthquake? Third, what if there is a fire? And fourth, are the roads capable of supporting a full evacuation?"

"Begin with number four," said Mouttet.

"Well, sir, as you know, there is only one road along the coast, the Trace Road, and you are aware of its condition. And, with all due respect, sir, you know how it gets when it rains. And the rainy season is just beginning."

"And the implications?"

"The road would never hold up under the wagon traffic of a full evacuation," said Léonce. "It would become a quagmire, vehicles would get stuck, and you would have a procession of thirty thousand people grinding to a halt. You might be able to evacuate most of the residents if they walked, but they couldn't take many of their belongings. And with all the hills on that road, only the people in good physical condition would make it all the way to Fort-de-France."

"So if we evacuate the city, people will need to abandon their personal belongings?" mused the governor. "And the very old and the very young may have to stay behind?"

"Yes, sir."

"What are the other issues on your list?"

"Well, sir, there is the weight of the ash. Most of the public buildings, commercial buildings, and the gable-roofed houses should be all right. But if the ash gets too deep, many roofs on the poorer homes might collapse. That is, unless someone keeps them shoveled off."

"Of course, that means that whoever does the shoveling does not evacuate."

"That is correct, sir."

"Go on."

"Then there is the earthquake matter. There are some multistory masonry buildings here, and they could collapse. But the situation on that score is no different than that in Fort-de-France, and historically the most serious earthquakes have struck there, not here. So it doesn't seem justified to evacuate because of the possibility of an earthquake."

Mouttet nodded thoughtfully. "And you mentioned fire?"

"Yes, Your Excellency. Fire could be an issue. Not so much the tile-roofed masonry buildings, but the smaller places and the homes in the outskirts. And the issue with fire in a city is always whether there is a means to extinguish it. In other words, is there sufficient water, and are there enough people to carry and pump it? Now at present, with all the streams flooding, there is obviously plenty of water. So if there is a fire, the best chance of containing it will surely be if people *don't* evacuate."

"So," said Mouttet, "from an engineering perspective, if I understand correctly, you think that an evacuation would actually *increase* the risk of property loss?"

"More than that, sir. An evacuation would virtually guarantee some property losses. In fact, *major* losses would be likely if the city were evacuated."

"Does anyone disagree with Monsieur Léonce's report?" the governor asked.

No one responded.

"I had hoped that Monsieur Mirville would be here tonight," he continued, "to give us an assessment of the issue of the chemistry of the atmosphere. In his absence, can you, Professor Doze, offer us any insights on that matter?"

Eugène Doze was a man who loved a forum, and he rose to the occasion. "Your Excellency, and gentlemen," he began. "We have all seen the birds falling dead from the skies. We have heard about the snakes slithering from the mountain, and we have seen our fellow citizens coughing and covering their faces with handkerchiefs. And we have all heard the tales of horses snorting too deeply, then dropping dead in the street!" Everyone nodded. "But before we draw any rash conclusions about the poisonous atmosphere, gentlemen, I must ask you this: who among you has actually seen a horse drop dead in the streets?"

Raised eyebrows.

"As I thought," continued Doze. "A few birds fly into a cloud of fumes that rise, as fumes always do, away from the ground we ourselves inhabit. These birds become dizzy and plummet to their deaths. A bystander witnesses this incident and figures: if birds, why not horses? And before you know it, the story of horses dropping dead is all over town. No matter that horses don't fly into ash clouds. And neither, may I point out, do humans!"

The governor suppressed a smile at the mental image. "In summary, Professor Doze?"

"In summary, Your Excellency and gentlemen: If the atmosphere were poisonous, people would be dying. But they are not dying. They are indeed coughing, sneezing, and some are complaining, but to my knowledge no one has yet died of asphyxiation. It would be a rash action to evacuate the city just because people are wheezing and spreading stories about dead horses."

"I see," said Mouttet, releasing his smile. "However, I trust you will keep a sharp eye and inform this commission immediately should you witness one of St. Pierre's horses flying into an ash cloud."

Eugène Doze smiled back and bowed.

When the laughter subsided, Mouttet turned to Gaston Landes. "And you, Professor Landes, what is your scientific assessment of the risk?"

"Your Excellency," said Landes, "I have been observing the volcano every day since early April. I have read every book related to volcanoes on the shelves in the Lycée and the Schoelcher Library. If you had asked me your question a week ago, I would have assured you that there is virtually no risk. But now I am not so sure. As you know, the volcano has recently caused numerous deaths and considerable property damage."

"But that was from the flooding and the mudflows," said the governor. "Surely you must agree that those incidents will not expand beyond the ravines and valleys."

"Yes, sir," Landes agreed, "the mudflows will stay in the valleys."

"And if there should be a flow of molten rock, would that follow a path any different than the mud?"

"Any molten lava will also follow the valleys," Landes agreed.

"Then," said the governor, "it would seem that we simply need to warn the people to move away from the streams and the ravines."

Gaston Landes shook his head. "My point, Your Excellency, is that a week ago no one would have thought that such devastating mudflows could result from a volcanic eruption. None of the books mention such a phenomenon. And if the books are all silent about mudflows, what else might they be silent about? There may be other mysterious phenomena, horrible beyond our imagination, in store for us. To me, sir, it would seem prudent to begin an orderly evacuation of the entire city."

"Professor," said the governor, "I must ask you to be more specific. What other life-threatening phenomena could there be?"

"I don't know," said Landes. "But Mont Pelée has already surprised us repeatedly. It seems presumptuous of us to think that it won't do so again."

Colonel Gerbault interrupted. "I believe it's clear, gentlemen, that we must reach a conclusion. And in my view, we have but two alternatives. We either organize an evacuation, or we do not. If we do, we create immense hardships not only for the forty thousand evacuated, but also for the seventeen thousand citizens of Fort-de-France who must cope with the presence of so many refugees. But if we do not evacuate, we create no more discomfort than Mother Nature herself has already delivered to the people of this fair city and the surrounding villages. If we do evacuate, many personal possessions will be looted or otherwise lost, and the civil upheaval will have effects that continue long after Mont Pelée has returned to slumber. But if we do not evacuate, St. Pierre's citizenry will be on hand to preserve their personal properties and possessions. If we do evacuate, we will need to provide food and public services in Fort-de-France. But if we do not evacuate, we will need to provide no greater a quantity of food and services here in St. Pierre. So I ask you, gentlemen, is this really an issue?"

Louis Mouttet looked around the table. The only one not nodding in agreement was Gaston Landes. Instead, the professor was staring out into space, his mind grasping for he knew not what.

Mouttet turned to him. "Professor Landes," he said, "I hope you will think about what additional surprises Mont Pelée can possibly send our way. And as soon as you have the answer, I trust you will inform this commission immediately. In the meantime, this body must develop a report that I can forward to the Ministry of Colonies. I have no choice but to report the majority opinion."

He called in his secretary, who had been listening to the proceedings from the hall. As he dictated a draft of the commission's findings, deferring to an occasional suggested rewording, only Gaston Landes sat silent.

The draft complete, Mouttet stood. "Gentlemen," he said, "I thank you for your valuable input. But our deliberations tonight have dealt only with the safety of St. Pierre. Clearly, we must also consider the other towns of North Martinique, and the place of most immediate concern to me is Precheur. I will arrange for a skiff to carry us there tomorrow morning for a firsthand investigation. Please plan to meet here at seven o'clock tomorrow morning."

With that, he adjourned the meeting.

• • •

Mouttet went to the front steps of the hotel and greeted the gathered crowd. He announced that his Scientific Commission had duly deliberated all aspects of the issue. What St. Pierre was experiencing, he said, was no less yet no more than could be expected from a volcano in eruption. He assured those assembled that they had already seen the worst that could possibly happen. He looked to his notes. In the words of the commission, he read,

La position relative des cratères et des vallées débouchant vers la mer permet d'affirmer que la sécurité de Saint-Pierre reste entière.

Translation: the relative positions of the craters and valleys opening toward the sea assure the complete safety of St. Pierre.

CHAPTER 10

WHIRLWIND OF FIRE

•

A s the governor soothed the throng outside the hotel, Gaston Landes mounted his horse. He had no need to listen to the rhetoric that a committee of human experts could guarantee the cooperation of the forces of nature. Yet he cursed himself, as one who normally prided himself on his scientific objectivity, that he had been able to offer the commission no more than an ineffective emotional appeal for why St. Pierre should be evacuated. He would need to do better at the commission's next meeting.

The sun had just set, and its waning rays cast a pink glow onto Pelée's towering ash cloud. The volcanic summit itself was veiled by a swirling mist, and low dark clouds were moving in from behind. Lightning flickered in the east. It was the beginning of the rainy season, and the expected rains were on their way.

The city sidewalks were clogged with poor wretches camped outdoors. What few belongings they had, and what makeshift bedding they lay on, were about to be drenched. A young mother sat forlorn against a wall, suckling her infant. A thin gray-haired woman lay on a bed of banana leaves someone had lovingly provided for her. Another group of women knelt on the pavement, praying the rosary. A beehive of humanity swarmed through the crowded corridors, bustling about with no obvious destination. His horse's progress slowed to a snail's pace, Landes watched the scared children, the tired old men, the young men exchanging bravados. Clusters of expatriates and upper-class folk somberly viewed the confusion from their balconies. Were they more concerned about the forces of nature or about civil order? Maybe they themselves couldn't say.

Landes thought about Colonel Gerbault's argument that evacuating St. Pierre would be the worst possible decision, and how persuasive that rationale had been. Yet his gut kept telling the professor that something ominous lurked beneath the colonel's logic. Was the chaos in the streets affecting his own scientific judgment? Or, after having watched the volcano for so long, was it possible that he had developed a level of intuition about the eruption? Maybe, Landes thought, there are some questions about nature that simply can't be decided scientifically.

The traffic thinned only slightly at the outskirts of town. A long line of simpler folk was still entering the city from the hills, even as carriages were evacuating some of the wealthier citizens to those same hills. One convoy of heavily laden carriages was taking twenty-six people to the country home of Monsieur Raybaud, managing director of the St. James Rum Company. Dr. Guérin had already moved to the south of the island with the surviving members of his family. The word in town was that other families were planning to leave. Yet the number of people that had actually left so far did not come close to offsetting the influx. The population of St. Pierre was actually swelling!

Professor Landes's home stood on a foothill northeast of the city. The site commanded a magnificent panorama—the Caribbean to the west, then the city of St. Pierre, the Plaine de la Consolation, the town of Morne Rouge to the east, and, towering above everything, the majestic Mont Pelée. Tonight, however, the weather was beginning to obstruct that view. As Landes dismounted and handed the reins to his stable-boy, the first drops of rain began to fall. He went inside, lit an oil lamp, and sat gazing out the window into the dusk.

He had no doubt that he and his servants were safe, situated here on a grade facing the volcano across a broad valley. But what about the masses downslope of the eruption? The geographic relationship of St. Pierre to Mont Pelée was almost identical to that of ancient Pompeii to Mount Vesuvius, and at Pompeii several thousand people had been killed. The climax of that ancient disaster must have come on suddenly, for recent excavations there revealed that many folk were going about their daily business when they were struck dead. But what killed those victims? Surely it wasn't the ash alone, for how could thousands simply sit around and allow themselves to be buried in ash? Something additional must have happened. But what? Meanwhile, thousands of others apparently had evacuated Pompeii. What warning signs had led them to evacuate? And were those warning signs any different from the ones Pelée had been serving up this past week?

The rainfall grew into a torrential downpour. Thunderclaps drowned out the rumbling of the volcano, and the visibility, even with the lightning, decreased to a few dozen feet. Yet Landes continued to gaze into the storm. He cursed himself for not having been more forceful with the Scientific Commission. For not reminding everyone about Pompeii. He thought about the poor refugees in the streets of St. Pierre. And about the people of Precheur, who must be truly terrified now that their only road out of town had been swept away.

Tomorrow the commission was to take a boat to Precheur. For what? To deliver more rhetoric? No, Landes decided, he would not be part of that. He would stay home and prepare himself to make a more compelling presentation to the governor when everyone returned in the afternoon. Precheur needed to be evacuated, and so did St. Pierre, regardless of how difficult a process that would be.

•   •   •

The downpour brought a miserable night to the people of Precheur. After dozens of roofs had collapsed during the ashfalls of the previous week, the displaced families had taken refuge, along with their salvageable belongings, in the homes of friends and neighbors. Tonight many of the roofs of these crowded surviving homes were leaking like sieves. Without stone sidewalks or paved gutters, the streets of this working-class community became impassable. Freshets poured down the steeper paths into town, and water streamed in under front doors. Outside it was pitch-black; the meager street lighting had gone out with the rest of the power three days earlier. Lamp oil and candles were in short supply. The thunder was incessant, and strange rumblings seemed to come through the ground. And, unbeknownst to the masses that huddled in fear that night of May 7, the Precheur River that bisected the town was turning violent.

As the rain tapered off in the morning twilight, the first to venture outside were struck by a horrible sight. The church was badly damaged, its foundation precariously undermined by the rampaging river. Worse, much worse—during the night there had been another devastating mud-flow. Riding the storm's floodwaters, it had destroyed nearly sixty homes and swept their four hundred occupants out to sea.

Mayor Grelet and Father Desprez, themselves astounded at the loss of lives, struggled to calm the frantic villagers. It was obviously too late for those four hundred victims to evacuate, but what of the remaining four thousand? There were two cable-repair ships within sight of Precheur, both sturdy vessels that could each carry off hundreds of refugees at a time. To the south, not far offshore St. Pierre, floated the aptly named *Grappler*, which was attempting to locate and raise the ends of the severed cable between St. Pierre and Guadeloupe. Farther out, some eight miles off the coast of the Rivière Blanche, the even larger *Pouyer-Quertier* was repairing another cable that ran directly to France. It was astonishing to the community's leaders that these two French ships that might have begun a timely evacuation of Precheur were instead fussing about fixing telegraph cables. Did the governor value cablegrams more than human lives? Or had he just made a terrible misjudgment?

As the mayor and the abbé did their best to reassure their remaining constituents that the government was aware of the plight of the people of Precheur, twenty-year-old Chavigny de la Chevrotière volunteered to lead a party of eleven friends in a pirogue to carry a message directly to Governor Mouttet. That message was simple: Precheur had to be evacuated. Immediately! At 7:30 a.m., Chevrotière's party started paddling toward St. Pierre.

Another group of townspeople, frustrated with the false promises and hollow assurances of the previous week, set off up the mountainside toward the semaphore at Morne Folie. To hell with the governor; they would signal the cable ships themselves. Although that task would re-quire but a couple of men, hundreds of villagers followed. By 8 a.m., some

four hundred people had crowded onto that hillock on the side of the volcano above Precheur.

• • •

May 8, Ascension Thursday, dawned bright and sunny in St. Pierre.
News of the presence of the governor and his wife, along with the reas-
surances of the Scientific Commission, had quickly spread through the
city the night before. The night's cloudburst had washed the dust from
the streets and had driven most of the homeless refugees into out-of-sight
nooks and crannies. By conventional wisdom, the huge release of volcanic
energy that had taken place a hundred miles to the south could only mean
that Pelée had been defused. And indeed this morning, as the rainclouds
drifted off, Pelée's rumblings had waned to a restful snore. What could be
more reassuring?

Shortly after 6 a.m., the steam ferry *Topaze* departed for Fort-de-
France with only thirty-four passengers. Its nominal capacity was eighty,
and in a pinch it might have evacuated one hundred. But this fateful
morning, all but a handful of the thirty thousand in St. Pierre chose to
stay put. Most of those with intentions to leave had put those plans on
the back burner.

Volcanoes in eruption have a dangerous habit of teasing. They spout,
they fume, they bluster, they raise apprehensions, then they calm down
and seduce people into thinking the worst is over. Sometimes a quiet note
signals the onset of an extended period of dormancy that will continue for
decades or even centuries. Other times, however, a volcano becomes still
because its ejecta have temporarily clogged its vent. In those instances,
the subterranean pressure continues to build, and a short silence is but a
prelude to a cataclysmic explosion.

As the *Topaze* steamed off, St. Pierre's harbor began bustling with activity. Around 6:30 a.m., the *Roraima* of the Quebec Line arrived from
New York with forty-seven crew and twenty-one passengers. Although
its decks were covered with a dusting of ash, Chief Officer Ellery Scott
noted in his journal: "The sun was now shining out nice and bright, and
everything appeared to be pleasant and favorable." As the *Roraima* anchored, the company agents, Messieurs Plessoneau and Testart, climbed

aboard and reassured Captain George Muggah that the volcano had done no damage since the destruction of the Guérin sugar factory a few days earlier. Unloading the cargo could commence that afternoon, after all the church services were over.

Shortly before seven, the steamer *Roddam* arrived from St. Lucia. Having just steamed through the raging thunderstorm, and aware that communications with St. Pierre had been severed days earlier, Captain Edward Freeman entered the harbor with more trepidation. Later he would say:

> I did not like the look of Pelée. I asked Chief Officer Campbell whether he thought we should stay clear of the island. We decided to approach the harbor, reasoning that as other steamers were there, it was an indication it was safe, as they would know the situation better than we would.

Yet he would make a distinction between the appearance of the volcano and the appearance of the city:

> How pretty and gay St. Pierre managed to look in spite of the ash. The cathedral glistened in the sun. Then from its towers came the sound of the bells summoning the faithful for morning mass.

At 7 a.m., the *Diamant* chugged in from Fort-de-France with a boatload of passengers eager to use their Ascension Thursday holiday to see the volcano for themselves. Among those on board was the young writer René Bonneville, who waved from the deck to his father, who was leaving on the *Topaze*. It was the last time the elder Bonneville would see his son.

At 7:05 a.m., the telegrapher in St. Pierre began dispatching a lengthy message from the governor to Secretary-General Georges L'Heurre in Fort-de-France. It read:

> The commission that was charged to study the volcanic phenomena of Montagne Pelée assembled yesterday evening, May 7, at the Hotel Intendance in St. Pierre, with the Governor presiding. On examination of all the facts collected since the beginning of the eruption, the Commission concluded:

1. That all the phenomena that have occurred until this date are nothing abnormal and are, to the contrary, identical to the phenomena observed in all volcanoes.

2. That the craters of the volcano being largely opened, the vapor and muds will continue to flow as in the past without causing earthquakes or projections of eruptive rocks.

3. That the frequent audible detonations are produced by localized vapor explosions in the chimney, and are by no means due to the collapse of the ground.

4. That the hot water and mudflows are localized in the Blanche Valley.

5. That the relative positions of the craters and valleys opening toward the sea assure the complete safety of St. Pierre.

6. That the black waters of the Rivière des Pères, Basse-Pointe, Precheur, and others, have returned to their normal temperature and owe their abnormal color to the ash they carry.

The Commission will continue to follow all further phenomena attentively, and it will keep the population informed of the slightest changes it observes.

—MOUTTET

By the time Georges L'Huerre would read these words a few hours later, Governor Mouttet would be dead.

• • •

Fernand Clerc awoke at his St. Pierre residence and began to dress for church. As was his custom, he checked his aneroid barometer to get some idea of the upcoming weather. He heard a strange burping sound from the volcano, then a few seconds later the barometer needle began to oscillate wildly. He was shocked at the sight, for he had never seen atmospheric pressure fluctuate like that. He dashed to the window. Although there was no wind at ground level, a massive ash cloud was speeding through the sky over the city. Clerc wasn't exactly sure what to make of it all, but he did know it wasn't a good omen. He roused his servants and the two dozen guests who had spent the night and advised them all to quickly get out of St. Pierre. Then he hurried his wife and four children into the family carriage and raced off toward his country home near Parnasse, three miles out of town.

At 7:15 a.m., Louis Mouttet boarded a steam launch for the short trip to Precheur. Accompanying him were several officials and three members of his Scientific Commission: Colonel Jules Gerbault, Eugène Doze, and William Léonce. Gaston Landes was nowhere in sight. As they waited for the professor, Pelée belched another dense black cloud that raced westward over the city. The vent at L'Etang Sec had started to blast sideways, and with such force that cinders were arcing over St. Pierre and falling out at sea. Around 7:40 a.m., Mouttet concluded that Landes was not going to show up, and he gave the captain the go-ahead to shove off for Precheur. None on board had recognized the implications of the volcano's lateral ejections.

On a hill at Parnasse, Roger Arnoux was getting his first glimpse of Pelée's activity. Although a member of the French Astronomical Society, and therefore one whose scientific opinion might carry some weight, for the past few weeks he had been in southern Martinique recuperating from an illness. "I knew as surely as I stood there," he would later report, "that Pelée was on the verge of total eruption. But I could not foresee, and nobody could have, just how devastating that eruption would be." Indeed, from his higher vantage point, Arnoux could see something that was not visible from the city or the shoreline: in two different places, the summit of the volcano was glowing incandescently.

A few minutes before 8 a.m., Arnoux was distracted from the volcano by the sight of a carriage racing up the road. As the vehicle braked to a stop in a cloud of dust, the Clerc family "literally tumbled out" and Fernand Clerc drove them up the hillside, in Arnoux's words, "not unlike a sheep dog urging its flock to safety."

At 8 a.m., the telegraph operator at St. Pierre keyed "Allez" to the station in Fort-de-France. The latter asked for the news of the morning. At 8:02, Fort-de-France received a short trill over the wire from St. Pierre. Then nothing more.

At the same instant, a businessman in Fort-de-France was on the telephone to a friend in St. Pierre. "He had just finished his sentence," he would later tell journalists, "when I heard a dreadful scream, then another much weaker groan, like a stifled death rattle. Then silence."

Mont Pelée had exploded.

• • •

There were two blasts, virtually simultaneous. One discharged vertically, driving a billowing mass of ash and steam to an altitude of seven miles. The second exploded sideways, sending a monstrous pyroclastic surge down the volcano's southwestern flanks.

It was the lower crater, L'Etang Sec, that coughed out the ground-hugging cloud. But unlike the mudflow of May 5 that had erupted from that same area, the nuée ardente did not limit its course to the valley of the Rivière Blanche. Instead, it exploded outward over a great fan-shaped region, quickly obliterating the villages of St. Philomene and Fonds-Coré and barely missing Precheur. To the south, the maelstrom of hot ash and superheated steam thundered toward St. Pierre. No matter that the terrain along the way was corrugated with ravines and ridges; this agent of destruction was too powerful to be deflected by such topographical features. Everyone in the region heard its roar, and given that it took two minutes to cover the four miles to the city, all of the victims in St. Pierre's streets certainly had a chance to see it bearing down on them.

Some ran toward the waterfront, others dashed into the nearest buildings, and many others dropped to the ground and covered their heads. But for those unfortunates in the path of the nuée ardente, all attempts to shield themselves or to escape were futile. Racing in at 120 miles per hour, the massive cloud struck the city with an avalanche-like impact that flattened even the stoutest of the north-facing masonry walls and buried thousands of victims in the rubble. Those who tried to outrun the onslaught were caught from behind and catapulted through the air as though shot from a cannon. With most of the cloud at a temperature near 700°F and pockets as hot as 1,300°F, it took only a single breath to fatally sear the lungs. Those engulfed by the lower-temperature regions received fatal steam burns, while flesh seared by the hotter gases was charred black. The pyroclastic current roared through St. Pierre continuously for three minutes, and even the east- and west-facing walls began to collapse. During those minutes, anyone who might have escaped being crushed, catapulted, seared internally, or burned externally, was left with no oxygen to breathe.

As the gases diffused upward, a gale-force wind rushed in to fill the vacuum. Combustible material in the rubble burst into flame, thousands of barrels of rum exploded, and within minutes the ruins of the grand city were engulfed in a firestorm. Meanwhile, the tons of rising steam began condensing overhead, and for the next hour it rained, covering the region with a thick paste of volcanic mud. Even this mud, however, could not extinguish the roaring fire; it would burn for three days.

• • •

The Clercs and their children had barely caught their breath from running up the hillside at Parnasse when the disaster unfolded below. In Véronique Clerc's words:

> We saw a sea of fire cutting through the billowing black smoke and advancing along the ground toward the town. What could we do? We held each other close. We wanted to die together, and we were waiting for death. It was a moment of anguish. Fear, lack of air, I know not what was the cause of the fearful choking in my throat. It was raining stones and mud, lumps of mud as big as coils of rope. St. Pierre was doomed. Our friends were doomed. Our world was doomed.

Fernand Clerc was to add:

> [There was a] continuous roar blended with staccato beats like the throbbing, pulsating sounds of a Gatling gun. It grew so dark that I could only be sure of the presence of my wife and children by groping for them and touching them with my hands.

Three miles south of the Clercs, Father Alte Roche watched with horror from the higher ground of Morne Verte.

> A column of fire, which I estimated to be at least four hundred meters in height, descended upon the town. It engulfed the statue of Christ and the cemetery. Then with a great roaring, it encircled the mulatto quarter, leaping over the Pont Basin, moving across L'Centre, where only a short time before I had conversed with the American Consul

and his lady. Then it doubled back on itself, traveling the way it had come, but this time extending into the roadstead, reaching out for the ships berthed there. Before my eyes the *Grappler* disappeared, and then the whole town vanished under the great wall of fire.

Eight miles off the coast, Captain Thirion of the cable ship *Pouyer-Quertier* watched the disaster unfold:

The fireball's forepart became luminously brilliant as it approached the sea. In an instant everything was ablaze, and flames shot from seemingly all points of the city as if from a single brazier. Light detonations followed one another in rapid succession, marking the passage of the cloud. One flash of lightning was observed, and that seemed to traverse the cloud from the ground upward. The further incidents of the cataclysm were unobservable, inasmuch as the land was immediately veiled in an impenetrable cloud of fiery smoke, and the *Pouyer-Quertier*, itself under threat, was obliged to flee for safety. In the roadstead every ship seemed to be ignited, and a number, including the *Grappler*, had disappeared.

In the town of Morne Rouge, parishioners arriving for mass at the church of Notre Dame de la Délivrande had dallied in the street outside, watching the volcano. Leaving the sacristy to investigate the distraction, Father J. Mary got to the overlook across the street just in time to witness the disaster. In his words:

I beheld the black vapor leap from the side of the mountain. Looking down on it as it rolled on to St. Pierre it seemed to me as if all Martinique was sliding into the sea. A great tongue of fire seemed to detach itself from the vapor to lick up all the water from the Roxelane River. The British Government's Residency was engulfed, as was every building around. Only the towers of the Cathedral of St. Pierre remained untouched, and they only for a brief moment, for the fiery mass enveloped them, too, as it spread itself over all of St. Pierre. The mass was being constantly refueled by a huge stream of fire pouring out of the side of the crater to ravage an already devastated town. The cane fields were on fire, as were the plantations around the town. There must be so many victims, hundreds, possibly thousands, and from here there was nothing to be done.

The owner of the Lagarrane estate, one Monsieur Albert, had a more personally harrowing experience:

I was in one of the fields of my estate when the ground trembled under my feet, not as it does when the earth quakes, but as though a terrible struggle was going on within the mountain.

As I stood still, Mont Pelée seemed to shudder and a moaning sound issued from its crater. Then there was a rending, crashing, grinding noise. It was deafening and the flash of light that accompanied it was blinding. It was like a terrible hurricane, and where a fraction of a second before there had been a perfect calm I felt myself drawn into a vortex. The mysterious force leveled a row of trees nearby, leaving bare a space of ground fifteen yards wide and more than 100 yards long.

Transfixed I stood, not knowing in what direction to flee. I looked toward Mont Pelée, and above its apex formed a great black cloud which reached high in the air. It literally fell upon the city of St. Pierre. It moved with a rapidity that made it impossible for anything to escape it. From the cloud came explosions that sounded as though all of the navies of the world were in titanic combat. Lightning played in and out in broad forks, the result being that intense darkness was followed by light that seemed to be of magnifying power.

That St. Pierre was doomed I knew, but I was prevented from seeing the destruction by a spur of the hill that shut off the view of the city. It is impossible for me to tell how long I stood there inert. Probably it was only a few seconds, but so vivid were my impressions that it now seems as though I stood as a spectator for many minutes. When I recovered possession of my senses I ran to my house and collected the members of the family, all of whom were panic stricken. I hurried them to the seashore, where we boarded a small steamship, in which we made the trip in safety to Fort-de-France.

I know that there was no flame in the first wave that was sent down upon St. Pierre. It was a heavy gas, like fire damp, and it must have asphyxiated the inhabitants before they were touched by the fire, which quickly followed. As we drew out to the sea in the small steamship, Mont Pelée was in the throes of a terrible convulsion. New craters seemed to be opening all about the summit and lava was flowing in broad streams in every direction. My estate was ruined while we were still in sight of it.

Monsieur Albert and his family had the good fortune to have been just outside the fringe of the nuée ardente.

Another eyewitness who was even luckier to have survived was a French aristocrat, Comte de Fitz-James. In the words of the comte:

> Baron de Fontenilliat and I had been in French Guiana on a business trip relating to some mining property in which we are interested. It became necessary for us to leave Cayenne before the regular mail steamer, and we hired a sailing vessel to transport us to Martinique. It happened that when we left Cayenne there was something of a scare prevailing because of an outbreak of yellow fever. For that reason we were not certain what would be our reception in Martinique, and instead of going at once to Fort-de-France or to St. Pierre, we decided to go to Carbet, a suburban village a little way outside of St. Pierre, there to remain until the quarantine regulations were complied with. Carbet is on the opposite side of the bay from Mont Pelée and there some of the wealthiest, as well as some of the poorest, citizens made their homes.
>
> We learned upon our arrival [the evening of May 7] that an eruption of Mont Pelée had destroyed a part of the village of Precheur, on the other side of the harbor. That was the eruption [of May 5] which ruined one of the best sugar factories in the island, killing scores of workmen. We made immediate arrangements to visit the scene of the disaster. Two boatmen were employed to take us across the bay, and it was the fact that we made an early start the next morning that saved our lives.
>
> After breakfast, we were in the boat and had started across to Precheur by 6 o'clock in the morning of May 8. We had no thought of what was to come. Not having been in St. Pierre, we had not an opportunity to share the panic which had been caused by the ugly temper betrayed by Mont Pelée.
>
> It was such a morning as it is almost impossible to describe. Low-hanging clouds gave the scene a dismal appearance, and this was heightened by the fine volcanic dust which filled the atmosphere,

making respiration difficult. This dust was next to impalpable. It could not be seen as it floated in the air, but it settled so rapidly that my hand, resting upon the edge of the boat, was covered completely in less than three minutes.

As we made our way across the water we more than half faced Mont Pelée, which was throwing off a heavy cloud of smoke, steam, and ashes. No flames were to be seen. On shore the inhabitants were making their way about the waterfront. The city was to our right. Small craft plied about the harbor, some trading with the ships that were at anchor, while in some fishermen were going out to the fishing grounds, just off Carbet.

Leaving shore, we first passed the *Roddam*, which was at quarantine, a fact to which the salvation of that ship was due. A little farther out in the roadstead was the *Roraima*, its passengers on deck observing the laboring of the volcano. Still farther off was the ill-fated *Grappler*. Then there were numerous sailing vessels at anchor.

I should have said that the calm of the morning was almost abnormal. Not a ripple was to be seen upon the face of the sea. Not a breath of air was stirring, which made it more difficult for us to breathe. But in spite of our discomforts we were glad that we had made the trip, as it was an opportunity not often given to man to see a volcano in active eruption.

The rumblings from the bowels of the mountain were majestic in tone. I cannot tell you just how they sounded, but perhaps you can imagine a mighty hand playing upon the strings of a harp greater than all the world. The notes produced were deep and full of threatenings. There was a jarring sensation, and every now and then there was a commotion of the waters that caused a swell without making the surface break. . . . Out from the shore put a small launch carrying the pennant of Governor Mouttet. The Governor at the last moment had realized that the situation was filled with a terrible danger.

While we were talking [about the governor], there came an explosion that was beyond any that ever before happened. I can only liken it to a shot from a mammoth cannon. The breath of fire swept down upon the city and waterfront with all of the force that could have been given to it by such a cannon. Of this comparison I shall have more to say later. For the present it will do to add that the explosion was without warning and that the effect was instantaneous. Cinders were shot into our face with stinging effect.

The air was filled with flame. Involuntarily we raised our hands to protect our faces. I noted the same gesture when I saw the bodies of victims on shore; arms had been raised and the hands were extended with palms outward, a gesture that in a peculiar manner indicated dread and horror.

When the frightful explosion came, our two boatmen were either thrown from the boat or with a quick impulse they sprang overboard. It was the one thing to do to save their lives; but, unfortunately for them, they lost their presence of mind and, instead of staying by the side of the boat, they swam away in the direction of Precheur, which we were approaching when the disaster came. It was impossible for them to land at Precheur, so they were compelled to put back. They then struck out across the bay, evidently hoping to reach Carbet. We saw neither of them again, and I have no doubt they were drowned.

My brave companion had the same impulse that actuated the boatmen. He sprang into the water, and when he saw that I did not move he reached up and, catching me by the shoulder, dragged me from the boat. I was stunned at first, and, though it was not a physical injury, I could not move of my own volition until the cold water restored my senses. It was thus that we could see all that happened about us.

The *Grappler* rushed through the water as far as her anchor-cable would permit. Then she seemed to rise by the bow, and when she settled back she sank almost before the force of the explosion had spent itself.

The *Roraima* was all a mass of flames for several seconds. We could see the poor wretches aboard of her rushing about in a vain attempt to escape from the fire that enveloped them. Captain Muggah—or, at least, I suppose that it was he—made an attempt to give orders to the maddened crew. Then he staggered to the railing and fell overboard.

The *Roddam* was also overcome. Her gangway was over the side. Her upper works were wrecked, but by heroic effort those on board were able to let slip the anchor chain, and, after many attempts, the ship began to move. She literally crawled away. It was a splendid display of courage. At least three hours elapsed after the explosion before the *Roddam* cleared the harbor.

On shore all was aflame. The city burned with a terrible roar. We realized that the inhabitants had all died, as not one was to be seen making an attempt to escape. Not a cry was heard save from the ships that were in the harbor.

Our own condition was desperate in the extreme. The heat was intense. We were able to keep our faces above the surface of the water for a second at a time at the most. We would take a mouthful of air and then sink into the water to stay there until forced to come to the surface again. This lasted only about three minutes. After that we were able to float by the side of the boat, dipping only occasionally.

The water began to get so warm that I feared we had escaped roasting only to be boiled to death. But the water did not grow so hot as to be life-threatening. That at the surface was many degrees warmer than that a foot below.

When we gave our attention to the panorama that was spread before us, the entire city of St. Pierre was mantled by a dense black cloud. Our eyes could not penetrate it, but it lifted a few seconds, revealing below it a second cloud, absolutely distinct from it. The second cloud lifted as did the first, both rising like blankets, and in a similar manner they floated away. Then, we saw the flames devouring the city, from which all show of life had disappeared.

When we could sustain the heat that filled the air we clambered into the boat and rowed back to Carbet. The *Roddam* had just gone out from the harbor, the *Roraima* was a smoking wreck, the *Grappler* had disappeared entirely, and little was to be seen of the other craft.

At Carbet we found the village absolutely deserted. Two portions of it had been ruined. That which was down by the water's edge had been swept by the great wave which followed the explosion. I have neglected to refer to that wave before, but it was of terrific force, and it added to the confusion all along the shore. Part of Carbet had been struck by the wave of fire from the volcano, but the greater portion of the village was left uninjured.

When we got ashore we called aloud, and only the echo of our voices answered us. Our fear was great, but we did not know which way to turn, and had it been our one thought to escape we would not have known how to do so. It was about one o'clock in the afternoon when we reached shore. Our weariness was beyond description.

• • •

Anyone following the events of the previous week would have figured that the most vulnerable spot in all of Martinique was *not* St. Pierre, but rather the town of Precheur. A mile closer to the volcano than St. Pierre, Precheur was where the ashfalls had crushed homes and where lahars had swept whole families into the sea; where refinery workers had been buried beneath tons of volcanic mud. A town caught between the volcano, the Caribbean, and two wildly misbehaving rivers, with all overland escape routes destroyed. More than four thousand souls were trapped there, short on food, lacking electricity, with even their leaders cut off from telegraph contact with the outside.

Yet the forces of nature can be capricious. Those who stayed in Precheur that terrible morning would be spared. Those who left would only swell the casualty list.

The nuée ardente missed Precheur by a mere one hundred yards. It did not, however, miss Morne Folie; the four hundred villagers who had crowded there around the semaphore, frantically trying to gain the attention of the cable ships, were mowed down and incinerated on the spot. The pirogue on its mission to reach the governor fared only a little better. The blast struck the small boat broadside and dumped all twelve young men into the bay. The five who eventually managed to reach shore were scalded, in the words of one Dr. Berté, "as if by a steam jet." Chavigny de la Chevrotière, leader of that failed mission, was swept more than a mile north to Les Abymes, where two days later he was rescued and taken to a hospital in Fort-de-France. He was to recover. Seven of his eleven friends died in St. Pierre Bay.

• • •

At 8 a.m. on May 8, Gaston Landes sat outside in his garden with his two servants and two visiting students. His thoughts were on meeting the governor that afternoon and convincing him to evacuate the threatened masses from Precheur and St. Pierre. It never occurred to the professor that his own life might be in danger that moment, for he was situated well above the city and across a broad valley from the volcano. Shielded by the lush tropical vegetation, he barely heard the explosion. And he did not see the nuée ardente.

An hour later, a dazed and injured neighbor, one Madame Montferrier, stumbled into Landes's garden as she frantically sought someone still alive who could help her find her missing children. She discovered the professor and his four companions writhing on the ground, all dreadfully burned and bleeding from their noses and mouths. They begged for water, yet none could swallow. Around noon, as he thrashed in his final agony, Gaston Landes moaned, "What on earth has happened? Will someone please tell me what happened?"

• CHAPTER 11 •

DEATH IN THE BAY

•

Most of the roughly thirty thousand victims died instantly or within minutes of the onslaught. Some less fortunate, including those like Gaston Landes who had been near the fringe of the blast, were to linger for hours or sometimes days in excruciating pain before they succumbed. Remarkably few of the victims received the kinds of injuries the human body is capable of surviving: the hospitals in Fort-de-France admitted only 151 patients (counting victims of floods and collapsing buildings over the previous few days), and of this number 40 soon died. Just 69 of those hospitalized would recover from burns, and they had all been outside the region of total devastation. Only later would it be learned that just *one* man had survived at the core of the holocaust: a prisoner in solitary confinement.

The exact death toll could not be tallied, for this was not a situation where body counts were possible. After the disaster, migrations and resettlements made it impractical to proceed by subtracting the remaining Martiniquian population from the population count before. Compounding matters, records of births and deaths were kept by the churches, and every church in St. Pierre was destroyed. Estimates at the time ranged from twenty-five thousand to forty thousand fatalities, but Father Alte Roché's figure of thirty thousand is probably the best informed. Of St. Pierre's population of 26,500, the relatively few who evacuated were more than offset by the many hundreds who poured into the city in its last few days. To this figure must be added the approximately three thousand victims from outlying villages and the foreigners on the ships in the bay.

The catastrophe devastated approximately twelve square miles, and no single person could have witnessed it all. Those just outside the fringes of the blast, including Roger Arnoux and the Clercs, saw the initial surge, then were engulfed in a cloud of dust that prevented them from seeing much else. Those farther to the east saw the event from the back side, where it was soon obscured by the rising plume. For other eyewitnesses, the view was partially blocked by the terrain. The report of a few observers that the cloud exploded upward, then collapsed onto the slope, may have represented a visual confusion of the two near-simultaneous blasts. Some thought they saw lightning; others did not. And surely, in the confusion of the moment, all missed some aspects of the event that they would have noticed under calmer circumstances.

On numerous details, however, most eyewitnesses did agree. The front of the surge, for instance, had a rolling motion superimposed on its internal turbulence. Its color was not uniform; it varied from dark gray or black in some spots to white in others, suggesting that it was a heterogeneous mixture of gas and ash of different compositions and temperatures. Although the cloud did not glow incandescently as does molten rock, numerous observers did report flashes of flame, particularly in the portions of the cloud that followed the initial surge. Just as with a snow avalanche, the nuée ardente drove a high-pressure blast of air ahead of it. And finally, it seemed to draw the oxygen from the surrounding air, leaving those who had been closely missed gasping for breath.

· · ·

There is nothing about a pyroclastic surge that forces it to stop at a coastline; it rumbles along as far as it must go to dissipate its kinetic energy. It makes little difference if water happens to lie in its path. And if there happen to be ships in that water, they will experience a force of nature that no marine vessel could possibly be designed to withstand.

Because the St. Pierre customhouse was consumed in the disaster, no official record was ever assembled of the shipping lost in St. Pierre Bay that terrible morning. It seems, however, that seventeen or eighteen sizable ships were struck broadside and destroyed. The cable-repair ship *Grappler* was one of the first. It rolled over and sank almost immediately, apparently with all on board.

The ferry *Diamant* had just unloaded its passengers and the ship's boy, Jean-Baptiste Innocent, was on the quay. As the *Diamant* capsized and its boiler exploded, Innocent dove into the water. He stayed submerged as long as he could hold his breath, then surfaced to find everything on shore ablaze. He would cling to a floating plank for some seven hours until he was rescued. Of those who had arrived in St. Pierre on that last ferry from Fort-de-France, Innocent was the only one to survive.

The impact of the blast dismasted the schooner *Gabrielle* and threw it on its side, but the buoyancy of its empty holds apparently kept it from sinking immediately. First Mate Georges Marie-Sainte and four crewmen were able to jump into the sea, where they clung to floating debris for six hours until they climbed into an abandoned canoe and paddled to Carbet.

The Italian bark *Teresa Lo Vico* was moored near the southern end of the city. Captain Ferrara was killed immediately by the falling mainmast, and most of the others on board were burned horribly. Below deck, the ship's boy plunged his head into a bucket of water to protect himself from the intense heat. As the ship burst into flames and began sinking, engineer Jean-Louis Prudent and the boy managed to float a boat and take off the engineer's wife and her maid, nine burned sailors, and the captain's widow. Prudent was later to describe the nuée ardente:

> That cloud was bigger, it seemed, than the mountain. The fire burned the city everywhere at once. Near me I saw only dead men, but on the shore I saw men and women rushing back and forth amid the flames. Then came that choking smoke and they dropped as though vitally shot.

Other ships sunk included the Italian barks *Albanese, Nord America,* and the *Sacro Cuore;* the American schooner *Anna E. J. Morse;* the British schooner *Canadian;* the British bark *L. W. Morton;* the French bark *Misti;* the French iron bark *Tamaya;* and the *Raisinier,* the *Clementina,* and the *Dalhia.* The two largest vessels in the bay that morning were the steamships *Roddam* and *Roraima,* both of which had the misfortune of arriving less than an hour before the disaster. The *Roddam* managed to limp to St. Lucia, badly damaged. The *Roraima* went to the bottom.

• • •

Built in Glasgow, Scotland in 1883, the *Roraima* was 340 feet long with a 38.2-foot beam and a displacement of 1,764 tons. On April 26, under Captain George Muggah, it left New York with a crew of forty-seven and twenty-one passengers. Its cargo included kegs of varnish and barrels of tar, ten thousand board feet of spruce lumber, hundreds of mattresses, several thousand cases of kerosene, and hundreds of puncheons of temper lime, a substance that burst into flame when touched by water.

Assistant Purser Thompson described what happened:

> Our boat, the *Roraima,* of the Quebec Line, arrived at St. Pierre early Thursday morning. For hours before we entered the roadstead we could see flames and smoke rising from Mont Pelée. No one on board had any idea of danger. Captain G. T. Muggah was on the bridge, and all hands got on deck to see the show.
>
> The spectacle was magnificent. As we approached St. Pierre, we could distinguish the rolling and leaping of the red flames that belched from the mountain in huge volumes and gushed high into the sky. Enormous clouds of black smoke hung over the volcano.
>
> When we anchored at St. Pierre I noticed the cable steamship *Grappler,* the *Roddam,* three or four American schooners and a number of Italian and Norwegian barks. The flames were then spurting straight up in the air, now and then waving to one side or the other for a moment and again leaping suddenly higher up.
>
> There was a constant muffled roar. It was like the biggest oil refinery in the world burning up on the mountain top. There was a tremendous explosion about 7:45 o'clock [*sic*], soon after we got in. The mountain was blown to pieces. There was no warning. The side of the volcano was ripped out, and there was hurled straight toward us a solid wall of flame. It sounded like thousands of cannon.
>
> The wave of fire was on us and over us like a lightning flash. It was like a hurricane of fire. I saw it strike the cable steamship

Grappler broadside on and capsize her. From end to end she burst into flames and then sank. The fire rolled enmass straight down upon St. Pierre and the shipping. The town vanished before our eyes and the air grew stifling hot, and we were in the thick of it.

Wherever the mass of fire struck the sea the water boiled and sent up vast clouds of steam. The sea was torn into huge whirlpools. One of these horrible hot whirlpools swung under the *Roraima* and pulled her down on her beam ends with the suction. She careened way over to port, and then the fire hurricane from the volcano smashed her, and over she went on the opposite side. The fire wave swept off the masts and smokestack as if they were cut with a knife.

Captain Muggah was the only one on deck not killed outright. He was caught by the fire wave and terribly burned. He yelled to get up the anchor, but before two fathoms were heaved in, the *Roraima* was almost upset by the boiling whirlpool, and the fire wave had thrown her down on her beam ends to starboard. Captain Muggah was overcome by the flames. He fell unconscious from the bridge and toppled overboard.

The blast from the volcano lasted only a few minutes. It shriveled and set fire to everything it touched. Thousands of casks of rum were stored in St. Pierre, and these were exploded by the terrific heat. Before the volcano burst, the landings of St. Pierre were crowded with people. After the explosion, not one living being was seen on land. Only twenty-five of those on the *Roraima* out of sixty-eight were left after the first flash.

The French cruiser *Suchet* came in and took us off at 2 p.m. She remained nearby, helping all she could, until 5 o'clock, then went to Fort-de-France with all the people she had rescued. At that time it looked as if the entire north end of the island was on fire.

Engineer C. C. Evans of Montreal, a man of fewer words, had the following to add:

I can never forget the horrid, fiery, choking whirlwind which enveloped me. Mr. Morris and I rushed below. We are not very badly burned, not so bad as most of them. When the fire came we were going to our posts (we are engineers) to weigh anchor and get out. When we came up we found the ship afire aft, and fought it forward until 3 o'clock, when the *Suchet* came to our rescue. We were then building a raft.

Mate Ellery Scott was to write the most comprehensive accounts of the destruction of the *Roraima*. Following is one of the shorter versions of his story.

We got to St. Pierre in the *Roraima* at 6:30 o'clock on Thursday morning. That's the morning the mountain and the town and the ships were all sent to hell in a minute.

All hands had had breakfast. I was standing on the forecastle head trying to make out the marks on the pipes of a ship way out and heading for St. Lucia. I wasn't looking at the mountain at all. But I guess the captain was, for he was on the bridge, and the last time I heard him speak was when he shouted, "Heave up, Mr. Scott; heave up!" I gave the order to the men, and I think some of them did jump to get the anchor up, but nobody knows what really happened for the next fifteen minutes. I turned around toward the captain and then I saw the mountain.

Did you ever see the tide come into the Bay of Fundy? It doesn't sneak in a little at a time as it does 'round here. It rolls in in waves. That's the way the cloud of fire and mud and white-hot stones rolled down from that volcano over the town and over the ships. It was on us in almost no time, but I saw it and in the same glance I saw our captain bracing himself to meet it on the bridge. He was facing the fire cloud with both hands gripped hard to the bridge rail, his legs apart and his knees braced back stiff. I've seen him brace himself that same way many a time in a tough sea with the spray going mast-head high and green water pouring along the decks.

I saw the captain, I say, at the same instant I saw that cloud coming down on us. I don't know why, but that last glimpse of poor Muggah on his bridge will stay with me just as long as I remember St. Pierre and that will be long enough.

In another instant it was all over for him. As I was looking at him he was all ablaze. He reeled and fell on the bridge with his face toward me. His moustache and eyebrows were gone in a jiffy. His hat had gone, and his hair was aflame, and so were his clothes from head to foot. I knew he was conscious when he fell, by the look in his eyes, but he didn't make a sound.

That all happened a long way inside of half a minute; then something new happened. When the wave of fire was going over us, a tidal wave of the sea came out from the shore and did the rest. That wall of rushing water was so high and so solid that it seemed to rise up and join the smoke and flame above. For an instant we could see nothing but the water and the flame.

That tidal wave picked the ship up like a canoe and then smashed her. After one list to starboard the ship righted, but the masts, the bridge, the funnel and all the upper works had gone overboard.

I had saved myself from the fire by jamming a metal ventilator cover over my head and jumping from the forecastle head. Two St. Kitts negroes saved me from the water by grabbing me by the legs and pulling me down into the forecastle after them. Before I could get up, three men tumbled in on top of me. Two of them were dead. [Inexplicably, Scott would omit this explanation of how he survived from most of the other articles he would write about his experience.]

Captain Muggah went overboard, still clinging to the fragments of his wrecked bridge. Daniel Taylor, the ship's cooper and a Kitts native, jumped overboard to save him. Taylor managed to push the captain onto a hatch that had floated off from us and then they swam back to the ship for more assistance, but nothing could be done for the captain. Taylor wasn't sure he was alive. The last we saw of him or his dead body it was drifting shoreward on that hatch.

Well, after staying in the forecastle about twenty minutes, I went out on deck. There were only four of us left aboard who could do anything. The four were Thompson, Dan Taylor, Quashee, and myself. It was still raining fire and hot rocks and you could hardly see a ship's length for dust and ashes, but we could stand that. There were burning men and some women and two or three children lying around the deck. Not just burned, but burning when we got to them. More than half the ship's company had been killed in that first rush of flame. Some had rolled overboard when the tidal wave came and we never saw so much as their bodies. The cook was burned to death in his galley. He had been paring potatoes for dinner and what was left of his right hand held the shank of his potato knife. The wooden handle was in ashes. All that happened to a man in less than a minute. The donkey engineman was killed on deck sitting in front of his boiler. We found parts of some bodies—a hand, or an arm or a leg. Below decks there were some twenty alive.

The ship was on fire, of course, what was left of it. The stumps of both masts were blazing. Aft she was like a furnace, but forward the flames had not got below deck, so we four carried those who were still alive on deck into the forecastle. All of them were burned and most of them were half strangled.

One boy, a passenger and just a little shaver [the four-year-old son of Clement Stokes] was picked up naked. His hair and all his clothing had been burned off, but he was alive. We rolled him in a blanket and put him in a sailor's bunk. A few minutes later we looked at him and he was dead.

My own son's gone too. It had been his trick at lookout ahead during the dog watch that morning, when we were making for St. Pierre, so I supposed at first when the fire struck us that he was asleep in his bunk and safe. But he wasn't. Nobody could tell me where he was. I don't know whether he was burned to death or rolled overboard and drowned. He was a likely boy. He had been several voyages with me and would have been a master some day. He used to say he'd make me mate.

After getting all hands that had any life left in them below and attended to the best we could, the four of us that were left halfway shipshape started in to fight the fire. We had case oil stowed forward. Thanks to that tidal wave that cleared our decks there wasn't much left to burn, so we got the fire down so's we could live on board with it for several hours more and then the four turned to knock a raft together out of what timber and truck we could find. Our boats had gone overboard with the masts and funnel.

We made that raft for something over thirty that were alive. We put provisions on for two days and rigged up a make-shift mast and sail, for we intended to go to sea. We were only three boats' length of the shore, but the shore was hell itself. We intended to put straight out and trust to luck that the *Korona*, that was about due at St. Pierre, would pick us up. But we did not have to risk the raft, for about 3 o'clock in the afternoon, the *Suchet* came along and took us all off.

We thought for a minute just after we were wrecked that we were to get help from a ship that passed us. We burned blue lights, but she kept on. We learned afterward that she was the *Roddam*.

Daniel Taylor, the *Roraima*'s cooper, gave an independent account that adds some details to Scott's story:

Hearing a tremendous report and seeing the ashes falling thicker, I dived into a room, dragging with me Samuel Thomas, a gang-way man and fellow countryman, shutting the door tightly. Shortly after, I heard a voice, which I recognized as that of the chief mate, Mr. Scott. Opening the door with great caution, I drew him in. The nose of Thomas was burned by the intense heat.

We three and Thompson, the assistant purser, out of sixty-eight souls on board, were the only persons who escaped practically unin-jured. The heat being unbearable, I emerged in a few moments, and the scene that presented itself to my eyes baffles description. All around on the deck were the dead and dying covered with boiling mud. There they lay, men, women and little children, and the appeals of the latter for water were heart-rending. When water was given them they could not swallow it, owing to their throats being filled with ashes or burnt with the heated air.

The ship was burning aft, and I jumped overboard. The sea was intensely hot. I was at once swept seaward by a tidal wave, but the sea receding a considerable distance, the return wave washed me against an upturned sloop to which I clung. I was joined by a man so dread-fully burned and disfigured as to be unrecognizeable. Afterwards I found he was Captain Muggah. He was in dreadful agony, begging piteously to be put on board his ship.

Picking up some wreckage which contained bedding and a tool chest, I, with the help of five others who had joined me on the wreck, constructed a crude raft, on which we placed the captain. Then, see-ing an upturned boat, I asked one of the five, a native of Martinique, to swim and fetch it. Instead of returning to us, he picked up two of his countrymen and went away in the direction of Fort-de-France. Seeing the *Roddam*, which arrived in port shortly after we anchored, making for the *Roraima*, I said goodbye to the captain and swam back to the *Roraima*.

The *Roddam,* however, burst into flames and put to sea. I reached the *Roraima* at about half-past two, and was afterwards taken off by a boat from the French warship *Suchet.* Twenty-four others with myself were taken on to Fort-de-France. Three of these died before reaching port. A number of others have since died.

On board was a nurse from Barbados, Miss Clara King, accompanying the three Stokes children (aged three, four, and nine) and their mother. Many years later, in 1945, she would give the following interview to the volcanologist Dr. Thomas A. Jaggar:

We had been watching the volcano sending up smoke. The Captain (who was killed) said to my mistress, "I am not going to stay any longer than I can help." I went to the cabin and was assisting with dressing the children for breakfast when the steward (who was later killed by the blast) rushed past and shouted, "Close the cabin door— the volcano is coming!" We closed the door and at the same moment came a terrible explosion which nearly burst the eardrums. The vessel was lifted high into the air, and then seemed to be sinking down, down. We were all thrown off our feet by the shock and huddled crouching in one corner of the cabin. My mistress had the girl baby in her arms, the older girl leaned on my left arm while I held little Eric in my right.

The explosion seemed to have blown in the skylight over our heads, and before we could raise ourselves, hot moist ashes began to pour in on us; they came in boiling splattering splashes like moist mud without any pieces of rock. In vain we tried to shield ourselves. The cabin was pitch dark—we could see nothing.

A sense of suffocation came next [but] when the door burst open, air rushed in and we revived somewhat. When we could see each other's faces they were all covered with black lava, the baby was dying, Rita, the older girl, was in great agony and every part of my body was paining me. A heap of hot mud had collected near us and as Rita put her hand down to raise herself up it was plunged up to the elbow in the scalding stuff.

The first engineer came now, and hearing our moans carried us to the forward deck and there we remained on the burning ship from

The ruins of St. Pierre from Morne d'Orange, late May 1902.
(Heilprin 1903)

Artist's rendition of panic outside the cathedral. (Morris 1902a)

Destruction of the shipping in St. Pierre Bay. (Morris 1902a)

Death of the captain of the Roraima. *(Morris 1902a)*

Rue Victor Hugo shortly after the disaster. (Heilprin 1903)

Ruins of the cathedral. (Heilprin 1903)

*St. Pierre's hospital. These remaining walls were destroyed
in the blast of May 20. (Morris 1902a)*

Angelo Heilprin with bodies in a St. Pierre basement.
(Heilprin 1903)

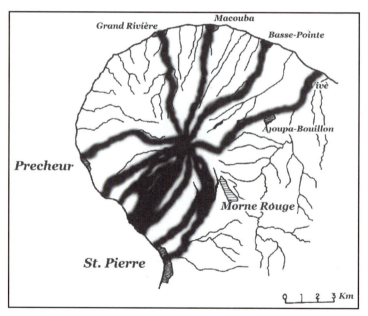

Paths of the lahars preceding the eruption of May 8, 1902.
(Adapted from Chrétien and Brousse 1988)

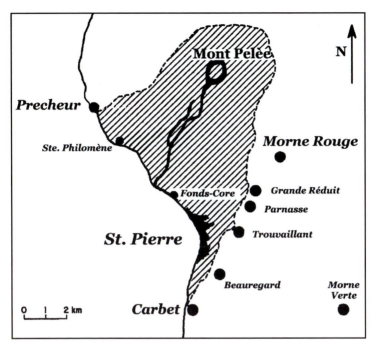

Region destroyed by the pyroclastic surge of May 8, 1902.
(Adapted from Heilprin 1903)

Precheur after the mudflow of May 8. (Heilprin 1903)

Artist's rendition of the cremations. (Morris 1902a)

George Varian's sketch of the night eruption of May 26.
(Kennan 1902)

The upper gorge of the Rivière Falaise.
(Drawing by Varian in Kennan 1902.)

*The mudflow in the valley of the Rivière
Blanche. (Drawing by Varian in Kennan
1902.)*

*Mont Pelée from Vivé on May 27. (Drawing by
Varian in Kennan 1902.)*

Father J. Mary, pastor of the church of Notre Dame de la Délivrande in Morne Rouge. (Kennan 1902)

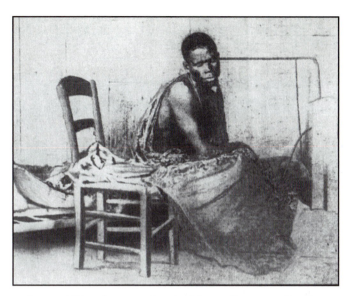

*Augusté Ciparis recovering in Morne Rouge on Sunday,
May 25, 1902. (Drawing by Varian in Kennan 1902.)*

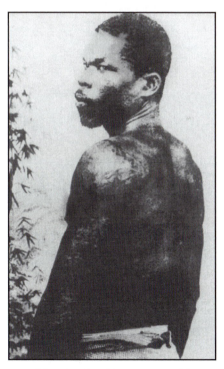

*Augusté Ciparis after his recovery. (Bureau du
Patrimoine du Conseil Régional, Martinique.)*

Ciparis in front of his cell before the removal of the ash. (Billings 1915)

Circus poster from the 1903 season, featuring "Ludger Sylbaris."
(Circus World Museum)

Ciparis's cell as it appears today.

A dissipating pyroclastic surge. (Heilprin 1903)

Mont Pelée viewed from the north, June 1902. (Heilprin 1903)

A cauliflower eruption column. (Heilprin 1903)

The volcano from Morne Rouge, late August 1902. (Heilprin 1903)

View from the outskirts of Morne Rouge, late August 1902.
(Heilprin 1903)

A pyroclastic surge reaching the sea. (Heilprin 1903)

The ruins of Morne Rouge, September 1902. (Heilprin 1903)

The church in Morne Rouge after the pyroclastic surge
of August 30, 1902. (Heilprin 1903)

The Tower of Pelée and the ruins of Morne Rouge, late 1902.
(Heilprin 1903)

The Tower of Pelée. (Heilprin 1903)

Mont Pelée and St. Pierre today, as viewed from Morne d'Orange.

8:30 a.m. until 3:00 p.m. The crew was crowded forward, many in a dying condition. The whole city was one mass of roaring flames and the saloon aft as well as the forward part of the ship were burning fiercely.

My mistress lay on the deck in a collapsed state; the little boy was already dead, and the baby dying. The lady was collected and resigned, handed me some money, told me to take Rita to her aunt, and sucked a piece of ice before she died.

The *Roraima* would burn furiously for the next three days before it sank. Its wreckage now rests upright at a depth of 165 feet, an underwater attraction for adventurous divers.

• • •

At 1,506 tons, the *Roddam* was only slightly smaller than the *Roraima*. Its captain, Edward Freeman, would dictate the following account from his hospital bed as he recovered from his burns:

St. Lucia, British West Indies, May 11.—

The steamer *Roddam*, of which I am captain, left St. Lucia at midnight of May 7, and was off St. Pierre, Martinique, at 6 o'clock on the morning of the 8th. I noticed that the volcano, Mont Pelée, was smoking, and crept slowly in toward the bay, finding there among others the steamer *Roraima*, the telegraph repairing steamer *Grappler* and [a number of] sailing vessels. I went to anchorage between 7 and 8 and had hardly moored when the side of the volcano opened out with a terrible explosion. A wall of fire swept over the town and the bay. The *Roddam* was struck broadside by the burning mass. The shock to the ship was terrible, nearly capsizing her.

Hearing the awful report of the explosion and seeing the great wall of flames approaching the steamer, those on deck sought shelter wherever it was possible, jumping into the cabin, the forecastle and even into the hold. I was in the chart room, but the burning embers were borne by so swift a movement of the air that they were swept in through the door and port holes, suffocating and scorching me badly. I was terribly burned by these embers about the face and hands, but managed to reach the deck. Then, as soon as it was possible, I mustered the few survivors who seemed able to move, ordered them to slip the anchor, leaped for the bridge and ran the engine for full speed astern. The second and the third engineer and a fireman were on watch below and so escaped injury. They did their part in the attempt to escape, but the men on deck could not work the steering gear because it was jammed by the debris from the volcano. We accordingly went ahead and astern until the gear was free, but in this running backward and forward it was two hours after the first shock before we were clear of the bay.

One of the most terrifying conditions was that, the atmosphere being charged with ashes, it was totally dark. The sun was completely obscured, and the air was only illuminated by the flames from the volcano and those of the burning town and shipping. It seems small to say that the scene was terrifying in the extreme. As we backed out we passed close to the *Roraima,* which was one mass of blaze. The steam was rushing from the engine room, and the screams of those on board were terrible to hear. The cries for help were all in vain, for I could do nothing but save my own ship. When I last saw the *Roraima* she was settling down by the stern. That was about 10 o'clock in the morning.

. . . The escape of my vessel was miraculous. The woodwork of the cabins and bridge and everything inflammable on deck were constantly igniting, and it was with great difficulty that we few survivors managed to keep the flames down.

FREEMAN, Master British Steamship *Roddam.*

Captain Freeman, just as all the other survivors of the disaster, was to relive the incident over and over in his mind. And each time he replayed his mental screenplay, it would strike him that he ought to have reported various other details. A few months after the disaster, he would tell the following story:

Above the roar of the blast I could hear the awful shrieks of those trapped on deck. They were weird, inhuman sounds, like the crying of sea birds in distress. I knew that people were being roasted to ashes, but there was nothing I could do, nor anybody else could do. In a trice the ash had penetrated every corner of the ship, and my own hiding place was like a furnace. You can imagine what it was like if you think of going to a blacksmith's forge, and taking up handfuls of fine red-hot dust to rub over your hands and face. Finally I could bear it no more, and I made my way back to the deck. It was a shambles. Bodies everywhere, some burning, some throwing themselves into the sea to drown rather than face further agony. I did not know if a crew could be mustered to work the ship.

I caught sight of the first engineer and told him to go and see if the anchor chain held fast. He replied that he could not move as he was so badly burned. I was helpless. I turned and looked toward the shore, just a couple of hundred yards away, for the ship was drifting all over the place as the blast had in fact uprooted the anchor, and we were a hulk. From end to end the town was ablaze, with the fiercest fires at the north end where the mulattos had lived. In the Rue Victor Hugo I could discern people running with flames clinging to them. They looked like effigies which had been set alight. Above the roar of the flames, their shrieks carried clearly, joining those coming from the deck around me, until a solid wall of demented sound stretched from the shore to the *Roddam*. As I watched, hundreds of people ran into the sea, their scorched flesh sizzling as it entered the hot water.

Then the *Roddam* was caught up in a new current, and we drifted back into the blackness which hung over most of the roadstead. By now I had a boatswain and five sailors at my service. I placed two men at the wheel, and I told the others to throw every burning thing overboard. I ran down to the engine room, and heard over the pipe that the second and third engineers had survived. Using my elbows to steer the wheel, for the flesh had been completely burned to the bone off my hands and wrists, I tried to get the ship under way.

All the time the dust continued to rain. It was so hot that the soles of my boots were burned through, and I sent a man to bring me a pair of thick snowshoes that I had bought in Hamburg last winter. They proved to be just the thing. The ship struggled like a wounded monster. Groans and curses and cries for help came from all quarters. But there was nothing I could do. Then from one of my crew came a shout that the *Roraima* was but a few cables away. Somehow I backed away from her and started to move out into the roadstead.

That afternoon, under its own power, the *Roddam* limped into the port of Castries, St. Lucia. As the badly burned Captain Freeman was helped from his ship, he whispered words that would quickly circulate through that town, and which in one or another variation would later be scooped up by visiting journalists:

"I have come from hell."

CHAPTER 12

CLOSE ENCOUNTERS

•

Martinique's vicar-general, Monseigneur Gabriel Parel, would later write that his guardian angel had been watching over him. After offering Sunday mass and spending Monday and Tuesday in St. Pierre, he caught Wednesday's 2:30 p.m. ferry to Fort-de-France so he could supervise preparations for the Ascension Thursday services at the Cathédrale Saint-Louis. He was there in the capital, some thirteen miles from the volcano, when he heard the first news of the disaster. He wrote his impressions in his journal:

Thursday, May 8, Ascension Day.
This date should be written in blood. Toward four o'clock in the morning a violent thunderstorm burst over Fort-de-France. Toward eight o'clock the horizon on the north and in the direction of the volcano was black as ink. The clouds raced across the sky toward the northwest. The sky grew darker and darker. Suddenly I heard a noise as of hail falling upon the roof and on the leaves of the trees. A great murmur arose in the city [of Fort-de-France].
At the church, where eight o'clock mass had begun, a frightful panic took place. The priest remained alone. At the same moment . . . thunder pealed, pealed continuously, appallingly. The sea receded three times for a distance of several hundred meters. The boat which was leaving for Saint Pierre returned affrighted. I went out on my balcony to see what was happening, and I noticed it was being covered by a hail of stones and ashes still hot. People stood petrified at

their doors, or rushed distractedly through the streets. All this lasted for about a quarter of an hour, a quarter of an hour of terror.

But what was taking place at St. Pierre? No one dared to think. . . . Communication by telephone had been cut off abruptly in the middle of a word. Some asserted that they saw above the mountains which separated us from St. Pierre a column of fire rising to the sky, and then spreading in all directions. The most terrible anxiety filled our hearts. At eleven o'clock the ship *Le Marin* set out to reconnoiter, and was witness to the most appalling spectacle imaginable. Saint Pierre was a vast brazier of fire. The news which burst upon the city at about one o'clock sounded like the funeral knell of all Martinique and evoked an indescribable cry of horror.

• • •

The Girard Company's steam ferries had been following their regular schedule the morning of the disaster. It was a simple enough schedule: boats leaving every hour, approximately on the hour, from both Fort-de-France and St. Pierre. To allow an hour for the actual trip and another hour for disembarking, refueling, and boarding at each end, three boats were in service simultaneously. On the morning of May 8, the *Diamant* left Fort-de-France at 6 a.m., the *Rubis* followed at 7 a.m., and the *Topaze,* which had been the last boat to leave St. Pierre before the disaster, left Fort-de-France on its return trip to St. Pierre at 8:15 a.m.

The *Topaze,* however, got only halfway to its destination when it was stopped by a hail of hot stones and ash. As its captain tried to decide whether to forge ahead or to turn back, the *Rubis* emerged from the haze ahead and chugged up alongside. Its crew reported that an impenetrable rain of ash was falling on St. Pierre Bay, the sea was littered with flotsam, and that it was currently impossible to get beyond Carbet. As the two ferries chugged in tandem back to Fort-de-France, the sight of their un-scheduled returns triggered a wave of worry and speculation through the crowd on the waterfront. Not only had the *Topaze* and *Rubis* been unable to get to St. Pierre, but apparently the *Diamant* had been unable to leave there. The truth, of course, was that the wreckage of the *Diamant* already lay at the bottom of St. Pierre Bay.

Meanwhile, Georges L'Heurre had received no communication from Louis Mouttet since before the rain of hot cinders fell on the capital. When he learned that it was no longer possible to communicate with St. Pierre even by ferry, he began exercising his authority as acting governor. Although it might have been more tactful to first establish the fates of Louis Mouttet and Colonel Gerbault (who was by appointment the deputy governor), the state of affairs was such that someone needed to be making decisions. L'Heurre immediately sent word to Commander Le Bris of the *Suchet* and the other ships in the harbor that their assistance was urgently needed in St. Pierre. And then, to the Ministry of Colonies in Paris, he sent this cable:

> All communications with St. Pierre lost. It is believed St. Pierre on fire following eruption this morning. Governor Mouttet at scene since yesterday evening. I have sent all available steamships to save population.
> — L'HEURRE.

Given the breaks in the various cable links, no one at the telegraph office could offer any guarantee of when or if that message might arrive in Paris. L'Heurre's only assurance was that he was on record as having tried to send it.

Commander Le Bris had spent the night in his own quandary, for it was not clear to him who was in charge. Had this been an enemy action, he would be expected to assume authority himself, and that he knew how to do. Had it been a civil insurrection, he would be expected to co-operate with the governor until specific orders arrived from the naval ministry. But a volcano? Was he to call the shots, or was Mouttet? Yesterday, L'Heurre informed him that the governor had asked Paris to put the *Suchet* at his disposal, and Le Bris agreed that he would prepare to sail to St. Pierre at daybreak pending the expected arrival of that order. In fact, he got up a full head of steam before six o'clock with the intention of getting to St. Pierre by seven, order or not. Then, as dawn broke sunny and clear on May 8, he demurred.

Le Bris would later explain that his planned departure was delayed not by any lack of leadership on his part but by engine trouble. Fortunate engine trouble, for had the *Suchet* arrived in St. Pierre as he had planned, it would have suffered the same terrible fate as the other ships anchored in the roadstead that morning. The cruiser's mechanical problem was miraculously solved soon after the first news of the disaster arrived in Fort-de-France. Le Bris and the *Suchet* steamed for St. Pierre around 11 a.m.

The scheduled 10 a.m. ferry departure from Fort-de-France already had a passenger list that included the thirty militia Mouttet had promised Mayor Fouché; Paul Mirville, the wayward member of the Scientific Commission; and Monsieur Labat, deputy mayor of Fort-de-France, who planned to discuss the refugee problem with Mayor Fouché. Because the scheduled *Diamant* had not returned, they boarded the *Rubis*, which then departed on its second attempt of the morning to land at St. Pierre. Atmospheric conditions had improved by then, only a fine dusting of ash was falling, and St. Pierre came into view shortly after 11 a.m.

To the astonishment of everyone on board, the bay was a mass of wreckage, ships were ablaze, and the city itself was an inferno. The captain stopped a mile from shore and passed around a pair of field glasses so his stunned passengers could take turns looking for signs of life. If anyone saw the desperate survivors in the water or on board the flaming *Roraima*, those lips stayed sealed. All agreed that it would be impossible to set foot on the flaming shore. The *Rubis* swung around and chugged back toward Fort-de-France. On the way, it passed the cruiser *Suchet*, outbound for St. Pierre.

It was 12:30 when the *Rubis* docked again at Fort-de-France. Hundreds of people now crowded the quays, representing thousands more who had friends or relatives in St. Pierre. Mirville forced his way through the throng to convey the news to L'Heurre. His fellow passengers passed the word that rapidly spread through the capital: St. Pierre had been obliterated.

Meanwhile, Commander Le Bris attempted a landing in St. Pierre, but the heat was of such intensity that none of the landing party could even step onto the shore. Others from the *Suchet* set out in its launches to pick up survivors from the waters and from the flaming *Roraima*. A wind kicked up the sea, tossing about the ship's boats and complicating the transfer of survivors to the cruiser. The victims who slowly trickled into the cruiser's sick bay exhibited a wide range of reactions to their ordeal:

some were speechless, others rambling, some crying, a few actually singing. All had raw oozing burns. And all seemed to have an unquenchable thirst, even though many found it impossible to swallow. Nine of those who had "swallowed the fire" would die before reaching Fort-de-France.

The cable-repair ship *Pouyer-Quertier* and the ferry *Topaze* showed up to assist with the rescues, and when there were no more living souls to be taken from the debris of the harbor, the three ships moved south to Carbet to evacuate the terrified crowd that had gathered on that shore.

• • •

The day's work was far from over for the *Rubis* and its crew. That afternoon, the ferry set off for St. Pierre for the third time that day, this time carrying the vicar-general Monseigneur Parel and another priest, the same thirty militia who had been on the ten o'clock ferry, and a delegation of officials. One of this group, Monsieur Lubin, the *procureur* of Martinique, would describe his approach to the devastated city:

> I left by the steamer *Rubis* at half-past two in the afternoon, with a company of thirty men of the troop commanded by Lieutenant Tessier. After we had passed Case-Pilote we observed that the sea was strewn with wreckage, and the *Rubis* was obliged to slacken its speed in order to avoid breaking the helm.
>
> We approached Carbet; to our great astonishment there were comparatively few people on the shore. Saint Pierre was enveloped in a cloud of smoke and flames, especially in the northern portion, known as the Fort.
>
> Saint Pierre and its suburbs seemed to us a heap of ashes and ruins. The roadstead contained nothing but an immense quantity of drifting wood. Two iron-clad steamers, completely dismantled, tilted toward the land, with their boats partly lifted from their pegs, had become the prey of the flames. Not a trace of the hull of any sailing-vessel; not a boat; we saw only three or four coasting vessels of Basse-Pointe, *pirogues*, their keels out of water capsized; on the coast and in the surrounding country not a living soul!
>
> A dozen people took refuge on the rocks between Saint Pierre and Carbet; the launches of the *Suchet* went to their relief. We knew at once that these people belonged to the crews of the lost boats.

I asked the captain to approach as near as possible to Saint Pierre, and then, having a boat lowered, the lieutenant, the ensign [Ensign Hébert from the *Suchet*], and I steered for the city itself. We landed a little beyond the Place Mouillage; the desolation there is complete and we had to force our way to the Rue Bouillé. In this neighborhood we found bodies scattered everywhere. It is impossible to penetrate into the interior and to reach the main street of the city, the Rue Victor Hugo. In fact, to do so would be to walk over a glowing brazier.

The quays exist no longer; the trunks of the trees are no more. The lighthouse of the Place Bertin, about twenty meters in height, is razed to within three meters of the ground. The grating of the fountain is twisted; a distorted spout still gives out water. We attempted to make our way through the Rue Lucie, but the heat was so suffocating that we were obliged to abandon the effort. Returning to our ship, we set out to pick up the refugees of Carbet.

From our examination of the ruined city I conclude that the phenomenon which destroyed it was produced with such suddenness and intensity that there was no chance of escape; the ships in the roadstead, which were under high pressure, notably the two cargoboats and the Girard-line steamer *Diamant*, which had just arrived from Fort-de-France, could not evade it, and foundered or burned. The absence of any massing of bodies in the Rue Bouillé and the Place Bertin, a street and square surrounded by extremely populous houses, obviously prove that no panic preceded the destruction; if it had been otherwise, the entire population would have hurried to the streets. Everyone died on the spot where he was overtaken by the cataclysm.

The appearance of our boats off Carbet attracted to the shore about four hundred people, among them a score of injured. I found on inquiry that not a single one of them had come from St. Pierre; all were from Carbet. That town was not set on fire, but seemed to have been devastated by water. The people all along the shore implored to be taken along.

The vicar-general was on the same ferry that afternoon, and he got his first glimpse of the devastation around 3 p.m. In describing what he saw, Monseigneur Parel's chronicle turns into a eulogy for the lost city:

St. Pierre, in the morning throbbing with life, thronged with people, is no more. Its ruins stretch before us, wrapped in their shroud of smoke and ashes, gloomy and silent, a city of the dead. Our eyes seek out the inhabitants fleeing distracted or returning to look for the dead. Nothing is to be seen. No living soul appears in this desert of desolation, encompassed by appalling silence. When at last the cloud lifts, the mountain appears in the background, its slopes, formerly so green, now clad in a thick mantle of ash, resembling an Alpine landscape in winter. Through the cloud of ashes and of smoke diffused in the atmosphere, the sun breaks wan and dim, as it is never seen in our skies, and throws over the whole picture a sinister light, suggestive of a world beyond the grave.

With profound emotion I raise my hand [to give blessing] above these thirty thousand souls so suddenly mowed down, buried in this terrible tomb to sleep the sleep of eternity.

Beloved and unfortunate victims! Priests, old men and women, Sisters of Charity, children, young girls, fallen so tragically, we weep for you, we the unhappy survivors of this desolation; while you, purified by the particular virtue and the exceptional merits of this horrible sacrifice, have risen on this day of the triumph of your God to triumph with Him and to receive from His own hand the crown of glory. It is in this hope that we seek the strength to survive you.

If it ever occurred to Monseigneur Parel that his own actions, inactions, and sermons might have contributed to the terrible loss of life, he kept such thoughts secret to his grave. In everything he was to ever speak or write, the death and mass destruction were acts of God, and of God alone.

Around 9:30 p.m., the haphazard convoy of relief vessels steamed into the harbor of Fort-de-France with about thirty survivors from the waters of the bay and seven hundred terrified refugees from Carbet. Nobody had been rescued from St. Pierre itself. At 9:55 p.m., Commander Le Bris sent a terse cablegram to the naval ministry in Paris:

SUCHET TO NAVY PARIS:
Back from St. Pierre, city completely destroyed by mass of fire about 8 in the morning. Suppose all population annihilated. Have brought

back the few survivors, about thirty. All ships in the roadstead burned and lost. Eruption of volcano continues. I am leaving for Guadeloupe to get supplies.

—LE BRIS

. . .

By the next day, stories of strange and terrible deaths began to circulate. The charred corpse of one victim was found with an unburned silk handkerchief held to her lips. The remains of several young girls were burned to a crisp, but the shoes they wore were scarcely scorched. Many bodies in the streets lay facedown and contorted into the grotesque shapes indicative of broken bones; they had apparently been caught from behind and propelled forward by the blast. Horses and dogs lay incinerated and half buried in the debris alongside the corpses of those unfortunates who had sought safety in the streets of the city. In the Rue St. Jean-de-Dieu, a gruesome tangle of bodies bore mute testimony to the last moments of terror of a dozen prostitutes. Some bodies did not even appear human and could have been mistaken for charred fireplace logs. Of the few doorways left standing, most were clogged with corpses. Yet of the thirty thousand who had died, only a small fraction lay exposed in the streets. Most were entombed in the rubble of the collapsed buildings.

Some of the deceased, however, did not appear burned at all. A man and a blond girl with a blue ribbon in her hair sat dead at a table set for a meal, not a mark apparent on either body. A woman with a one-year-old child lay lifeless in a garden yet without an external burn. One man died with his daughter's arms around his neck and his son at his knee. A stable lad was found dead where he slept.

The edge of the nuée ardente did not always cut a clean slice between life and death. Madame Montferrier, the woman who had discovered Gaston Landes in his death throes, was in the kitchen of her home northeast of St. Pierre when her husband shouted from outside. She ran to the door just in time to meet the blast. Although both were burned, the couple immediately set out to look for their children, who had gone to Ascension Thursday services at the church at Trois-Ponts. There, they found the church a smoldering ruin. Her husband could go no farther, but Madame

Montferrier pressed on herself in the hope that their children had some-how escaped; for the rest of the day she continued her futile search from one ruined house to another. Her husband would die of his burns five days later. She would survive but remain scarred for life, both physically and emotionally.

According to one widely circulated story, Edouard Lasserre, owner of an estate near Morne Rouge, was in St. Pierre that morning to attend his daughter Hélène's First Communion at the cathedral. Before the service started, his estate manager arrived with the news that a herd of livestock had escaped from the plantation. Driving off at once to tend to the prob-lem, Lasserre, his manager, and their coachman barely reached the hills near Grand Réduit when they heard the explosion. Before they had time to react, the nuée ardente overturned their carriage and tossed them onto the road, where it took them several minutes to regain their senses. When they got up, they found that all of the exposed parts of their bodies had been terribly burned. Meanwhile, two pedestrians just thirty feet behind them had been killed.

This story is particularly interesting in that it is so similar to two other widely circulated stories, one involving a man named Lasserne and his friend, the other involving two men named Lassère and Simonut. All were purported to have been in carriages in the same general area, but for different reasons and with different destinations. In all of the versions, the carriage was wrecked, the mules (or horses) were killed, and the two men were burned. One version mentions that the driver, who sat forward of the two men but behind the mules, miraculously escaped unsinged. Later, George Kennan would report that he found the wreckage of a carriage on that particular road near Grand Réduit, then interviewed a man named Lassère in a hospital in Trinité.

Although at least one writer treated two of these stories as indepen-dent experiences, there can be little doubt that only one man with a name of that approximate spelling could have been in a carriage on the road near Grand Réduit at the instant of the catastrophe. Given human nature, it is not surprising that such stories will acquire different details as they circulate. Where there are elements of agreement, however, truths may easily be lurking. The relevance of these accounts lies not so much in their specifics, which are today beyond any hope of authentication, but rather in the broader picture they present of the human impact of the catastrophe.

The incredible good fortune of Fernand Clerc's family, standing exposed on that hill near Parnasse, became even more apparent after the story of Simon Taudilas began to circulate. Taudilas was one of a party of six—three men and three women—taking a holiday morning stroll to Parnasse when the Clerc family's speeding carriage drove them off the road and showered them with dust. Just a few minutes later, when they had barely finished cursing and brushing off their clothes, the volcano exploded. The three men immediately began running for higher ground, trying to drag their female companions along. At the sight of the advancing cloud, however, the women in their long dresses decided that flight was not for them. There happened to be a building near the road, and in that manner in which women sometimes seem to communicate telepathically, all three ladies simultaneously pulled away from their partners and bolted for that shelter. Realizing that it wasn't a good time to debate the relative merits of running versus hiding, the three men continued their mad dash up the hill. The nuée ardente mowed them down less than 1,500 feet from where the Clerc family stood unprotected. Simon Taudilas would recover, but one of his friends would die of his burns within the hour and the other three days later. All three women survived. For the rest of their lives they would tell the story of their experience to everyone who would listen.

On Morne d'Orange, the bluff south of St. Pierre that today still draws photographers seeking a panoramic view of the city and the volcano, two unnamed women watched the mountain explode. When the nuée ardente began to annihilate St. Pierre before their eyes, they ran into the Laugier shop and barricaded the door. That modest structure turned out to be at just a sufficient distance and altitude to shield them from the heat. Terrified, they huddled inside as the steam and ash churned around the building and its roof burst into flame. When the cloud dissipated, they bolted from the burning building unharmed. The ground outside was littered with dead bodies.

On the Trace Road just north of Carbet, Passioniste Lesage was talking to two women selling wares. The blast sent him tumbling down the road and drove two large rocks deep into one of his legs. When he struggled to his feet several minutes later, he was choking on ash. His body was covered with wet volcanic mud, and his hands and feet were burned. He survived, yet the two women he had been talking to died on the spot.

A young man, Joseph Bonnet-Durival, who many years later would become curator of the tiny museum that would be built to house a collection of artifacts of the disaster, would describe his own escape from Carbet:

> I was at the very spot where the eruption stopped, between St. Pierre and the next village, Carbet. In the next cottage, our neighbors were killed, we not. We ran away driven by fear, for there was no time to lose; in half a minute the town was destroyed. It was an explosion. The eruption was a cloud of steam carrying stones and ashes, with a heat of a thousand degrees and rolling over the ground with a speed of 500 [kilometers per hour]. I saw very well the eruption coming down to St. Pierre and toward us, with a dreadful noise. The cloud, running on the ground, passed at some distance from us, but from its edge extending above us we received little hot pieces of ash, stones, and much water from its condensation. Running to the village, we were stoned hard, and covered as if by wet cement. The eruption was over, but while running we were afraid, seeing the houses in the country burning behind us with high flames. Not ours, because by the best blessing, it was the first cottage safe towards the south. And in the evening, when I was going to Fort-de-France by sea from Carbet, I saw in the harbor of St. Pierre the liner *Roraima* still burning with a high flame, ten hours after the eruption.

Others who had been between Carbet and St. Pierre told their own stories of how they survived.

From Beauregard, Emilie Dujon watched the initial surge engulf St. Pierre, then swell outward and upward into a monstrous billowing cloud, flashing with lightning. The noise was deafening. Her husband, Charles, immediately grabbed her hand and started pulling her toward higher ground. Then, with the cloud still expanding toward them, he realized that his parents had not been keeping up, and he returned to help them, ordering Emilie not to follow. Screams could be heard from the lower slopes, and for the young woman it was a terrible moment. Charles returned with the old couple, but they got only a little farther before both fell to their knees exhausted and began praying. Emilie's thought was that only a miracle could save any of them. The miracle came in the form of a gale-force counterblast of wind that halted the approaching whirlwind of fire.

For the next seven hours, the family struggled through the hills above Carbet, finally arriving at a stable on the Lajus Plantation where some 150 people had already taken refuge. "We threw ourselves on the straw," Emilie said. "Our throats were on fire." A priest gave everyone absolution, for no one knew what horrors might still lie ahead. Then, around 5 p.m., they heard the whistle of the *Suchet*. Although it was much easier to run downhill to Carbet than up from Beauregard, by the time they reached shore the cruiser was already departing. They were ready to despair when the two other ships pulled in near shore and sent out rowboats. All four of them made it to Fort-de-France that evening. Shortly after, Emilie and Charles left Martinique for good; Emilie never saw her home again. Fifty-seven members of her family had died in the disaster.

A twenty-eight-year-old shoemaker, Léon Compère-Léandre, was to give the following account of his own miraculous survival:

On the eighth of May, about eight o'clock in the morning, I was seated on the doorstep of my house, which was in the southeastern end of the city and on the Trace Road. All of a sudden I felt a terrible wind blowing, the earth began to tremble, and the sky suddenly became dark. I turned to go into the house, made with great difficulty the three or four steps that separated me from my room, and felt my arms and legs burning, also my body. I dropped upon a table. At this moment four others sought refuge in my room, crying and writhing with pain, although their garments showed no sign of having been touched by flame. At the end of ten minutes one of these, the young Delavaud girl, aged about ten years, fell dead. The others left. I then got up and went into another room, where I found the father Delavaud, still clothed and lying on the bed, dead. He was purple and inflated, but his clothing was intact. I went out and found in the court two corpses interlocked; they were the bodies of the two young men who had been with me in the room. Re-entering the house, I came upon the bodies of two men who had been in the garden when I returned to my house at the beginning of the catastrophe. Crazed and almost overcome, I threw myself upon a bed, inert and awaiting death. My senses returned to me in perhaps an hour, when I beheld the roof burning. With sufficient strength left, my legs bleeding and covered with burns, I ran to Fonds-Saint-Denis, six kilometers from St. Pierre. With the exception of the persons of whom I have spoken, I heard no human cries; I experienced no degree of suffocation, and it was only the air that was lacking to me. But it was burning.

The cobbler would recover from his burns. Two women who were taken alive from the city would not. One, named Fillotte, would be found in a cellar a few days later, burned almost from head to toe; she would die soon after arriving at the hospital in Fort-de-France. The second, a woman named Laurent who worked as a servant in the household of Monsieur Gabriel, survived in the same hospital long enough to tell her brief story. She had heard the explosion, she said, then lost consciousness. When she awoke, apparently a few hours later, she was terribly burned and incapable of doing anything to comfort the two members of the Gabriel family who lay dying. Madame Laurent's burns were extensive, and despite the best efforts of the physicians and nurses, she too soon died.

• • •

Although the devastating pyroclastic surge had exploded to the south, the towns to the north of the volcano—Ajoupa-Bouillon, Basse-Pointe, Macouba, and Grand Rivière—had also suffered terribly from the ashfalls and the lahars that had swept down their adjacent streams. After the disaster in St. Pierre, many of the people of these communities lost faith in the government in Fort-de-France. Every seaworthy rowboat and canoe was mobilized, and within a day after the disaster at least three hundred refugees of Martinique's northern towns and villages had paddled to the British island of Dominica, where there was no active volcano. And the exodus continued.

After watching the destruction of St. Pierre firsthand from the main street of Morne Rouge, Father Mary advised his parishioners that when God sends signs, it is man's responsibility to pay attention. At his urging, eight hundred people from his parish hiked the fifteen miles through the mountains to the safety of Fort-de-France. Father Mary, however, did not join them; he remained in Morne Rouge to minister to those who could not, or would not, make the journey.

Others who had been spared in the hillside villages of the Pitons du Carbet carried what belongings they could to the coast and frantically begged passing ships to pick them up. Within a few days of the disaster, thousands of refugees arrived in Fort-de-France, all clamoring for food and shelter.

From the city of St. Pierre itself, however, there were only three refugees: the cobbler and the two women, who soon died. All of those miraculous stories of survival had come from people who had been at or beyond the fringes of the blast. And in fact, it was easy to dismiss the cobbler as a survivor from the city, for he had been about as far from the volcano as one could go and still be within the southern city limits. In fact, it was not even possible to see the volcano from Léon Compère-Léandre's home, for a hill blocked that line of sight. The early reports were therefore essentially correct in stating that St. Pierre had no survivors.

Meanwhile, however, one man still languished alive and undiscovered in the ruins of the center city: the prisoner.

CHAPTER 13

FRONT PAGES

•

Telegraphers and typesetters around the world worked night and day to spread the terrible news as it unfolded. On Friday, May 9, 1902, the *Chicago Daily News* ran the following front-page article:

EXTRA

REPORT 40,000 DEAD

St. Pierre, Martinique, Overwhelmed by a Volcano
and City is Ruined.

OFFICIAL NEWS IN PARIS

Heaps of Bodies Seen on Wharves
by Officers of a French Cruiser,
Who Attempt to Land.

[By the Associated Press.]
St. Thomas, D.W.I., May 9.—It is now estimated that forty thousand persons perished as a result of the volcanic eruption in the island of Martinique.

Paris, May 9. The colonial minister, M. Decrais, received at 6 o'clock this evening two cable messages from the secretary-general of the government of Martinique, J.E.G. L'Hurre [sic], sent respectively at 5 p.m. and 10:30 p.m. yesterday. The earlier cable reported that the wires were broken between Fort de France and St. Pierre, but it was added, in view of reports that the eruption of Mount Pelee had wiped out the town of St. Pierre, all the boats available at Fort de France were despatched to the assistance of the inhabitants of that place.

The second dispatch confirmed the reports of the destruction of St. Pierre and its environs and shipping by a rain of fire, and said it was supposed that the whole population had been annihilated with the exception of a few injured persons rescued by the cruiser Suchet.

Immediately after the receipt of the above dispatches the flag over the colonial office was draped with crepe and hoisted at half-mast.

Awful Story Confirmed.

Paris, May 9.—The commander of the French cruiser Suchet has telegraphed to the minister of marine, M. De Lanessan, from Fort de France, Island of Martinique, under date of Thursday, May 8, at 10 p.m., as follows:

"Have just returned from St. Pierre, which has been completely destroyed by an immense mass of fire which fell on the town at about 8 in the morning. The entire population (about 25,000 souls) is supposed to have perished. I have brought back the few survivors, about thirty. All the shipping in the harbor has been destroyed by fire. The eruption continues."

News of Disaster Confirmed.

St. Thomas, D.W.I., May 9, 9:30 a.m.— The French cruiser Suchet arrived at Pointe-a-Pitre, island of Guadeloupe, French West Indies, from Fort de France, Island of Martinique, this morning, bringing several refugees. She confirmed the report that the town of St. Pierre, Martinique, was entirely destroyed at 8 o'clock on Thursday morning by a volcanic eruption. It is supposed that most of the inhabitants of St. Pierre were killed, that the neighboring parishes were laid waste and that the residue of the population of St. Pierre is without food or shelter.

Passing Boat Covered with Ashes.

The British royal mail steamer Esk, which arrived at St. Lucia this morning, reports having passed St. Pierre last night. The steamer was covered with ashes, though she was five miles distant from the town, which was in impenetrable darkness.

A boat was sent in as near as possible to the shore, but not a living soul was seen ashore. Only flames were visible. The Quebec Steamship company's steamer Roraima was seen to explode and disappear.

The commander of the Suchet reports that at 1 o'clock on Thursday the entire town of St. Pierre was wrapped in flames. He endeavored to save about thirty persons, more or less burned, from the vessels in the harbor. His officers went ashore in small boats seeking for survivors, but were unable to reach the town.

Heaps of Bodies on Wharfs.

They saw heaps of bodies upon the wharfs and it is believed that not a single person resident in St. Pierre at the moment of the catastrophe escaped. The governor of the colony and his staff colonel and wife were in St. Pierre and probably perished. The extent of the catastrophe cannot be imagined.

Nearly All Roddam's Crew Dead.

The captain of the British steamer Roddam was very seriously injured and is now in the hospital at St. Lucia. All of his officers and engineers were dead or dying. Nearly every member of his crew is dead. Supercargo Campbell and ten of the crew of the Roddam jumped overboard at St. Pierre and were lost.

The first news was brought here by the British steamer Roddam, which was badly damaged and which lost seventeen men in the disaster. Captain Freeman was himself badly hurt.

Showers of Boiling Mud.

Early in the week a great shower of boiling mud overwhelmed and destroyed the Guerin factories, killing 150 men. This, it is believed, was the beginning of the great disaster.

The Quebec Steamship company's Roraima is among the lost, with all on board. It left New York on April 26 for St. Thomas and sailed from there on May 2 for St. Croix, stopping at St. Pierre two days later.

Death List May Be Swelled.

It is feared that adjacent islands have been badly damaged and that there has been a fearful loss of life.

For several days earthquake shocks have been reported by cable on the islands of St. Vincent, St. Lucia, Dominica, Antigua, and St. Kitts and Guadeloupe.

Fire and smoke from the volcanoes at St. Pierre, St. Vincent, and Dominica have been visible from the island of St. Lucia for several days. The cable line to Martinique was suddenly broken on Wednesday and since then no word came from the island until the British steamer Roddam arrived to-day.

M. Bouguenot, a sugar planter of the island of Martinique, received a cable dispatch this morning from Fort de France, sent by the manager of the Francais factory, announcing that he had "tried to reach St. Pierre, but found the coast covered with ashes and the town enveloped in dust and could not land."

Further Details Requested.

The commander of the French cruiser Suchet, now at Fort de France, has been ordered to return to St. Pierre, Martinique, with all the speed possible, and to forward details of the disaster to the French government. He cannot, however, be heard from for twenty-four hours, as the Suchet has gone to the island of Guadeloupe in order to obtain provisions.

It is feared that M. L. Mouttet, the governor of Martinique, is among the dead. He telegraphed May 7 that he was proceeding to St. Pierre. Senator Knight is also supposed to have been at St. Pierre.

Earthquake of Wide Extent.

Kingston, Jamaica, May 9.—All the islands in the neighborhood of Martinique are isolated, apparently by an earthquake. Cable communication with St. Vincent, Barbados, Grenada, Trinidad, Demerara, and St. Lucia is interrupted. Fears are entertained for the safety of the cable-repair steamer Grappler, which was at Martinique prior to the disaster.

Report by Consul Ayme.

Washington, D.C., May 9.—United States Consul Ayme yesterday cabled the state department from Guadeloupe that great consternation prevails in that locality in consequence of earthquakes and volcanic activity. Loud noises are heard continuously, which are ascribed to volcanic action. Telegraphic communication with Martinique is broken in every direction. He says he is informed that many hundreds of people have been killed in and about Martinique.

Three Passengers on the Quebec.

New York, May 9.—There were three passengers on the Quebec Steamship company's steamship Roraima, which is supposed to have been lost with all on board in the harbor of St. Pierre. These passengers were: F. Ince, Mrs. H. J. Ince, and Mrs. Stokes. All lived in the West Indies.

At the Quebec Steamship company's office here no news had been received, either from Capt. Muggah, the commander of the vessel, or from any of the West Indian agents of the line. At the offices of the Danish and French consuls nothing had been heard directly of the present conditions in the destroyed district.

St. Vincent Volcano Still Active.

London, May 9.—The colonial office here has received a dispatch from Sir Robert Llewelyn, governor of the Windward Islands in the Caribbean sea, dated from Kingston [*sic*], St. Vincent, yesterday, in which the governor says that the Soufriere volcano, in the northwestern part of the island of St. Vincent, continued in activity. Earth shocks had recurred for a week past, but not actually in Kingston [*sic*]. On Wednesday a big cloud of steam hung over the Soufriere, and the inhabitants, who were greatly alarmed, were flocking to Chateau Belairo. There were already 300 refugees there who were being fed by the authorities.

With the exception of a dispatch repeating the news brought to the island of St. Lucia, yesterday afternoon, by the British steamer Roddam, which announced the total destruction of the town of St. Pierre, by a volcanic eruption, the English merchants and shippers here having trade relations with Martinique have received no direct news of the catastrophe. Even the owners of the Roddam, which was forced to slip her anchors at St. Pierre in order to escape and which was badly damaged, seventeen of her crew being killed, have not heard from the vessel's captain.

London Is Cut Off.

At this hour (6:25 p.m.) London is quite cut off from communication with the island of Martinique. The cable companies have received nothing except vague messages saying the cable is interrupted owing to the volcanic eruptions.

The colonial office is without word from Martinique, except that a grave disaster, the extent of which is not mentioned, has occurred, and the receipt of a repetition of the steamer Roddam's news. The belief now exists that the British West Indian islands of Dominica and St. Vincent have also suffered severely. All messages to these islands are sent at sender's risk and no cipher dispatches are accepted. It is expected that possibly news will reach England to-night through steamers arriving at ports in the other West Indian islands.

• • •

The next issue of the *Chicago Daily News*, Saturday, May 10, included the following:

[By the Associated Press.]
Fort de France, May 10, 1:46 p.m.—The earthquakes have ceased, but the volcanic eruptions continue.

[By the Associated Press.]
Washington, D.C., May 10.— Secretary of the Navy Moody has cabled the commander of the cruiser Cincinnati, now at San Domingo city, to proceed to Martinique and render such aid as is possible.

SPECIAL CABLE TO THE DAILY NEWS.
St. Thomas, D.W.I., May 10.—As fuller reports of the Martinique disaster arrive the catastrophe grows in horror. It now appears that the immediate cause of the terrific explosion that blew off the top of the Mont Pelee crater and overwhelmed the town of St. Pierre in fiery ruin was the presence of a large lake in the heart of the old crater. The intense and sudden rise of temperature converted the mass of water into steam, with the result that the whole top of the mountain was blown away. It is now estimated that the loss of life in Martinique is 40,000.

Graphic Account of Disaster.
A schooner from the island of St. Vincent which reached Dominica to-day gives a graphic report of the scene. The schooner left St. Vin-

cent hurriedly on Wednesday because of the threatening state of matters there. A heavy fall of sand from the volcano on that island covered the vessel's decks inch deep. Steaming to within a mile of St. Pierre the crew of the St. Vincent vessel witnessed on Thursday morning at 8 o'clock a terrific explosion from Mont Pelee. The explosion seemed to lift the cap of the mountain completely off. At the same time the land heaved and swelled and a terrible convulsion took place at sea. The waters rose in a huge, threatening mass as though they would engulf every living thing on the ocean. Then a mass of fire descended on the doomed city and a pall of smoke covered the catastrophe from sight.

The Grappler First to Take Fire.

The captain of the St. Vincent vessel says that the British cable repairing ship Grappler was the first to take fire. It was lying nearly opposite the volcano.

The survivors of the Roraima crew, eight in number, tell a similar story. Molten lava fell in showers on their vessel. The sailors say that earthquake shocks had been felt at intervals for several days before the great disaster on Thursday. The upheaval of the waters seemed to pick the steamer up, throw it at the sky, and then drop it into the seething waters. The steamer was dashed to pieces. The eight sailors rescued were thrown into the water, where they clung to pieces of wreckage.

Many Sailors Leap Overboard.

All the crews of the eighteen vessels in the harbor were so suddenly surprised that they had barely time to leap into the sea. There most of them perished. It was impossible to escape from the pitiless rain of fire and only thirty were saved. The French cruiser Suchet picked them up, having arrived on the scene after the explosion of the crater. The inhabitants of St. Pierre, along with the thousands who had flocked into the town from the surrounding districts, as far as could be seen rushed down to the harbor looking for means of escape by sea. There, as in the case of the memorable disaster in Lisbon in 1755, they perished miserably, all escape being cut off.

Great clouds of ashes and smoke from the crater covered the sea for a distance of several miles, shrouding the town of St. Pierre and the country round about in impenetrable darkness.

The eruption still continues. Cable communication is broken and it is feared the relief sent to the survivors may not be able to reach them.

• • •

A rival Chicago newspaper, the *Chicago Daily Tribune,* offered an additional dispatch beyond the other widely circulated articles:

[BY CABLE TO THE CHICAGO TRIBUNE.]
ST. LUCIA, Windward Islands, May 9.—It is feared that there has been great loss of life and property on the Island of St. Vincent. The volcano that nearly destroyed the island in 1812 has been in active eruption for several days. Great clouds of dust, steam, and smoke have compelled the people to flee from the vicinity of the crater, and shipping has been driven from the harbor.

St. Vincent May Be Destroyed.

There is no news from the Island of St. Vincent, where the crater Soufriere has been active for several days. Cable communication has been broken since early in the week. There is no cable communication with Grenada or Dominica.

It is feared that both islands, St. Vincent and Dominica, have suffered severely.

St. Vincent Volcano Erupting.

The last message from St. Vincent was dated on Wednesday, May 7, at 3 o'clock in the afternoon. At that hour dense clouds of steam and smoke were pouring out of the crater of Soufriere, and there had already been four violent outbursts from the volcano.

The people from the surrounding country were swarming into the Chateau Belair for safety.

Driven from St. Vincent.

The British schooner Ocean Traveler of St. John, N.B., arrived at the Island of Dominica, British West Indies, at 3 o'clock this afternoon. The schooner was driven from the Island of St. Vincent during the afternoon of Wednesday, May 7, by a heavy fall of sand from the volcano in eruption there.

The schooner tried to reach the Island of St. Lucia, but adverse currents prevented it from so doing, and the vessel arrived opposite St. Pierre on Thursday morning, May 8.

Sees Mount Pelee Explode.

While about a mile off the volcano, Mount Pelee was seen to explode, and fire from it swept the whole City of St. Pierre, destroying the town and the shipping there, including the cable repair ship Grappler of the West India and Panama Telegraph company of London, which was engaged in repairing the cable near the Guerin factory. The Ocean Traveler, while on its way to Dominica, encountered a quantity of wreckage.

• • •

The *San Francisco Chronicle*, consistent with the international interests of its readership in a major port city, blared banner headlines of the catastrophe. In its issue of May 10, the paper reported:

FORTY THOUSAND BELIEVED TO HAVE PERISHED IN MARTINIQUE DISASTER.

Not a Single Inhabitant of St. Pierre Thought to Have Escaped.

Sudden Outburst of Molten Lava Gave the People No Chance for their Lives — Only Meager Reports of the Catastrophe Yet Received.

Although most of the edition's stories duplicated those appearing in other papers across the nation, one related a local impact:

STOCKTON WOMAN LOSES SISTER IN THE DISASTER

Says She Lived in Portion of City
Exposed to the Flow of Lava.

STOCKTON, May 9.—Mme. Louise Louit, a teacher of French in
this city, is prostrated over the news of the terrible disaster at St. Pierre,
Martinique, as her sister and family resided in that city. On learning
of the volcanic eruption this morning she swooned, and has been in
a serious condition for hours, though at times she would discuss the
terrible loss of life. Her sister, Mme. Gentile, her husband, two sons,
George and Raoul, and two daughters, Alice and Anais, are believed
to have been killed, as she says they lived in a portion of the city
where they would be greatly exposed to the molten lava which flowed
down the mountain side.

Raoul Gentile was rated as one of the most brilliant lawyers and
orators on the island, and, like his father, has held many prominent
positions of trust. For the past two years he has been one of the representatives from the island to the French Chamber of Deputies.

Mme. Louit says that the island has been swept by earthquakes,
floods, droughts, yellow fever, cyclones, and insurrections till the majority of the inhabitants were too poor to emigrate. If her relatives are
alive she expects to hear from them at any hour.

Certainly, what happened to Madame Louit's sister and her family
was no less terrible than if they had indeed been engulfed by "molten
lava." Yet her contention that the Martiniquians were "too poor to emigrate" reflected Mme. Louit's economic status in San Francisco more than
the true sentiments of the Martinique natives. In fact, most of that island's
natives probably would have politely declined any offer to help them emigrate, for Martinique was (and still is) a pretty nice place to live. It is
doubtful that Madame Louit ever reflected back on her conjecture four
years later, when almost nobody chose to emigrate from her own city of
San Francisco after the terrible destruction of the great earthquake and fire.

One strange geographic error, duplicated in newspapers across the
United States, ran in the *Chronicle* under the headline "HISTORY
CONTAINS MANY SUCH STORIES." Here, the reader learned

that "there was an earthquake in 1839 which destroyed nearly half of Port Royal, the present capital of the island [of Martinique], and killed 700 persons."

In 1839, however, the capital of Martinique was actually Fort-de-France, and prior to 1794, this city was called Fort Royal, not Port Royal. But, on June 7, 1692, the then-capital of Jamaica was destroyed by an earthquake and a tsunami that claimed thousands of lives (not merely seven hundred). And the name of that city, which was never rebuilt, happened to be Port Royal. This journalistic mistake had a ripple effect, for it led a number of later authors to associate Martinique with the site of a prior major disaster that had actually struck a different island two centuries earlier!

· · ·

The *New York Tribune* also ran banner headlines:

FORTY THOUSAND LOST

Rain of Fire Blotted Out St. Pierre, Martinique, in Three Minutes.

FRENCH WARSHIP VISITS THE SCENE

FEARS FOR THE OTHER ISLANDS

Not surprisingly, considering that the sources were distant and limited, many of the *Tribune*'s articles duplicated those of the *Chicago Daily News* and other U.S. daily newspapers. A few of the *New York Tribune*'s articles did, however, bring new titbits to U.S. readers on May 9 and 10, some of them well-informed, some not:

CONSUL PRENTIS [*SIC*] AND FAMILY LOST. INFORMATION SENT TO THE STATE DEPARTMENT BY THE CONSUL AT GUADELOUPE.

Washington, May 9.— The following cable dispatch has just been received by the State department:

Point a Pitre, May 9, 1902.

Secretary of State, Washington.

At 7 o'clock a.m. on the 8th instant a storm of steam, mud and fire enveloped the city and community. Not more than twenty persons escaped with their lives. Eighteen vessels were burned and sunk with all aboard, including four American vessels and a steamer from Quebec named Roraima. The United States Consul and family are reported among the victims. A war vessel has come to Guadeloupe for provisions, and will leave at 5 tomorrow.

AYME, Consul

PARIS DUMFOUNDED

APPALLED AT THE MAGNITUDE OF THE WEST INDIAN CALAMITY.

PRINTING OBITUARIES OF ITS COLONY OF MARTINIQUE—WAITING FOR DETAILS OF THE DISASTER.

(Special to the Tribune by French Cable.)

Paris, May 9.—News received in Paris today by way of St. Thomas and a telegram from Fort de France of May 8, sent by Captain Lebris [*sic*], commanding the French cruiser Suchet, announcing in a few brief words that the town of St. Pierre, its twenty-five thousand inhabitants and all the shipping in the harbor were last Thursday wiped off the face of the earth by combined earthquake and volcanic eruption, is the sum total of all that has yet reached Paris concerning the terrible seismic convulsion that can only be compared with the destruction of Lisbon in 1755 or that of Herculaneum and Pompeii in the year 79. People here are simply dumfounded at the catastrophe, the magnitude of which they have not yet grasped.

The "Figaro" to-morrow will publish a leading article recounting at length the topography of and history of Martinique in a sort of obituary of that colony, together with an interview with the Bishop of Martinique, who has nothing to say beyond deploring the sad fate of his diocese. The "Figaro" concludes as follows:

"Not only France, but humanity, is in mourning, for such commotions break down the barriers of nations, and in a few seconds unite all who think and love."

The "Matin" says the whole world trembles with emotion at the gigantic disaster, and the French nation can at present only express ardent pity and sympathy for the survivors.

The "Gaulois" says that in the face of this appalling misfortune the nation's subscription must at once be raised under the auspices of a syndicate of the Paris press.

At theatres, clubs, and on the boulevards all seem simply dumfounded, but as the details are lacking, the facts are not yet appreciated.

● ● ●

One curious front-page article in the *New York Tribune*'s May 10 edition was a quagmire of misinformation and wild speculation guised in the rubric of scientific observation and theory. One has to wonder what the contemporary reader made of this:

EARTHQUAKE PREDICTED.

THE MARTINIQUE DISASTER NO SURPRISE
TO WASHINGTON SCIENTISTS

[BY TELEGRAPH TO THE TRIBUNE.]
Washington, May 9.—Research into scientific works and records develops that it was long ago foreshadowed that there would be an earthquake in the Lesser Antilles about this time. The prophecy was made soon after the earthquake which devastated parts of the West Indies in 1851, it being said by scientists then that the volcanoes on those islands, though quiescent, would be likely to upturn the earth

in that region in about fifty years. While this intelligence was widely known, the modern "sharps" were inclined to disregard its potency in a large measure, believing that the volcanoes of the Antilles were nearly extinct. At the same time, the government experts in Washington expressed no surprise this morning when the news was published that St. Pierre had been destroyed by an earthquake, attributing the cause, however, to overloading, which is widely different from the process of volcanic explosion. Since the days when the belief was held that big catfish lived under the earth, whose chief function was to swallow wholesale the inhabitants of sections of the globe, superstition with respect to seismic disturbances has been reduced to more reasonable theories, the important two being that earthquakes are the result of spasmodic acceleration of the secular folding of rocks and masses having their centrum at the mouths of large rivers, where prodigious quantities of silt are deposited, and to [sic] volcanic explosions. The former cause produces the more disastrous earthquake, is further reaching in its effect and therefore is regarded as of more scientific importance. According to this theory, regions near water basins at the foot of long, sloping territory are peculiarly susceptible to subterranean explosions, in view of the natural overload of sediment which is continually being dumped therein. There are few lands more exposed to the danger of this natural evil than the West India Islands, including Martinique, as the surrounding waters are the dumping ground for the sediment washed down the Mississippi and Ohio Rivers, together with other bodies of water flowing into the Gulf from other directions. Other places known to geologists as susceptible to earthquakes from this cause are the lands near the mouth of the Po, where other rivers empty great deposits of silt; the Bay of Bengal, which is the receptacle for the washings of the Ganges and other rivers; the Yellow Sea, into which deposits are made from the Yanktse [sic] River, and the mouth of the Amazon. Perhaps the territory near the Mississippi River and the Yellow Sea is most liable to earthquake from overloading. It is estimated by scientists that if freight cars coupled in a line sixty miles long from Cumberland, Md., to Washington, were kept hauling continually for one year it would not be possible to unload at Washington half as much silt as the Potomac River deposits in six months. From scientific observations it is learned that a large majority of earthquakes are results of this cause, while only a few are caused by volcanic explosion.

Of course, no one is able to tell at this moment the exact cause of the earthquake at Martinique. But experts here think that it was probably from overloading, and this opinion was expressed by Professor W. J. McGee this afternoon. From trustworthy geographical descriptions of Martinique it is gleaned that the island is rocky and volcanic, containing five or six extinct craters. Heretofore earthquakes there have been exceedingly disastrous. Of three mountains in the interior the highest is Mount Pelee, which is 4,438 feet above the sea. By recognized authorities, the island has been pronounced susceptible to earthquakes, the last serious one occurring in 1851, as a result of the eruption of Mount Pelee. At one time there was an earthquake in one of the Antilean group, when all of the inhabitants of a town except one man were killed. He was swallowed by the earth, but lived in the chasm which held him until another upturning of the earth opened the inclosure and let him out again. He lived to be an old man, a monument was raised to his memory, bearing an epitaph telling of the phenomenon, and his character has a place in books on the West Indies.

The entire archipelago between Northern and Southern Asia, like the archipelago of Eastern Asia, is a distinctively volcanic region, being a continuous link of volcanic manipulation. Yet most volcanoes in these islands are extinct, or have been quiescent during the historical period.

No, no one has ever fallen into a fissure and later been ejected, nor has a monument ever been raised to such a person. No, "overloading" by silt is not a major cause of earthquakes; in fact, the Mississippi delta region with its extensive silt deposits is one of the *least* seismically active regions in North America. No, the last serious earthquake in Martinique did not occur in 1851, but in 1839, and it was not associated with any volcanic activity. No, earthquakes have *not* been common or particularly disastrous in Martinique. No, the volcanic islands of Eastern Asia were not extinct by a long shot (it had been less than two decades since the cataclysm at Krakatau). The concept of extinction is based on a geologic, not a human, timescale.

Most scientists simply shrugged at this kind of ignorance and un-founded speculation (and maybe a few wished that the *Tribune*'s editor had himself studied a bit of science in high school). But the *Tribune*, after all, was not a scientific journal. Given that even publications in scientific forums were often wrong, most scientists were not likely to waste their time correcting the errors and misconceptions that appeared in newspapers. Meanwhile, the reading public was subjected to a heterogeneous mixture of fact and fiction, substantive theory and wild speculation about the twin disasters in the French West Indies.

• CHAPTER 14 •

AFTER THE END

•

Friday, May 9. With the unthinkable catastrophe verified as true, no longer could anyone debate whether the northwest coast of Martinique should be evacuated. At 8 a.m. on May 9, the cable-repair ship *Pouyer-Quertier* dropped anchor off Les Abymes, the village just north of Precheur, and blew its horns. With the volcano still rumbling less than three miles away, the villagers did not wait for the ship's landing boats to beach; they immediately launched every floatable pirogue they could find and paddled out to meet their rescuers. In less than two hours, 456 people crowded onto the decks of the *Pouyer-Quertier,* and not even the ship's winches and coils of cable remained visible through the carpet of humanity.

Although none of Precheur's evacuees were seriously injured, all were distraught and hungry. The ship's crew handed bowls of milk to the children and passed bread and cheese into the crowd. There were about thirty bottles of wine on board, and Captain Thirion ordered that they be opened and diluted so each adult could have a few deciliters. It may have been the only incident in history where hundreds of Frenchmen were given watered-down wine and not a one complained.

On its way back to Fort-de-France, the *Pouyer-Quertier* steamed past Precheur. Although that town's shoreline was packed with people waving and shouting for the ship's attention, there was no way to fit another soul on the vessel. Captain Thirion also knew it would be folly to return that afternoon to try to rescue as many as 4,000 people when he could accommodate no more than 450 at a time; a whole flotilla of ships and boats would clearly be needed to evacuate Precheur. He gave his signalman a message to semaphore to shore: all of Precheur would be evacuated no later than tomorrow. Then Thirion looked up at the still-smoldering volcano and said a silent prayer that Pelée would cooperate with those semaphore flags.

That evening, Captain Thirion sighed with relief when he saw that the *Suchet* had returned from Guadeloupe and was docking. The cruiser was capable of carrying as many as seven hundred evacuees at a time. Thirion immediately went on board to discuss the coordination of Precheur's evacuation with Commander Le Bris. There, in the captain's cabin, he was startled to find Senator Amédée Knight, whom everyone had assumed dead.

The senator was circumlocutory about how he had personally escaped the disaster. He was, however, insistent that he participate in tomorrow's evacuation of Precheur. His personal yacht, which would hold up to three dozen people, was now in the service of the public welfare.

Both Thirion and Le Bris went to sleep that night muttering about the senator's audacity and the man's blatant attempt to garner publicity for himself. But they both knew that they were trapped. How could they possibly turn down a senator's offer of personal assistance?

• • •

Saturday, May 10. The *Korona,* of the Quebec Line, arrived at St. Pierre two days later than scheduled. One of its passengers, Herman Rosenberg of Philadelphia, would later describe his observations:

> As far as the eye could see inland, the utmost desolation prevailed. If there is any word that will describe the appearance of the landscape it is "whitewash." A vast field of slaking lime might have resembled the scene, with the thick, steamy fumes rising continually from it. Not a living human being was to be seen, and not a tree, nor a shrub, nor a blade of grass. Nothing was visible but that awful vaporous white, and overtopping all the devilish Pelée, still vomiting lava, which flowed thickly down its white sides into the sea.
>
> In the harbor every vessel was stripped of masts and deck housings. We could do nothing. Captain Carey had the *Korona* steam about for an hour or so, and then we left for Fort-de-France. As we were com-

ing into the harbor we picked up a small boat in which were four men. Two of them spoke English. They were sailors from our sister ship the *Roraima*, which had touched at St. Pierre, bound for Barbados.

[Based on other accounts, these two English-speaking men were probably the *Roraima*'s First Officer Scott and Assistant Purser Thompson.]

It is true that it is foolish to send more money or supplies to Martinique. It would be a waste and could only serve to foster pauperism. St. Pierre is dead. All its inhabitants are dead, and it will never arise from its ashes. Nobody would live there now. Outside of St. Pierre the people are not in want. When all the bodies are taken care of there will be little more to do. The volcano left little to be done.

Rosenberg, of course, was very wrong about there being little to be done. Thousands of people remained threatened by the continuing eruption, and the refugees swarming into Fort-de-France with only the clothes on their backs were overwhelming all public efforts to meet their needs.

Meanwhile, the planned evacuation of Precheur was late getting started. A predawn cablegram had arrived from Paris directing the acting governor to secure St. Pierre's ruins against looters, and Le Bris was told to cooperate. Considerable sums of money lay locked in bank vaults in the rubble, gold chalices and other religious hardware were buried in the ruins of the churches, and many personal items of considerable value were expected to be salvageable from wrecked private homes. What the cablegram did not say was that the French banks had been telling nervous European depositors and investors that all of their Martinique books and funds had been transferred to the *Suchet* prior to the disaster!

Commander Le Bris dutifully put a party of gendarmes ashore at St. Pierre that morning. By the time the *Suchet* and the *Pouyier-Quertier* arrived at Precheur, Senator Knight was already on shore enthusiastically establishing himself as the leader of the town's evacuation. Le Bris and Thirion, knowing enough not to raise a challenge in front of thousands of agitated people, allowed Knight to direct the chaotic operation. It took five long hours for forty oarsmen to transport 1,200 women and children across Precheur's choppy bay to the two ships and Knight's yacht. As they sailed off to Fort-de-France, Thirion and Le Bris left most of their ships' boats in Precheur as an assurance to the remaining 3,000 that their ships would indeed return. One of the exhausted oarsmen shouted to Knight as he sailed off, "See you tomorrow, Senator—if we are not dead!"

• • •

Sunday, May 11. A small fleet of ferries and boats landed more gendarmes and infantry in St. Pierre, along with firewood, petroleum, and quicklime to cremate the bodies. The heat from the burned city was still suffocating, and the stench of burning flesh made more than a few sailors vomit over the rails before even reaching shore. Meanwhile, the volcano rumbled, and a great cloud of volcanic dust continued to shroud the site from the sun. The hulk of the *Roraima* still burned in the bay; the ship would go to its watery grave that afternoon.

The cremation of the dead was an immediate priority. Fires were begun on the beachfront, and corpses were heaped on the burning wood. To facilitate the combustion and help mask the awful odor of burning flesh, the impromptu crematories were soaked with coal tar and petroleum.

Meanwhile, the Danish ship *Valkyrien* joined the *Suchet*, the *Pouyer-Quertier*, and Senator Knight's yacht to complete the evacuation of the last 3,000 people from Precheur. In three days, a total of about 4,600 people were successfully taken from Martinique's northwest coast to Fort-de-France.

• • •

Fifty miles away at Castries, as his steamer *Etona* was being coaled, Captain Cantrell wrote in his log:

> At St. Lucia, on May 11th, I went on board the British steamship *Roddam*, which had escaped from the terrible volcanic eruption at Martinique two days before. The state of the ship was enough to show that those on board must have undergone an awful experience.
>
> The *Roddam* was covered with a mass of fine bluish gray dust or ashes of cement-like appearance. In some parts it lay two feet deep on the decks. This matter had fallen in a red-hot state all over the steamer, setting fire to everything it struck that was burnable, and, when it fell on the men on board, burning off limbs and large pieces

of flesh. This was shown by finding portions of human flesh when the decks were cleared of the debris. The rigging, ropes, tarpaulins, sails, awnings, etc., were charred or burned, and most of the upper stanchions and spars were swept overboard or destroyed by fire. Skylights were smashed and cabins were filled with volcanic dust. The scene of ruin was deplorable.

The captain [Edward Freeman], though suffering the greatest agony, succeeded in navigating his vessel safely to the port of Castries, St. Lucia, with eighteen dead bodies on the deck and human limbs scattered about. A sailor stood by constantly wiping the captain's injured eyes. I think the performance of the *Roddam*'s captain was most wonderful, and the more so when I saw his pitiful condition [in the hospital]. I do not understand how he kept up, yet when the steamer arrived at St. Lucia and medical assistance was procured, this brave man asked the doctors to attend to the others first and refused to be treated until this was done.

My interview with the captain brought out this account. I left him in good spirits and receiving every comfort. The sight of his face would frighten anyone not prepared to see it.

· · ·

That same day, May 11, a survivor was discovered in the ruins of St. Pierre. His curious story and eventual recovery would make news around the world.

He was an unlikely celebrity, an illiterate twenty-eight-year-old with a fiery temper and a reputation for mayhem. Answering to the nickname Sanson (or Samson), he was not particular about his birth name, and neither were most of the contemporary writers who would spread his story. Ludger Sylbaris, Joseph Sibarace, Joseph Surtout, Ludger Morell, Raoul Sarteret, Ludgar Symbaris, Louis-Auguste Cyparis, or Augusté Ciparis—it made little difference. A cane cutter, a carpenter, a sailor, a criminal, a murderer—he would eventually learn to bask in his notoriety and tell his interviewers what they wanted to hear. Burned by ashes? Yes. Burned by lava? That, too. Witness to the deaths of scores of nuns and schoolgirls? Why not? Rescued by looters? Yes. Rescued by a kindly priest? Sure.

Although there were numerous other survivors, all but Sanson had been either on the ships in the roadstead or in a place singed only by the fringes of the fireball. Such survival at the periphery was understandable; in fact, it would be surprising if the disaster did *not* have a transition region where some were killed while others received nonfatal injuries. Ciparis was unique: he had been smack in the center of the holocaust. In jail.

The official records of Sanson's arrest went up in smoke along with the rest of St. Pierre. The warden and guards who might have told about the circumstances of his incarceration lay dead. Thus freed from the encumberances of verification, some chroniclers embellished the bare bones of Sanson's story with various imaginative details.

In one version, Sanson had a day job as a cane cutter at one of the hillside plantations. Walking home to Precheur one afternoon three weeks before the disaster, he encountered an acquaintance. The two men argued about a debt—it isn't clear who owed whom—and the matter escalated from a verbal confrontation to a shoving match to Sanson getting punched in the face. For the cane cutter, that was sufficient reason to abandon any semblance of self-restraint; he yanked his machete from his belt and swiftly put a slice across the man's chest. Meanwhile, the altercation drew the attention of a gendarme, who jumped into the fray and snatched away the machete before something more serious could happen. Sanson, not in a frame of mind to exercise his best judgment, threw a flurry of punches at the officer. Several other gendarmes ran to their comrade's aid and arrested the offender. According to this account, Sanson was remanded to a month's solitary confinement in the prison in St. Pierre, where he was still incarcerated when the volcano exploded.

A slightly different version of the story relates that in early April, Sanson overimbibed at a fiesta in Le Precheur and wounded a friend with a cutlass. For that, he was sentenced to a month in jail. Toward the end of his time, he was taken into St. Pierre on a laboring job and learned that there was another festival going on in Le Precheur. He escaped, dashed off to his hometown, danced all night, then remanded himself to custody the following day. That escapade earned him a week of solitary confinement in the stone cell where he would be discovered on May 11.

Another writer, however, claims that Sanson actually requested the solitary confinement. According to this story, he had been suffering from a fever and viewed the unoccupied thick-walled *cachot* as a way to get relief from the midday tropical heat.

An imaginative writer could improve on these kernels, and some apparently did. One said that Sanson killed a man in a barroom fight and was sentenced to die by hanging. He was placed in solitary confinement in a "death cell," awaiting execution. On Wednesday, May 7, the governor reprieved his death sentence but ordered that he remain incarcerated until he could be transferred to France to serve out his sentence.

In an even more melodramatic version of the story, Sanson's execution was scheduled to take place on the very morning of the disaster. In the ultimate irony (according to this account), Mont Pelée chose to obliterate all thirty thousand of the community that had sentenced Sanson to death and to spare this murderer instead.

The discrepancies led many to suspect that the entire tale was a concoction. In its essential features, however, Sanson's story would turn out to be true. Regardless of the reason for his incarceration, Augusté Ciparis was indeed in solitary confinement in St. Pierre's prison on the morning of May 8, 1902. His cell survives today in a small courtyard in the ruins of the prison complex. Its stone walls and arched roof are more than a foot thick, and its rear wall is contiguous with a tall stone abutment that retains a nearly vertical hillside. The cell, about nine feet high on the outside, has a single small west-facing window and a doorway a mere four and a half feet in height. In a photograph taken shortly after the disaster, more than three feet of ash was piled against the stout wooden door. If anyone were to have a chance of surviving the nuée ardente, this was the place for it to happen: the hillside shielded the cell from the direct impact of the blast, its arched construction and thick walls gave it a structural integrity unmatched by any other building in the city, its thermal mass protected its occupant from the searing heat, and the small barred window restricted the inflow of hot gases. The thick accumulation of ash outside provided further insulation and also helped prevent the door from being blown in by the blast.

Ciparis did not even hear the explosion. He got his first hint that something had happened when hot ash began pouring into the cell, billions of particles of grit adhering to his skin. He coughed up a sticky gray sputum, then took off his shirt, urinated on it, and draped it around his head as a mask. In a few minutes it was over, and outside all was silent. For the next three days he languished in pain from his burns, entombed alive with no food or water.

Then, on the morning of May 11, two men from Morne Rouge happened to be walking through the wrecked prison for reasons they would never quite explain. When they heard Ciparis's muffled cries, they pried open the cell door. Ciparis emerged into the scene of devastation and quickly collapsed. The men brought him water, which was still running plentifully through the city, and when he was sufficiently revived, they helped him walk the nearly four miles to Morne Rouge. There, Father Mary fed him, tended as best he could to his burns, and sheltered him in the vacated home of one of the parishioners. Distressed, exhausted, and in physical pain, it would be several weeks before Ciparis would venture outside again. And during those several weeks, even before Ciparis himself would say much of anything to anyone, rumors of his survival would gain enough of a foothold to generate wildly imaginative tales.

One particularly flagrant fabrication, which appears in several sources, was in the supposed words of the prisoner as he looked out the small window of his cell:

Right in front of me where the brick wall had stood [knocked down by a huge red-hot stone] I saw the large convent, and I could see that molten matter had come down the hill and had run into the grounds. I realized then that there must have been an eruption of Mont Pelee. To my horror I discovered that the lava had completely encircled the convent with its first rush and that all the [two hundred] girls and sisters who were in the building were doomed. ·

While I looked I saw another stone, even larger than the one which had fallen near my cell window and broken down the wall, strike on the convent roof and crash through its three stories, evidently plunging through to the ground. I had not seen any of the sisters until that time, and I suppose they had depended for safety on the building, seeking shelter from the rain of hot ashes which I could see falling.

In an instant after this huge stone crashed through I saw the poor girls flocking out in the utmost terror. Their actions looked as though they were screaming in an agony of fright, but I could not hear a sound owing to the hissing of the lava and the roar of the volcanic discharge. As the girls came running out I saw that they carried with them bodies of those who had been injured by the crashing of the stone through the building. Some they carried out were dead, while I could see that others were only injured.

The sisters came running out, too, bringing appliances for helping the injured, but those who had hurried out of the building were driven in again by the blinding ashes and the fumes which I could see rise from the lava.

A pit had been dug on the inside of the wall in order that none of the girls should be able to climb up from the inside, and this acted as a sort of moat, in which the lava floated, and thus made a complete circle round the convent, rendering escape impossible, even if it had been possible to live in the rain of hot stones and ashes from the mountain.

Again as I looked I saw another stone fall upon the building, and this time many more of the girls rushed out. A party of them broke down one of the doors, and holding this over their heads they tried to run for the gate, but were amazed to find their escape cut off by the river of lava.

The lava gradually rose and rose, and I could see the huddled group of girls growing smaller and smaller, as first one and then others succumbed to the poisonous fumes and the fearful heat. And as the group got smaller the lava rose . . . until there was but a small piece of land around the building.

Then with one great burst, it seemed to me, a fresh stream of lava flowed into the moat and overswept the building and the little island on which the girls were standing a moment before. I turned away my eyes in horror, and when next I looked nothing was to be seen of the convent but a heap of calcined stone, and here and there the blackened corpses of those who but a few moments before had been full of life and hope.

This purported eyewitness account belies all of the facts. Apart from the detail that Ciparis was virtually uneducated and would not speak so articulately, there is no way anyone could have possibly witnessed the events described. Standing in Sanson's cell today and peering out its tiny window, one gets a narrow view of only a few broken walls within the prison compound. Moreover, the window faces west, while the convent stood to the north, a quarter mile away across the Rivière Roxelane. The blast struck the convent only about eight seconds before it engulfed the prison, and even if there had been a view, all of the described actions could not have taken place in that short a time. The image of a group of school-girls tearing down a convent door and using it for protection is as far-fetched as their carrying out the bodies of their friends. Beyond this, there were few if any boulders falling from the sky in St. Pierre—and certainly none large enough to knock down a brick wall. The walls, moreover, were not even made of brick; they were made of stone. Finally, the flow of lava was total fiction. Not only was there no lava, but there was not even a mudflow that might have been mistaken for a lava flow.

When George Kennan met Ciparis two weeks later, he would do a better job of reconstructing what the prisoner had actually experienced. By then, however, a great deal of misinformation had already made its way to typesetters around the world.

$$\bullet \quad \bullet \quad \bullet$$

Steam burns are unlike those from open flames. In less time than it takes fire to char a victim's skin, steam will cook the underlying flesh. This rapid and usually lethal effect depends little on the steam's temperature, but instead on what physicists refer to as its "latent heat of vaporization." When a single ounce of steam condenses into an ounce of liquid water on a victim's body, it immediately gives up enough heat to raise nearly ten ounces of human flesh to the boiling point. If the steam is superheated—in other words, at a temperature above 212°F—this rapid and deep heating effect is even greater.

The great mass of steam in Mont Pelée's pyroclastic surge might have claimed thousands of victims by essentially flash-cooking them alive. Ashes covering the cooked flesh further retarded its decomposition, and many bodies that had not been charred too badly and had been coated with ash still had recognizable features several weeks after the disaster.

Toward the south, however, there had been less ashfall, and the ex-posed corpses, cooked or not, began to decompose in the tropical heat and humidity. There, salvagers tramping through the ruins couldn't help but notice that many of the bodies had exploded from the inside: internal organs spilled out of ruptured abdomens, and brains protruded from burst skulls. Some officers in charge of the cremation crews argued that the condition of the corpses proved that a great vacuum had followed the blast. The same physiological wreckage, however, could also be explained if the internal bodily fluids had been flash-heated to a boil. Regardless of the reason, the frailty of the human body in the face of this unbridled force of nature was sobering.

It was into this gruesome scene of hundreds of exposed decomposing and mutilated bodies, and many thousands more buried in the rubble, that Signor Paravicino, the Italian consul at Barbados, ventured to search for the remains of his daughter. The girl had been visiting friends near Carbet, where a ridge had shielded most of the town from destruction. Just behind that natural barrier was a stately residence, most of its windows and blinds blown out. Paravicino wandered through, finding furniture and personal items intact, but no living soul to ask about the fate of his daughter. Where such residences had survived, their occupants had invariably fled soon after. He had no choice but to begin looking at the grisly corpses that littered the road and the backyards yards of the burned homes by the sea. A man had died while praying at the foot of a statue of St. Mary. Several victims lay half submerged in the waters near the mouth of the Rivière du Carbet, where they apparently had attempted to quench their burns before they succumbed. A man was sprawled dead on the decaying carcass of his horse. A dozen servants lay dead outside the charred ruins of a seaside home. And then, to Signor Paravicino's horror, he found the partially decomposed body of a girl whose clothing and jewelry unmistakably established her as his own daughter. As his aides prepared the corpse for removal, a skeletal ox surrealistically stalked slowly through the wreckage, took a sip of sea water, then went back up the hillside.

• • •

Disasters bring out both the best and the worst elements of human nature. When Lisbon, Portugal, was struck by a terrible earthquake and tsunami in 1755, thirty-four looters were executed within the first week after the disaster. Although the twentieth-century French were more restrained, several fights did break out between looters and gendarmes that resulted in two scavengers being shot. Within a few days of St. Pierre's demise, several dozen others were arrested, including a few women. The men were sentenced to five years' imprisonment; the women, apparently, to two years. It does not seem overly speculative to suspect that the reason Sanson's rescuers didn't turn him over to the French authorities was that this would place them in the awkward position of having to justify their own presence in St. Pierre.

Although the volcano was still in eruption, dozens of opportunists boated in from other islands, hoping to sift through St. Pierre's rubble to recover items of value. There are always rationalizations for such behavior: the dead no longer own anything, the volcano would eventually destroy any unrecovered items anyway, and so on. One Englishman, apparently from St. Lucia, was arrested at the ruins of the cathedral with a sack full of gold candelabras and chalices. He was taken to Fort-de-France, where he offered the defense that he just wanted to ensure that the religious items would be safe from looters. The court formally accepted his explanation, confiscated the valuables, and ordered that he be immediately deported.

• • •

By the third week of May, journalists were arriving not just from neighboring islands but also from the United States. One correspondent of the *New York Herald* would eloquently describe his first impressions of the disaster's aftermath:

> St. Pierre is as dead as Pompeii. If men be found with hearts stout enough to build again beneath the steaming maw of old Pelée, a new city can rise only on the ruins of the old. St. Pierre is not only dead, but buried. Most of her people lie fathoms deep in a tomb made in the twinkling of an eye by the collapse of their homes, and sealed forever under tons of boiling mud, avalanches of scoria, and a hurricane of volcanic dust.
>
> Above the miles of piled debris rise here and there the relics of her ten thousand homes and commercial factories, ragged walls, rent, seamed, and seared by fire. Fit monuments they are to the myriads of

dead beneath, who are victims of the most heart-rendering calamity of modern times!

In other parts of the city not even a roof peak or chimney thrusts its top through the sea of scoria. In the section known as the new town, winding up the slope of the mountain from the crescent of the roadstead, many of the city's most pretentious homes have utterly vanished, as a Swiss chalet is swept from sight by the rush of an Alpine avalanche. At such points one is spared all the gruesome horrors of the scene elsewhere, for Pelée has covered them under a pall of ashen dust as soft, impalpable, and smooth as drifted snow, with only a scurry blown from the surface now and then into the blinking eyes of the explorer, blinded by the dazzle of the sunlight on the billowy gray-white surface of this volcanic grave.

Old Pelée breathed upon the city, and under his dragon breath fair St. Pierre shrivelled, crumbled, and burned, as the wing of the moth is scorched in the flame of the torch. He breathed again and shrouded the dead city under a pall that mercifully hides in spots the ghastly relics of her former comeliness.

Over the entombed city the volcano from a dozen vents yet pours its steaming vapors in long, curling wreaths that mount thousands of feet aloft, like smoking incense.

Another journalist from the *New York Herald*, whose name, unfortunately, was not identified, described his trek into the devastated city two weeks after the disaster:

With little difficulty a landing was effected directly in front of the ruin of the large rum warehouse of Lasser Frères. The wharves in front were littered with an inextricable tangle of rum casks, barrel hoops and staves, heavy iron anchor chains, piles of conch shells and other maritime debris. The heavy masonry walls of the building, falling outward, had tumbled great masses of stone and shattered machinery over the entire area, and the powdery coverlet of fluttering dust had swathed the whole in a cloak of neutral gray. Up to the second story above the ground the thick stone walls of the front still stood, though seamed and tottering.

Here in the main doorway, at the very threshold of the place where he had toiled, was seen the first mute relic of human tragedy—

a negro, broad-shouldered and strong; he had probably been a stevedore or warehouse porter. The stone arch of the doorway had saved him from being crushed under the falling walls and the masonry had shielded the body partially from fire. The sleeves of his shirt had been rolled up to the elbows. Death had found him at his daily task and struck him down where he stood, or, perchance, had caught him in one desperate effort at flight through the doorway toward the harbor so close beyond, whose waters were soon a seething caldron under the blast of fire that scourged both land and sea.

Along the waterfront the piled debris was not so formidable as to seriously impede a good climber, but the moment one sought to penetrate to Bouille Street, the next thoroughfare back from the shore, he encountered difficulties that called for the skill of an Alpine mountaineer. Mingled masonry, crumbled mortar, mud and ashes formed a foul, noisome series of hillocks, beneath which the dead lay in thousands. At every step the explorer encountered relics suggestive of the simple home life of the people. The wheels and pendulum of a mantle clock were kicked out from the debris as the party shuffled through the flying dust. The end of an old spring bed projected amid the ruins of a private house, and close beside it the relic of a human skull and the fragments of a spinal column indicated all that was left of its possible occupant.

Pushing through Bouille Street to the northward, the tangle became more and more intricate. Here and there the stone walls of the taller buildings, cracked and crumbling, leaned menacingly outward toward the center of the street. Seamed and rent with jagged cracks from base to top, they looked as though the slightest jar might bring them tumbling about the heads of those who ventured through. There had been commercial houses here, and in a dozen places iron boxes and small safes had been routed out of the ruins and their fronts torn open by means of crowbars and other heavy tools. In some cases this had been done by the legitimate heirs to the property. In too many instances there were evidences of the alert industry of the looters and ghouls who had come only to prey upon the city of the dead. In the deep gray powder that covered the surface of all things visible could be traced the footprints of the looters and of the rescuing parties who had traversed the ground before. Save for these, the only evidences of life in the stricken town were the footprints of the sea-birds along the strand.

Here on the left is heard at last a sound. In the deathlike stillness it strikes upon the ear strangely. It is the ripple of gurgling water. Tracing it to its source, we find a water pipe, the nozzle of which projects through the shattered wall of a private dwelling. From it the water, in pure, crystal, plenty, is pouring down and welding the masses of ashes and cement beneath into a sticky paste. St. Pierre's streets, with their trickling rivulets of mountain water, had been the pride of her citizens. Through all the blast of fire at least this remnant of her water system had survived.

One of the party approached the trickling water to lave from hands and face the choking accumulation of dust. As he did so he stepped back and paused. Directly below where the water fell lay huddled the grizzled remnants of a dead family.

From this point the party, with difficulties increasing at every step, pushed further up the slope toward the heart of the town and into Victor Hugo Street. Progress here was made rather by climbing than by walking. At every step bent and twisted iron girders, pieces of steel shafting, tons of tumbled masonry and piles of half-burned corpses barred the way. One sought instinctively to turn the steps so as not to desecrate the dead, but try as he might, at every footstep his feet scuffed up the dust that uncovered the ashes of another corpse.

Through Victor Hugo Street we penetrated to what had been the Cathedral de Moullage. Had it been hammered for a fortnight under the guns of a fleet of battleships its ruin could hardly have been more complete. . . . Even the altar was not spared, though one of the earliest rescuing parties succeeded in saving the candelabra, the chalice and other holy vessels, and persons of a deeply devout bent of mind soon found in this an evidence of miraculous intervention. . . . Immediately surrounding the cathedral, one could hardly so pick his way as to escape walking upon the dead. It was no exaggeration when Consul Ayme, of Guadeloupe, said that the streets of St. Pierre were paved with the corpses of her citizens.

Though many ghouls had already prowled through the catacombs of the ruined city, St. Pierre presented a profitable field for the would-be looter. It would have been easy for any member of our party during the hours in which we tramped over the entombed town to have filled barrels with silver spoons, coins, earrings, finger rings, jewelry and knickknacks of all kinds, many of them of intrinsic value, and others of interest solely as souvenirs. In the ruins of every house of the better residential quarters might have been picked up scores of such trinkets. In one place it was easy to recognize the steel framework of a bicycle. In another the iron portions of a sewing machine projected through a conglomerate mass of dust, ashes, kitchen utensils and human bones.

Some crude effort has been made to destroy by fire the gruesome relics spared by the original cataclysm, but the work had been done all too ineffectively. Faggots of driftwood, piled around and above heaps of the slain, had been fired by laborers employed for that purpose, but the work of cremation was only partly accomplished. From a sanitary point of view it is fortunate for Martinique that the vast majority of those who died when her chief city was annihilated are buried so deep as to need no better sepulchre.

· · ·

On May 20, the American cruiser *Cincinnati,* the U.S. naval tug *Potomac,* and the British cruiser *Indefatigable* left Fort-de-France for St. Pierre on a mission to recover the bodies of the American consul, Thomas Prentiss, and the British consul, James Japp. The men's bodies had been found in the ruins of their respective consulates after a long and difficult search, and the intent was to bring their remains to Fort-de-France for a proper military funeral.

As the ships arrived in St. Pierre Bay, they found the volcano to be in an agitated state of activity. The *Potomac* put a landing party on shore, but before the two cruisers could anchor, a series of detonations came from the volcano and a cloud of steam and ash thundered down the slope toward St. Pierre. Although it was a small event compared with the monstrous nuée ardente of May 8, everyone was now on edge and the British cruiser immediately put to sea. The party of rescuers ran along the beach and back to their landing boat. As they reboarded the *Potomac,* the volcano blasted another whirlwind of fire down its southern slope, and, almost simultaneously, a mudflow surged down the valley of the Rivière Blanche.

The three boats reconnoitered offshore as the officers studied the volcano. Although ash was now sifting down through the air, the blasts had not actually reached the city, and a couple of cremation crews on shore were returning to their grisly work. It would not look good for such a hefty expedition—three warships—to fail in the simple task of recovering two bodies. Ensign Miller of the *Potomac* volunteered to lead another party to the ruins of the American consulate, while a Lieutenant McCormick led a group a half mile farther north to the site of the British consulate. Each party carried a metal airtight coffin.

Progress over the piles of rubble was painstakingly slow. The second group had barely sealed James Japp's body in its coffin when Pelée again began to roar. There was no way to run through the ruins, let alone run while hefting a heavy coffin. McCormick saw the volcano belch a great column of black smoke just as the three ships simultaneously began blowing their whistles. The two cruisers were already backing away. "For God's sake, boys," he shouted, "forget the body and get to the shore quick!"

It took no further persuasion to unceremoniously drop Consul Japp's coffin. All began running as a deafening explosion rattled the air and a ground-hugging tornado of fire surged down the mountain toward them. Meanwhile, Ensign Miller's party had succeeded in getting Consul Prentiss's coffin to shore, but the sea had suddenly turned violent and there was no way to load it into the landing boat. They looked toward the mountain to see a churning cloud of ash and steam bearing down on them. When death appeared certain, a blast of wind came in from the sea and deflected the nuée ardente upward over their heads. All on shore hastily climbed into the boats and rowed through the troubled waters to the *Potomac*, which steamed full speed to sea as soon as they scampered aboard. The two cruisers were already far offshore. About five miles off the coast, the *Potomac's* captain stopped the engines, and all stood on deck to watch the most awesome sight any of them had ever witnessed.

It was as if the whole mountain had exploded. A monstrous funnel-shaped mass of ash surged several miles into the sky, its underside flickering in an orange glow from the volcanic vent below. Almost simultaneously, another blast surged down the mountain's southern flank, this one a dozen times larger and more violent than the one that had almost engulfed the landing parties a few minutes earlier. This pyroclastic surge swept through the ruined city and knocked down what few walls remained standing, then thundered into the bay. Had the ships not hastily put to sea, they would have been engulfed and incinerated. In fact, although they would not learn this until later, what the amazed seamen were witnessing was an event even more violent than the explosion that had claimed those thirty thousand victims on May 8.

As the dust settled, the two cruisers returned to Fort-de-France to find the city in a panic. Meanwhile, the crew of the *Potomac* was not about to give up. The tug circled to the south of St. Pierre's ruins, then turned and slowly maneuvered north along the coast through clouds of rising steam. When the captain confirmed through his spyglass that Consul Prentiss's coffin remained where it had been left on shore, a team of enlisted men volunteered to land and recover it. It was a foolish decision, but sometimes people get away with tempting fate. That night, the *Potomac* triumphantly steamed into the harbor at Fort-de-France, its mission accomplished. Consul Thomas T. Prentiss would be given a full military funeral and a proper burial.

The British consul's remains did not fare as well. James Japp's coffin was buried beneath tons of new rubble and was never recovered.

CHAPTER 15

THE OTHER SIDE OF THE MOUNTAIN

•

T he odor of the dried codfish in the hold gave the civilians on the relief ship an incentive to rise early. For days, it had been a running joke on board that the cablegram telling the Martiniquians that U.S. aid was on the way had been a waste of money, for everyone on that island would surely *smell* the *Dixie* coming!

On Wednesday, May 21, 1902—the day they would make port at Fort-de-France—George Kennan climbed out of his hammock at 4 a.m. and joined most of the other journalists on deck to catch their first glimpse of Mont Pelée. It was a warm starry tropical night, and the nearly full moon still hovered above the western horizon. To the east, the shadowy outline of a beautifully sculptured peak was barely visible. Pretty as it was, the sight was disappointing to Kennan, for he and most everyone else on board had hoped to see some sign of volcanic activity. "Looks like the show's over, boys," he said.

Robert Hill of the U.S. Geological Survey, who had visited Martinique before, told Kennan not to jump to a hasty conclusion. "We may be looking at one of the peaks of the Carbet group," he said. "If so, the volcano will be a bit to the left."

"All I see there is a big cloud," said one of the journalists. Big, indeed. It masked the background stars to a height of several thousand feet. As the *Dixie* steamed closer, it revealed itself as not a conventional cloud at all, but rather a churning column of steam. On the shoreline beneath it were two glowing fires. The show, in fact, was far from over.

At 7 a.m., just after the *Dixie* had anchored at Fort-de-France, an officer from the cruiser *Cincinnati* came alongside in a steam launch and delivered a telegram from Washington. Captain Berry read the message, then called his forty-four civilian passengers together. Because the refugees from Martinique's northern towns and villages had already been provided for, he explained, he had received orders to proceed to St. Vincent, where the suffering and destitution were apparently worse. The civilians on board would need to decide whether to disembark here or to continue on to St. Vincent Island on the *Dixie*. And they would need to decide within the hour.

The newsmen and scientists discussed their best course of action. Several pressed Captain Berry for a guarantee that if they stayed in Martinique, the *Dixie* would indeed come back to pick them up. Berry, of course, could offer no such assurance; he would return if he could, but depending on what further orders he received, there was indeed a possibility that anyone who went ashore would be stranded there. To Kennan and some of the other more seasoned travelers, this was but a minor glitch. To those who had never traveled abroad on their own, however, it raised a major concern. To some, the financial ramifications were paramount, for a mere hour was not enough time to contact their sponsors to confirm that the considerable cost of the return trip would be covered. Most of the forty-four civilians decided to stay on the *Dixie* and go on to St. Vincent.

George Kennan did not have to ponder his own decision. It was the Martinique disaster he had come to investigate, and if this turn of events cost the *Outlook* more than budgeted, that was the publisher's problem. George Varian and A. F. Jaccaci of *McClure's* magazine felt the same way, and the three men teamed up and went ashore in one of the ship's boats. The *Dixie* steamed off to St. Vincent with its cargo of codfish and the majority of the journalists and scientists.

Onshore, Kennan's trio discovered that hotel rooms were in short supply and decided to seek advice at the U.S. consulate. There they met Louis H. Ayme, U.S. consul at Pointe à Pitre, Guadeloupe, who was temporarily acting as consul to Martinique until a replacement for Thomas Prentiss could be appointed. Ayme pulled a few strings and got them rooms at the Grand European Hotel, where he was staying himself.

After checking in, Kennan and Jaccaci went to the military hospital and spent the afternoon interviewing some of the frightfully burned victims from the ill-fated *Roraima*.

That evening, Consul Ayme invited the three travelers to join him for dinner in the hotel dining room. The meal, however, was so embarrassingly unappetizing that Ayme registered a complaint with the management and refused to pay the full price. The next day, the owner retaliated by overcharging them all for breakfast. Later, Kennan would write, "It is a great mistake to eat too much in a hot climate, and for that reason I can confidently recommend the Grand European Hotel at Fort-de-France as a place where a northern man may hope to escape the disastrous consequences of intensive nutrition in a tropical environment."

On the afternoon of Thursday May 22, they rode the U.S. tug *Potomac* to St. Pierre to survey the destruction. They were told that the disaster of May 8 had left at least a few walls standing in the city, but after the explosion of May 20, virtually everything had been reduced to rubble. Parts of the ruined city were still smoldering from that tremendous pyroclastic surge—an event the trio would have witnessed themselves had the *Dixie* arrived twenty-four hours earlier. Pelée still rumbled, and steam and ash drifted overhead. Horrible visions of the burn victims still fresh in their minds, the men quickly abandoned what inclination they might have had to set foot on the devastated shore. Kennan muttered his disappointment that to attempt to climb the volcano from this site would be sheer folly. As George Varian pulled out a pad and began sketching the dismal scene in charcoal, Jaccaci unfolded his map of the island. Morne Rouge, which had been spared, was even closer to the summit than St. Pierre. They could cross the island from Fort-de-France, travel north along the eastern shore, and perhaps find some accommodations there. After observing the volcano in safety from that vantage point, they could then proceed to Morne Rouge, where it might be practical to make an ascent. After taking turns studying the map, Kennan and Varian both agreed.

Back in Fort-de-France, Jaccaci went off to arrange for horses, while Kennan inquired about accommodations near the eastern foot of the volcano. No one, however, knew of any hotels in that region. The best advice, offered independently by Consul Ayme and several natives, was that the party should go to the plantation at a place called Vivé, throw themselves upon the owner's hospitality, and take the consequences. The name of the planter? Fernand Clerc.

Assured that the hotel servants would wake them at four o'clock the next morning, and that a carriage and a team of mules would arrive by five, the optimistic trio turned in for the night.

• • •

It was almost six when the roosters woke them. The carriage was nowhere in sight, and the dining room tables were still covered with dirty dishes from the previous night. As it would apparently be impossible to get breakfast before eleven, they sat at a dirty table in the bar and munched on some of the provisions they had wisely brought with them from the *Dixie* while they waited for their arranged transportation. When Jaccaci's impatience reached its limit, he stalked off in search of the driver and his mules. It was almost nine when they finally started the journey.

The narrow flower-lined road wound through a billowing sea of hills, crossed ridges and snaked into deep ravines, and changed its direction so often that each two miles of travel advanced them no more than a mile toward the eastern coast. Kennan would liken their path to the "tracings of a seismograph in a Lisbon earthquake." It took them an hour and a half to get to the village of St. Joseph, just four miles from the hotel as the crow flies. Kennan resigned himself to the fact that they would never make Vivé before nightfall, and he decided to enjoy the trip on its own terms.

It struck him that there was very little vehicular traffic in Martinique. Oxcarts were used to carry cane from the fields to the sugar mills, and small donkeys brought sacks of charcoal into town, but it was barefoot women and girls who carried most kinds of merchandise, from ceramic tiles to farm products. Over and over again they encountered long lines of straight, vigorous women, beautifully attired in bright tropical dresses and native jewelry, walking swiftly with a long free stride while balancing loads on their head weighing as much as eighty pounds. It occurred to Kennan that those graceful women displayed more energy and endurance than did the mules pulling their carriage.

As the road descended toward the Atlantic, it grew straighter and they began to make better progress. They arrived in Trinité in the early afternoon, lunched, changed mules, and proceeded up the coastal road. Up to now, there had been nothing along the way to indicate that a volcano was in eruption on the island; Pelée had been hidden behind the Pitons du Carbet and the adjacent mountains and hills, all the vegetation visible from the road had sparkled under the tropical sky, the air was fresh and clear, and the natives were all going about their daily activities. As they headed north from Trinité, all that changed. Peleé was now visible in the distance, wrapped in a black mantle of storm clouds, a huge column of steam rising high into the clearer air above. Now a film of ash covered the road, and the vegetation was all a colorless gray. Beyond Marigot, the volcanic dust was a couple of inches deep, and the trees—particularly the breadfruit trees—had been so plastered with wet ash that limbs up to four inches thick had broken under the weight. And then they began to see the refugees.

No longer were the pedestrians carrying produce and merchandise for sale; they were now transporting personal possessions and furniture. And no longer was it just the women, but whole families. The man usually marched in front, leading a cow or a goat and balancing a trunk on his head, the rest of his family following behind. One woman held an infant in one arm while using her free hand to steady a large inverted table on her head, which she had filled with pots, pans, and dishes. Another had a live razor-backed pig lashed into a wooden tray, which she kept deftly balanced on her head. Everybody, down to the smallest child who could walk, was carrying a load of some sort. One five-year-old girl held a chicken by the wings in one hand while cuddling a kitten to her chest with the other. Half of the women and children had pictures of the Madonna pinned to their clothing. All were heading south. The violent explosion of May 20, two days earlier, had been enough for them.

It was evening when Kennan's group arrived in Lorrain. The long street running parallel to the sea was crowded with refugees, and municipal authorities were distributing food near the docks. As they continued through town on the road that led to Ajoupa-Bouillion and Morne Rouge, one woman excitedly pointed them out to the crowd. "Look at those foolish foreigners," she screamed, "they're going toward the mountain!"

Kennan smiled. "These poor ignorant natives," he said to his companions. "They know nothing about volcanoes, and they're frightened and running away because of the volcanic dust. They don't understand that there's no danger on this side of the island." That he himself might soon get frightened enough to run never entered his mind.

Overhead, the ash cloud formed a dismal canopy over the entire northern third of the colony. When night fell, it grew so dark that they could barely see the outlines of the road. Still, the procession of refugees continued silently in the opposite direction like a train of shadowy ghosts. The tired mules were going very slowly and could hardly be lashed into a trot even on the descending slopes. It occurred to Kennan that this would not be a comfortable night if they didn't find the plantation.

A light appeared ahead. As they drew closer, they found it to be a wayside shrine, where several candles burned in front of a plaster crucifix behind a glass door. A small group was kneeling around it, praying. Jaccaci apologetically interrupted and asked whether anyone knew how far it was to the house of Monsieur Clerc. One man replied, "It is here."

Until now, it had not been clear whether Vivé was the name of the plantation or the name of the village where it was located. As it turned out, the village and the plantation were essentially one and the same. They drove up a long avenue lined with hedges and mango trees, stopped in front of the estate's spacious mansion, and rehearsed the French phrases they would use to introduce themselves and ask for accommodations. But before they got to the front door, Fernand Clerc came out with a lighted candle to give them a cordial greeting. Their rooms were ready, he said, and dinner was waiting. Consul Ayme had succeeded in sending a telegram to Lorrain, and Clerc had been expecting them. Within twenty minutes, they were all seated around the dining table, drinking "cylone" wine (vintage 1891, the year of the great hurricane), and discussing that all-absorbing topic, the volcano.

After his family's harrowing near-death experience of May 8, Clerc explained, he had shipped his wife and children off to Guadeloupe. He likewise had advised most of his employees and their families to evacuate the region. Now he was here alone except for a few of his most devoted workers and house-servants, watching the volcano and trying to decide on his course of action. Kennan, Varian, and Jaccaci were welcome to stay at Vivé as long as they wished, and Clerc himself would be interested in participating in their explorations. However, with the exception of tonight, they should understand that Clerc would not be sleeping at Vivé.

Instead, he would keep his promise to his wife that he would spend the nights on higher ground, at a friend's estate at Acier.

Prior to Tuesday, Clerc continued, some people had believed that St. Pierre could be rebuilt. The streets and most of the water system lay intact beneath the rubble, and enough walls remained standing that a core collection of structures might be reassembled fairly quickly. These initial buildings could house the workers and authorities, and then the more difficult aspects of the reconstruction could be tackled. This would certainly be a monumental undertaking, but not impossible. And seemingly worth doing, considering that the disaster was a freak event that had not happened before in recorded history, and which would not be likely to recur for at least another five hundred years.

Then, twelve days after the catastrophe, Peleé unleashed another blast that actually exceeded the first in intensity. When that explosion of May 20 completed the destruction of St. Pierre, said Clerc, it became clear to him that the city could never be rebuilt. That eruption also threw thousands of tons of volcanic ash over the Vivé cane fields, and a new fissure had opened in the gorge of the Rivière Falaise, sending an avalanche of boiling water and mud into the Rivière Capot, which ran next to the plantation. Basse Pointe, a village on the northeastern coast less than three miles from Vivé, had been partially destroyed by a mud-flow and was now mostly abandoned. Farther up the mountain, Ajoupa-Bouillon had been largely evacuated but was being guarded by the priest, the mayor, and a few gendarmes patrolling the road. Morne Rouge was also virtually empty and was not considered a safe place to be. The world, said Clerc, seemed to be coming to an end.

• • •

The estate had recently been a magnificent place. Its stately two-story house with its broad, shady veranda had all the appointments of the best French colonial architecture. The formal flower gardens surrounding the house had been carpets of rich and glowing color, and the avenue to the main road was lined with perfectly groomed hibiscus bushes. In every direction the view was said to be spectacular: the sea, the vivid green hills, the gurgling streams. But when day broke on Saturday, May 24, Kennan and his companions saw nothing like this. The walls of the house looked as if splashed by "a mixture of mucilage and cement" that had trickled down in muddy lines, dried volcanic dust lay in great heaps where it had been shoveled from the walks and veranda, the ground under the mangos was littered with broken branches, and the flowerbeds were buried in gray mud. The streams and beach were littered with debris, and the hills were a ghostly gray devoid of plant life.

Although storm clouds were threatening, Clerc and the three journalists decided to make the short drive to the village of Basse Pointe. The going was slow, as the road was clogged with more fugitives heading south, including more women with brightly colored chromos of the Virgin Mary pinned over their hearts. At the village, the reason for this evacuation became terribly apparent: huge boulders lay strewn amid the wreckage of scores of homes near the tiny, trickling Rivière Basse Pointe. Volcanic mud was everywhere. If such a tiny brook was capable of carrying such stones obviously weighing many tons, who could say what other unlikely things might be about to happen? Kennan began to identify, at least a little, with the "ignorant" natives.

As Varian completed his sketches and Jaccaci his interviews, the rain began. They returned to Vivé, dried off, and spent the rest of the day smoking and drinking on a porch facing the sea as Clerc filled them in on more details of the disaster of May 8. The following morning, weather permitting, they agreed they would all proceed across the southeastern flank of the volcano to Morne Rouge, then go as far as possible down the road toward St. Pierre. This decided, Fernand Clerc rode off to Acier to spend the night, leaving his guests with the household servants at Vivé.

• • •

Sunday morning, May 25, dawned clear. Monsieur Chancel, the overseer at Vivé, hitched up two carriages; with the mountain roads buried in wet volcanic ash, he figured that the group would make better progress by splitting the load. Besides, he wanted to come along himself and didn't want to crowd the guests. When Clerc arrived, they headed up the north bank of the Capot, crossed the muddy stream on a stone bridge, then wound upward over several miles of gentle slopes to the nearly deserted village of Ajoupa-Bouillon. Beyond this point the terrain got more rugged, scoured by a seemingly interminable series of gorges and arêtes. The road snaked back and forth in narrow curves around the heads of profoundly deep ravines, which were filled with thick but scorched tropical undergrowth. A few weeks earlier, the scenery here would have been splendidly picturesque, but now everywhere the dying vegetation bespoke of the ravages of the volcano.

The dense forest ended just before Morne Rouge, where a life-size crucifix marked the divide separating the Atlantic watershed from that of the Caribbean. From this spot, they had a breathtaking view of the ruins of St. Pierre, the mud-clogged Coulée Rivière Blanche, Mont Pelée's smoking crater, the steep peaks of the Pitons du Carbet, and to the northeast, the blue Atlantic. The spire of the church of Notre Dame de la Délivrande lay directly ahead on the main street. They rode past the ash-plastered vacant houses and stopped in front of the parish rectory.

Father Mary, a middle-aged man with a friendly demeanor, came out to meet them in his cassock and an incongruous white pith helmet. The holy man showed no nervous strain or apprehension; on the contrary, he was as buoyant and lighthearted as a frolicsome boy. As he herded his visitors into his dining room, he laughed and joked with Clerc and Chancel. And when Kennan and Varian declined the stiff drinks of rum he poured for them, he exclaimed in feigned astonishment, "What? No rum? Is this, then, a temperance society?"

Father Mary was a man who immediately won Kennan's admiration; he was brave, rational, and too cheerful to be warped by fear or gloomy apprehensions. He might not have been able to reconcile the destruction of St. Pierre with the providence of a loving and merciful Creator, yet he trusted where he could not understand, and even in the threatening shadow of death he faithfully discharged his duties to his parishioners. Vicar-General Parel would be mistaken in reporting that "Père Mary has at length left Morne Rouge, being the last to abandon the place." In fact, the good father remained in the vulnerable town, and only when he was in no condition to protest a few months later would he be taken from the place.

Of the five thousand people who had populated Morne Rouge and its environs a few weeks earlier, fewer than two hundred remained. Father

Mary had established a house of refuge for those too old and infirm to evacuate, and along with a few brave parishioners he cared for those helpless souls. He was also, it turned out, tending to a burn victim who had survived the destruction of St. Pierre.

•   •   •

Kennan had heard the stories in Fort-de-France about a prisoner and his miraculous survival of the holocaust of May 8. Yet no one he interviewed had actually seen the man or knew where he was, and Kennan began to conclude that the "sole survivor" was simply the product of some news-paperman's overactive imagination. But Father Mary assured Kennan that Augusté Ciparis was a real person, and that he had been brought to Morne Rouge four days after the disaster by two men who had found him in the ruins of the city. He was now in an otherwise-abandoned home just down the street.

The group, of course, had to go and meet Ciparis. Kennan would write:

> He was sitting stark naked, on the dirty striped mattress of a small wooden cot, with a bloody sheet thrown over his head like an Arab burnoose and gathered in about the loins. He had been more fright-fully burned, I think, than any man I had ever seen. His face, strangely enough, had escaped injury, and his hair had not even been scorched, but there were terrible burns on his back and legs, and his badly swollen feet and hands were covered with yellow, offensive matter which had no resemblance whatever to human skin or flesh. The burns were apparently very deep—so deep that blood oozed from them—and to my unprofessional eye they looked as if they might have been made by hot steam.

As George Varian sketched, Ciparis told the men his story. He had been in solitary confinement in a stone cell with an arched stone roof, a single door, a small grated window, and a chimney for ventilation. As he waited for breakfast on May 8, wearing his hat, shirt, and trousers (but no shoes), it suddenly grew very dark. Then, without any noticeable blast or rush of wind, hot air and fine ash came in through the window grate and burned him. He breathed as little as possible until the intense heat subsided. He jumped about in agony and cried for help, but there was no answer. He heard no noise, saw no fire, and smelled nothing except "what he thought was his own body burning." Although his clothing did not catch fire, his back was severely burned under his shirt. He did not hear another sound until the following Sunday, more than three days after the disaster. Then he heard faint voices outside and renewed his cries for help. The two men outside cleared away the stones and several feet of ash that had piled up against the low door, and pried it open enough to allow Ciparis to squeeze himself out. He was weak from four days without food, not to mention the lack of medical attention, but a drink of water revived him sufficiently to stand. With the help of his rescuers, he was able to walk the nearly four miles up the valley of the Roxelane and over the Grande Reduit to Morne Rouge—a walk that terribly aggravated the burn damage to his feet. He had been in Morne Rouge ever since.

Ciparis impressed Kennan as an uneducated man of average intelligence, whose temperament (at least at that time) was stolid rather than excitable. He answered all of Kennan's questions simply and quietly, without making any attempt to heighten the effect of his narrative or to embroider it with dramatic or fanciful details. What happened outside he did not pretend to know, but his testimony as to what happened inside could not be shaken by any amount of cross-examination. He heard no explosion, saw no flames, smelled no sulfurous gases, and had no feeling of suffocation. He had been burned by hot air that came in through the window, and that pretty much was that.

To Fernand Clerc, there was no question of the man's identity; the planter had often seen him in the streets and waterfront of St. Pierre before the disaster and had in fact heard him called by the name Ciparis. But to Kennan, there was still a missing link. Given that all the police records had certainly been destroyed, how could they be sure that this Ciparis had indeed been imprisoned in the cell during the disaster? On their walk back to the rectory, Kennan mentioned the matter to Father Mary. The priest called over one of his parishioners from across the street and said something in unintelligible Creole. The man returned shortly with a companion—one of the two natives who had rescued Ciparis. The curé vouched for the veracity of the rescuer, and Kennan interviewed him to confirm that his story was consistent with that of Ciparis. Kennan would later write:

> Some doubt has been expressed as to the existence of any survivor of the St. Pierre disaster—or, at least, of any person who was actually in the city at the time of its destruction. Several American correspondents in Fort-de-France wrote their papers that the wild tale of the rescued prisoner was wholly imaginary, and one well-informed journal in New York said editorially: "Although the story of the only survivor of St. Pierre, the prisoner in the underground [*sic*] cell of the jail, has been proved to be a fake, it was published so broadcast [*sic*], and was so picturesque, that it would not be strange if it were incorporated in the permanent records of the disaster." The story of the rescued prisoner, however, is not a fake, and I think that it ought to be "incorporated in the permanent records of the disaster," not on account of its picturesqueness, but because it helps to throw light on the real nature of the catastrophe.

•   •   •

Meeting Ciparis had been fortuitous. Kennan, Varian, Jaccaci, Clerc, and Chancel climbed back into the carriages to continue their plan to examine the Roxelane valley, which the fiery blast had swept through before striking St. Pierre. Two miles below Morne Rouge, and a mile from the ruined city, they came to a bold promontory that ended in a high, steep bluff; here the road suddenly turned on itself in an inverted "S" and descended some five hundred feet. The place was called Grande Reduit ("grand retreat"). On the highest part of the bluff, and facing the volcano, stood a life-size statue of Christ crucified, now covered from head to foot with a sun-dried plaster of volcanic ash. Nearby stood a little chapel and four abandoned homes. This spot had been just outside the pyroclastic surge, the structural damage had been slight, and a number of trees were still standing. Behind one of the houses, however, was the rotting carcass of a mule, and a short distance down the road lay an overturned carriage, half buried in a pile of broken tree branches. Its leather top was torn but not burned. The group assumed that the carriage had not been in use at the time of the disaster and had been blown there. Some nine days later, while visiting the municipal hospital in Trinité, Kennan would meet the two men who survived a terrible experience while riding in this very carriage: Monsieurs Lassère and Simonut.

Passing the crucifix, they trudged through a thicket of leafless bushes to the western edge of the bluff, where they could get an unobstructed view of the valley of the Rivière Roxelane below. Kennan wrote in his notebook, "A more impressive picture of ruin and desolation would be impossible to imagine." The once-beautiful valley looked as if it had been swept by a violent hurricane that smashed houses and uprooted trees, then had been overwhelmed by a monstrous flood, which, after sweeping immense masses of wreckage into heaps, subsided and left everything covered with a thick layer of gray mud. Protruding from the surface of this muck were human corpses, carcasses of mules, wheels of dismembered carts, iron kettles, pieces of machinery from a wrecked sugar mill, timbers, boulders, roofs of houses, and huge numbers of uprooted trees that had been swept from the slopes above.

They continued to the base of the bluff in the carriages, but a quarter mile farther the road was blocked by a tangle of uprooted trees. Leaving the rigs and mules, they proceeded on foot with Fernand Clerc silently leading the way. In this part of the Roxelane valley there had been a large number of stately homes and villas belonging to wealthy residents of St. Pierre, most of whom Clerc had known. The area was now a chaos of boulders, smashed tiles, broken crockery, twisted iron bedsteads, sheets of metallic roofing, fire-scorched remains of pianos, chandeliers, farm implements, and ash-covered wreckage of every description. Nothing here of human construction had been strong enough to withstand the impact of the blast. Houses had been torn to pieces and scattered like children's kindergarten blocks. In many places, no trace of the road remained visible, and they had to pick their way across the heaps of debris. The breezeless tropical air was fetid with the stench of decaying bodies, and every now and then they came upon a swollen, blackened corpse lying in the open or half buried in the debris. In several places on the road or beside it, they saw human bodies that had been rolled, tumbled, and smashed by the blast until they were shapeless masses of torn bloody clothing and lacerated flesh, out of which stuck the splintered remains of arm and thigh bones.

Clerc stopped in front of a low shapeless mound of ash-plastered building stones. His voice trembling, he said, "This was the country house of Senator Knight's father. I knew him well." Kennan would not have guessed that there had recently been a house there; it was now no more than a random mass of stones half buried in ash. They turned from that ruin and continued down the road, but before they got much farther, Clerc became so overwrought with grief that he broke down in a fit of sobbing and walked away from the party until he could recover his self-control. When he returned, his bloodshot eyes met Kennan's. "Please excuse me," he said. "Let us go on."

At the spot where a small stream from the south joined the Rivière Roxelane, there had been a pretty little suburban settlement known as the Village of the Three Bridges. Although most of the place had been obliterated, four or five homes did survive in a lateral ravine sheltered by a high bluff. The front door of the first house was open, and the group ventured in. The lack of footprints in the ashes told them that no one had been in the place in the eighteen days since the catastrophe. Just inside, lying on a cot-bed, was a dead man, plastered with ashes except for a few places on his neck, face, and hands, where the rain had blown in and washed off the volcanic dust. Flies were crawling all over him, and blood from a wound in his head had run onto the mattress and dripped from there onto the floor. Just how he had died was anyone's guess; the only thing certain was that he had never moved after the disaster. In the next room were the bodies of a man, woman, and child, huddled on the floor and in such a state of decomposition as to render them unrecognizeable.

The adjoining house was also full of corpses, but they were so encrusted with ash that it was impossible to determine their age, sex, or race. Across the stream and closer to the bluff stood a pretty two-story country home whose front yard had been planted with geometrical flowerbeds. They explored it from top to bottom, but the only thing alive there was a huge black tarantula, which startled everyone when it ran out of a crevice over one of the second-story doors. The arachnid had survived where all the higher forms of life had perished.

Prowling through the silent houses, expecting at every moment to come upon the ghastly sight of rotting bodies in the semidarkness, began to grate on everyone's nerves. If the dead had looked like other corpses, they might not have made such a fearful impression. But in these gray dust-covered forms lay the horrors of a frightful end, somehow worse than death by sickness or even by murder.

In the lower story of the next house, where they had not yet found any bodies, Fernand Clerc stopped suddenly, listened with strained attention, then hoarsely whispered, "What's that? There's someone walking overhead!" Although Kennan had heard nothing, the words sent a shiver down his spine, as if it were actually possible for one of those grotesque gray figures with its swollen face and ash-plastered eye sockets to emerge from the shadows, groping its way down the stairs.

Obviously, they had all seen enough to satisfy everyone's curiosity for the day and were beginning to get unnerved. Weary and sickened with the stench of death, they climbed slowly and silently back over the rubble-strewn road to the carriages, then drove back to Vivé.

No one had much of an appetite for dinner that night. Jaccaci rode into Trinité and managed to send a telegram to the military hospital at Fort-de-France, asking that linseed oil, limewater, phenic acid, and aseptic bandages be delivered to Morne Rouge so the prisoner's burns could be properly treated. Meanwhile, the others retired early.

Fatigued as he was, however, Kennan found it impossible to sleep. The room seemed to be pervaded by a faint odor of decomposing flesh, and he began to imagine he could see gray ash-covered corpses swarming with flies in every dark corner of the room. Finally he got up and lit a candle. The smell persisted; it was not imaginary. He dumped out the small sack of items he had picked up during the trek through the devastation of the Roxelane valley. One item—a little etched calabash he had found in the ruins of the village of Trois Ponts—proved to be so saturated with the odor of a rotting corpse that it had tainted the air of the whole room. He put it out the window, blew out the light, and crawled back in bed.

Yet it continued to be a restless and feverish night. For the first time, Kennan had a terrible feeling of dread and foreboding about the volcano.

CHAPTER 16

THE CAULDRONS OF HELL

•

Monday, May 26. Kennan woke up with every muscle aching, a symptom of the low malarial fever that returned to haunt him every couple of years. Varian was even sicker, having apparently drunk some contaminated water during yesterday's hike along the Roxelane; he got up for a few minutes, emptied himself out, then returned to bed. Jaccaci, however, was a bundle of nervous energy and eager to conduct further explorations, and Monsieur Chancel, the overseer, was in like spirit.

Fernand Clerc had again spent the night at Acier. When he showed up at Vivé late in the morning, he suggested that they investigate the subcrater at the head of the Rivière Falaise on their side of the mountain. On several occasions he had seen clouds of steam rising from that region, but no one had visited it recently and today it appeared quiet. It was on one of the lower slopes of the volcano, a straight-line distance of about four miles from Vivé, and could probably be reached without much difficulty from a footpath he knew of. It would be worth visiting, Clerc explained, not only as a scientific curiosity but also to determine whether it presented a threat to the plantation.

Kennan was tempted but decided it would be more prudent to save his strength for tomorrow's planned climb to Pelée's summit. Varian, meanwhile, was in no condition to travel anywhere. As Clerc, Jaccaci, and Chancel rode off, Kennan confirmed through a field glass that there were no signs of disturbance in the gorge of the Falaise. Above, the main crater belched a continuous column of yellowish white vapor that rose several thousand feet before drifting slowly to the west under the influence of the trade wind. But there were no detonations or ground tremors, and the continuing eruption, though awe inspiring, did not strike him as menacing.

When the group returned five hours later, Jaccaci was particularly excited. He had been to Vesuvius, Stromboli, and Etna, he said, but the crater of the Falaise was the most frightfully unearthly place he had ever seen. It was a rugged gorge, deep beyond imagination, its craggy walls and all of the surroundings plastered in surrealistic gray. A stone tossed into the abyss never returned any sound of striking the bottom. One small slip, and the visitor would apparently plummet straight to the gates of hell. There was not a sign of life—not a leaf, nor an insect, nor even the footprints of a wayward gull. Clearly, there had been some serious volcanic activity here quite recently.

Most curious, however, was the fact that this fissure lay at such a low elevation relative to the summit, and on the opposite side of the volcano from the eruptions that had destroyed St. Pierre. Could it be that the whole island of Martinique was turning into a Swiss cheese of volcanic vents?

• • •

That evening, five additional guests showed up for dinner. Three of Clerc's friends stopped on their journey from Basse Pointe to Fort-de-France, his brother Josef arrived from Trinité for a short visit, and there was a journalist named Confiant who, it turned out, had lost twenty-eight relatives in St. Pierre. Mademoiselle Marie de Jahan, the plantation's affable hostess, managed to accommodate everyone on short notice without compromising the elegance of the meal or the plantation's reputation for hospitality.

George Varian was still pale and could bring himself to eat very little. Shortly after eight, he excused himself to retire for the night. He had just gone upstairs when the air reverberated with the sound of three heavy explosions.

"Le volcan! Le volcan!" Clerc shouted as he sprang from his chair and bolted out the front door. His guests all followed at his heels. They ran thirty yards to get beyond the mango trees, where they could get a view. In Kennan's words:

> When we got out into the open, it burst suddenly upon our startled eyes, and a more splendid and at the same time terrifying object I had never seen nor imagined. The whole mountain, from base to summit, was ablaze with volcanic lightning, and the air trembled with short, heavy, thunderous explosions, like the firing of thirteen-inch guns from half a dozen battleships in action. Straight up from the crater, clearly outlined against the starry sky, rose a column of inky-black vapor, a thousand feet in height, which looked like a shaft of solid ebony. Before I had time to breathe twice it had reached a height of two thousand feet; in thirty seconds it had grown three thousand feet more, without the least increase in width; and in less than two minutes it stood ten thousand feet above the crater and was still going up. In every part of this ascending column of black vapor there were bursting huge electric stars of volcanic lightning, which illuminated the whole mountain, while the accompanying roar of thunderous explosions sounded like a great naval battle at sea.

Fernand Clerc shouted in English, "Gentlemen, we must leave! This is a dangerous place! We will go to my friend's house at Acier." Then, in French, he gave a hasty order to the overseer Chancel. Kennan had been so absorbed in the magnificence of the spectacle that only now did he notice that a crowd had gathered behind them: a heterogeneous mass of fugitives, servants, and laborers from the sugar mill—all staring at the volcano in a daze of bewilderment and terror. Chancel's shout that everyone needed to evacuate jolted the gathering into a panic. The yard instantly became a scene of wild confusion; many of the bivouacking evacuees from Ajoupa-Bouillon and Basse Pointe broke into headlong flight, while employees of the estate rushed to their homes calling loudly to their wives and children as they ran. Dogs barking, children crying, and the screams of a couple of frantic women contributed to the tumult. Clerc, remembering that Varian was in bed but momentarily forgetting his name, ran into the house and shouted up the stairway, "Mr. Artist! Mr. Artist! It is time to go!"

Kennan wavered a moment, then took another look at the eruption, remembered the gruesome bodies of the dead in the valley of the Roxelane, and agreed that it was indeed "time to go." He ran up to his bedroom, succeeded in finding his notebook and camera in the darkness, but could not locate his cork helmet. To protect his head should a rain of volcanic rocks or hot cinders begin to fall, he grabbed a mackintosh that happened to be hanging on the back of a chair. There was no time to look for, or put on, his shoes, and he ran back outside still in his slippers. In that short time, the volcano had taken on an increasingly threatening appearance:

> A dull red glow, streaked with what seemed to be tongues of flame, rose two or three hundred feet above the main crater, forming a fiery base for a shaft of intensely black vapor, ten or twelve thousand feet in height, which had already begun to mushroom out at the top. Showers of incandescent stones were falling over the summit of the mountain, and the vapor-column was pierced incessantly by short streaks of volcanic lightning, which seemed to end in explosive electric stars of blinding brilliancy, like huge sparks from a gigantic Leyden jar. There was no rolling, reverberating thunder, but every starlike outburst at the end of a lightning streak was followed by a heavy jarring explosion, and as the stars were flashing out constantly in every part of a vapor column two miles high, the roar was like that of a continuous cannonade.

On hearing Clerc's shouts, Varian scrambled down the stairs and outside into the confusion, took a quick look at the thundering volcano, then ran back to get his sketchbooks. As Monsieur Chancel saddled the first horse, another series of detonations jarred him to the decision that the situation was too urgent to take the time to prepare horses for everyone. With Clerc leading and only Mademoiselle Marie on horseback, the group of houseguests and hosts fled on foot through a cane field. Kennan and Varian, juggling their notebooks, camera, and drawing materials, brought up the rear.

At the main road, they merged into a stream of refugees headed toward Lorrain. To keep from getting separated in the darkness, they repeatedly shouted to one another: "Kennan, where are you?" "I am still here, behind you." And so on. Varian, despite his illness, had somehow risen to the physical demands of their flight. Jaccaci, however, was the most stoic of the bunch. When, after one particularly terrifying series of detonations, a female refugee began to break down and cry, "Oh, mon Dieu! Oh mon Dieu!" Jaccaci soothed her with "Cheer up, Mother. It's not serious. Nothing is going to harm you."

It was a warm humid evening, and everyone was quickly dripping with perspiration. After a few miles, Chancel shouted: "Kennan, Varian, Jaccaci! Acier is up the road to the right! Follow me!" The only illumination was the weird explosive lightning, but a few flashes confirmed where Chancel was going. "We're coming!" Kennan shouted back. They veered off the main road and its river of refugees and trudged uphill.

A shower of ash and small hot volcanic stones began to patter through the trees like sleet. The old colonial mansion was in sight, and they scrambled to the protection of its veranda. There, as they caught their breath, drenched in perspiration, they realized that their group had dwindled to just five: Chancel, Kennan, Jaccaci, Varian, and Mademoiselle Marie. Although Clerc and the other houseguests had been just a short distance ahead on the main road, what had happened to them was anybody's guess.

The house was dark and empty; its owner and his servants had apparently taken off when they heard the first explosions. But the side door had been left unbolted, and the group went inside. Kennan lit a couple of candles and set them on the dining table. Attracted by the lighted windows, other refugees trickled into the house. Chancel found a couple of bottles of rum in a wine closet, took a bracer for himself, then passed the bottles. After a drink and a short rest, Kennan noticed that the pattering of stones on the metal roof had died down, and he went back outside to check on the volcano.

The explosions and the electric starbursts had ceased, the incandescent glow from the crater had disappeared, and the volcano was dark. The only activity was just above the summit, where bolts of smoke-reddened lightning danced in the clouds. Kennan had to watch awhile before assuring himself that that he was now witnessing no more than a raging thunderstorm. By the time he returned to the dining room, Mademoiselle

Marie had taken charge of the house. She had lit a dozen oil lamps, sent the motley bunch of refugees to the kitchen, and was getting bedrooms ready upstairs for her employer's guests. The fact that Clerc himself had disappeared had no effect whatsoever on her loyalty or commitment to her employer's standards of hospitality. It did not even matter that they were not on Clerc's property. It was her role to be a gracious hostess to Fernand Clerc's guests, and so she was. George Varian, overcome by fatigue and chills, soon went to bed. Jaccaci and Chancel began discussing the volcano, while Kennan sat at the dining table to write his notes.

The feature of the eruption that had surprised and impressed Kennan most was the "stellar" lightning. This strange phenomenon, he wrote, was distinguished from ordinary lightning by the shortness of the streak, the size and brilliance of the light-burst at its end, and the single booming report that always followed. Occasionally, three or four of these explosive bursts, connected by thin fiery streaks, had flashed together. At other times, the "stars" exploded far back within the cloud and lit up a circle of vapor. It seemed as if the ash column was carrying pockets of some high explosive, which were being detonated by electrical discharges.

When Kennan finished his notes around 11 p.m., the volcano was quiet and even the thunderstorm at the summit had dissipated. Jaccaci, having sat pensively for the last fifteen minutes, looked over at him and said, "What would you think about going back to Vivé?"

"Surely you don't mean tonight."

"Yes," said Jaccaci. "As soon as there's enough moonlight to see the road."

Kennan shook his head. "I don't see any particular logic," he said, "in going back to a place we've just run away from. Why wouldn't we be comfortable here?"

"I don't like running away from things," said Jaccaci. "If the three of us had been alone at Vivé, we surely would have stood our ground. It was Clerc and his other guests who stampeded us. Besides that, someone ought to look after Mr. Clerc's house. We simply abandoned it in our haste, leaving all the doors open, and it might be looted."

"Well, 'Field Marshal,'" Kennan smiled, "my underclothes are wet, I'm getting chilly, and I'd like to wash and change. So if you really want to head back to Vivé, I guess I'll go along."

Within a half hour, the moonlight was bright enough. Chancel, Jaccaci, and Kennan trekked back together. The return trip was mostly downhill, the road was now empty, and it was a much easier and quicker trek than it had been a few hours earlier in the opposite direction. When they arrived back at Vivé at midnight, they found a few frightened fugitives in the house with candles and lamps burning, but nothing else disturbed. They smoked and drank some rum, then went to their rooms.

Kennan peeled off his perspiration-soaked underwear, sponged himself, then climbed into bed. It had been an exhausting evening for a fifty-seven-year-old man, particularly one with malaria. But just as he was dozing off, he was jarred awake by the pounding of footsteps on the stairs. He bolted up, threw a towel around his waist in a gesture of modesty, and dashed down the hall to investigate. Jaccaci stumbled out of his own room half asleep, rubbing his eyes at the sight.

It was Fernand Clerc. The planter's hair, wet with perspiration, was plastered onto his forehead, and he was visibly anxious. "Well, gentlemen," he said, "wasn't that one hell of an explosion! Ai! Ai! Ai! I've come with two carriages to take you away."

Jacacci, still not quite awake, showed no empathy for Clerc's concerns, nor for the planter's behavior in having disappeared earlier without explanation. "Thank you," he said, "we prefer to stay here." At best, it was a presumptuous statement for any guest to make to his host.

"But you can't stay here!" Clerc shouted, too caught up in his apprehensions to take offense at Jaccaci's bad manners. "You don't know what that volcano is going to do next! I've seen four explosions—*four!*"—looking to Kennan for support, he held up four fingers—"and I don't want to see any more, God forbid! But I've put my personal safety secondary to coming back for you! You must come!"

"But we're very comfortable here," said Jaccaci, "and volcano or no volcano, I don't intend to get up again tonight."

Clerc continued his excited pleas, Jaccaci continued his recalcitrance, and Kennan, more than a decade older than the other two and with no enthusiasm for making another trip himself before a long rest, watched the exchange in bemused silence. "I felt satisfied," he would write later, "that nothing short of a Krakatoa explosion would drive Mr. Jaccaci away from Vivé again that night."

"Well, gentlemen," Clerc finally said, "you are my guests. It was only because I felt responsible for your safety that I came back here after midnight, with two carriages, to take you to Trinité. You won't go, and I obviously can't do any more. I must bid you good-bye. I am going, myself, to France. The conditions of life on Martinique have become impossible."

Kennan thanked Clerc for his warmhearted hospitality, for his kindness, and for the courage and devotion he had shown in coming back for them in the middle of the night. He reminded his host that he and Jaccaci had come to Martinique to study the volcano, and explained that they did not wish to run from their object of study twice in one night. Clerc shook their hands, wished them good luck, then departed for Trinité. A few days later, after settling his business affairs in Fort-de-France, Fernand Clerc sailed to Guadeloupe to meet his wife and children, and from there he and his family took the first transatlantic steamer for Le Havre.

● ● ●

Tuesday, May 27. Kennan awoke at dawn and went outside to marvel at the sight of a great column of yellow smoke rising against a dark background of cinders and ash falling to the west. George Varian and Mademoiselle Marie arrived at Vivé at 6:30 a.m., and Marie put together a cold breakfast. Varian was still too ill to have much of an appetite, and now Jaccaci also began complaining about some intestinal bug. Kennan, the oldest, found himself the only one still on his feet.

Over the next four hours, Kennan watched the volcano with increasing uneasiness. Here they sat, downslope of a violent geophysical phenomenon they did not understand, on the bank of a stream not unlike those that had already swallowed up scores of people in unexpected mudflows. The volcano was acting indecisively, just as it had done prior to the monstrous explosion of May 8 that had claimed thirty thousand lives. Maybe, amid its fluctuations, the eruption was gradually declining in intensity. On the other hand, maybe it was gradually escalating. There was, after all, no way to measure such things in 1902. But why were they taking chances by staying at Vivé? Kennan went to Jaccaci's bedside and said, "If you feel able to get up, I wish you'd look at the volcano."

Jaccaci stumbled to the side window of the second-story bedroom, where he could see the summit. He pondered in silence for a full minute. "It looks," he finally said, "as Vesuvius must have looked five minutes before the destruction of Pompeii. If you want to get out of this, I'm ready to go."

"I've been wanting to get out of this for the past four hours," Kennan said.

They summoned Chancel and held a volcano council. The consensus was to close the house and move. Chancel brought oxcarts to the door, and they loaded bedding, personal baggage, table linen, food, and wine. Then they departed for Acier, leaving the Vivé plantation house to its fate.

• • •

It was the first time the travelers saw Acier by daylight. It was an attractive old two-story house of yellow-washed stone and stucco, whose irregular roof was pierced by a series of small dormers. The wide front door opened on a narrow piazza leading to a grassy yard shaded by century-old trees. A low stone wall bound the yard on the two sides where it terminated at a steep precipice. From here, one got an unobstructed view of the ocean and a magnificent panorama of Mont Pelée from Morne Rouge to Macouba. The place had suffered much less from the ashfall than had Fernand Clerc's plantation. There was a deposit of powdery dust on the piazza floor and on some of the foliage, but only a few leaves had fallen, the grass was generally green, and flowers bloomed in a garden. The owner and his family were still absent. Kennan and the others—Varian, Jaccaci, Chancel, and Mademoiselle Marie—carried in their belongings and provisions and unceremoniously took possession of the place. In the upstairs hall hung a life-size chromolithograph of the Madonna with a sword-pierced heart. Varian lit a votive candle in front of it.

Then, just as they finished lunch, a man walked in the front door. Assuming he was another fugitive, Jaccaci greeted him cordially and offered him the best they had in the house. The new arrival, however, reacted with shock and anger; he began shouting in French so excitedly that Jaccaci couldn't follow the words. On hearing the commotion from the next room, Chancel and Mademoiselle Marie ran in to recognize the man as Lagarrigue de Meillac, the plantation's owner. When he learned that the foreigners were guests of Fernand Clerc, however, Meillac calmed down and extended them his hospitality. Everyone took turns laughing and apologizing for the misunderstanding. The American visitors, Meillac said, could have the use of the premises for as long as they wished.

This was to have been the day they climbed the volcano, but that was now out of the question. Pelée roared all afternoon, and both Jaccaci and Varian were still ill. When they begin to recover that evening, the trio of journalists sat in rocking chairs on the lawn and discussed the possibility that the conditions for exploration would be more favorable tomorrow.

It was not to be. On Wednesday morning, in Kennan's words,

about nine o'clock there was a sudden and tremendous outburst of dark-yellow vapor, which looked almost like a colossal geyser of liquid mud. I watched it as it swiftly ascended to a height of four or five thousand feet, then ran into the house to get my camera. When I returned to the yard the huge vapor-column had reached a height of ten thousand feet and was still going up. Every part of it was rolling, boiling, and unfolding in multitudinous convolutions, and its clearly defined top looked like an immense growing cauliflower, eight hundred or a thousand feet across.

Without a single rumble or detonation to indicate the Titanic power of the agency at work below, the great column of dark vapor rushed swiftly upward until it was more than three times the height of the volcano itself. Then, for a moment, it seemed to rest. The whole sky, at that time, was perfectly clear, and the gigantic pillar of cloud, standing nearly three miles vertically above the crater in bright sunshine, made a spectacle of almost unimaginable beauty and grandeur.

The most striking feature of this eruption was the rapid and noiseless evolution of immense volumes of dust-charged steam. There must have been a tremendous explosion to send that vapor column twelve or fifteen thousand feet into the air; but, if so, it took place far down in the depths of the earth, because I did not hear a sound of any kind until lightning began to flash in the cloud over the crater.

By the following day, Thursday, May 29, they found themselves getting restless sitting around waiting for the volcano to quiet down enough to permit an ascent. They decided to drive to Morne Rouge, where during their wait they might at least be able to interview a few more eyewitnesses to the May 8 disaster.

• • •

Father Mary was elated at their return. He herded everyone into the rectory and set out a loaf of brown bread, a bottle of rum, a saucer of limes, and a bowl of sugar. He was eager to talk about Monday's eruption—the night of the flight from Vivé. A party of American newspaper correspondents, he said, had arrived in Morne Rouge late Monday afternoon, and they were just finishing dinner with the priest when the explosions began. Panicked by the lightning and the shower of cinders, they had summarily abandoned their cameras, horses, personal baggage, and their host as well, and fled on foot toward the Carbet peaks. What happened to them afterward Father Mary did not know. Some of the natives said they had hiked back to Fort-de-France. Probably, the priest speculated, after such a poor display of courage they were too embarrassed to return to the parish house. Feeding their deserted horses, meanwhile, was presenting a bit of a problem, as the animals couldn't graze on the ash-covered pastures.

After hearing that character assessment from the good Father, Kennan and his companions were not about to disclose the details of their own frantic flight that Monday night. Yet it was with some satisfaction that Kennan scribbled in his notebook, "[A]lthough we, too, had been stampeded by the night eruption of the 26th, we are still in the field!"

Father Mary continued. On Tuesday, another American correspondent named Kavanaugh had arrived on horseback from Fort-de-France. He said he had started out in the company of Professor Robert T. Hill of the U.S. Geological Survey, but the professor, apparently a small frail man, had turned back well before reaching Morne Rouge. Kavanaugh had lunch at the rectory, then attempted to climb the volcano alone. He returned three hours later in a state of complete exhaustion, having gotten nowhere near the summit. Then, after the eruption Wednesday morning, he also returned to Fort-de-France.

Sometime during the chaos of the past few days—Père Mary couldn't say exactly when—a courier from the military hospital in Fort-de-France had delivered a couple of bags of medical supplies. The priest immediately passed them on to the women who were tending to Augusté Ciparis's burns.

And indeed, when Kennan, Varian, and Jaccaci checked once more on the condition of St. Pierre's "sole survivor," they found him much improved and in good spirits. Fortunately, the human body has a tremendous capacity to heal itself, and the ointments of carbolic acid (which served only to draw more fluids out of the flesh) had arrived too late to do much harm. Not only had Ciparis survived the disaster, but he would have the additional good fortune of surviving his medical treatment as well.

• • •

When day broke on Friday, May 30, the volcano was still emitting a plume but making no alarming noises. Varian stayed in bed, suffering from a relapse, and Kennan and Jaccaci found a native guide to lead them up the mountain. As they started up the old Calebasse Road, a tropical squall blew in and transformed the foot-deep blanket of volcanic dust into a mire of heavy slush. From that point on, the going was difficult, and it quickly became apparent that they would not get to the top that day. They decided, nevertheless, to slog on awhile and observe what they could. To their left, all the trees in the ravines were stripped naked and apparently dead. Hanging over the whole mountain was the gray stillness of universal death. Most notably, in some of the crevasses there was evidence of strange and violent subterranean turmoil. Kennan would write:

> [S]team began to rise from a deep gorge about half a mile away on our left, and ten minutes later there was a great uprush of brownish vapor from a mud-slope in the valley of the Rivière des Pères, or the Roxelane, followed by a roar like that of a big waterfall. Near the point where the old route to the main crater leaves the Calebasse road, at a height of about three thousand feet, fine ashes began to blow in our faces from the other side of the divide, and we noticed for the first time a strong, peculiar odor, which reminded me of the smell of a blacksmith shop when fresh coal has been put on the smoldering fire and the smoky products of imperfect combustion escape into the room.
>
> . . . [O]n the brink of a precipice, we looked down into the wild, gloomy, unearthly gorge of the Falaise — a chaos of tremendous cliffs,

landslides, enormous volcanic boulders, blackened forests, and narrow eroded channels, hundreds of feet in depth, through which were tumbling torrents of steaming water and hot mud. A great cloud of yellowish-brown smoke was rising from the crater a thousand feet below, and all up and down the bottom of the gorge we could see up-rushes of steam from fumaroles.

The distinctive characteristic of the whole scene was its absolute unearthliness. The wildness and ruggedness of the contours; the absence of all colors except white, gray, and black; the sudden and mysterious up-rushes of steam or smoke; the faint haze of falling dust; the storm-clouds that eddied around us and deepened the gloominess of the gorge; the drifts of volcanic ashes in the foreground, and the immense gray mass of the mountain, rising to unknown heights in the thick mist overhead, made up a picture that had no parallel in my experience. It might have been a scene from a Dantesque Inferno, or a glimpse of another planet in one of the formative stages of development, but it was like nothing terrestrial.

For a moment, they thought about descending into the gorge to see what the Falaise fissure was actually doing. But the weather was threatening again, and a sudden roar from the steaming abyss below warned them that the gorge would not be a good place to find themselves during an eruption or even a heavy rain. They returned to Morne Rouge, getting caught in another tropical storm along the way. Fortunately, they had no streams to cross, and they reached the rectory around three in the afternoon. The parish house was filled with the pungent smell of carbolic acid, which Father Mary had sprinkled around to counteract (or overpower) an odor of dead bodies that had drifted up from the valley of the Roxelane.

That evening, a glow of subterranean fire lit up the vapor column over the main crater. A few hours after dark, a ship somewhere off St. Pierre threw a powerful searchlight on the mountain, sweeping the beam down the mud-clogged slope of the Rivière Blanche to the site of the buried Guérin sugar mill, then south to the ruins of St. Pierre. For 1902, it was an impressive display of the power of human technology. Then the artificial illumination disappeared, leaving only the flickering reddish orange glow above the mountain and the distant stars to light the night.

• • •

There was another approach to the summit that all the natives said would be easier than the one from Morne Rouge, but it was by way of the Morne Balais Arête, which meant that they would need to backtrack. On Saturday morning, after taking a photograph of Father Mary and bidding him an appreciative good-bye, Kennan and his companions started down the sinuous road back to Acier.

At the high stone bridge spanning the mouth of the Falaise gorge, they encountered something unexpected. An immense mass of boulders, trees, and volcanic ash had clogged up the bridge and turned it into a dam, so that water was now running over it rather than beneath it. Trusting their own feet more than the wheels of their carriage, they waded the swift shin-deep stream that poured over the bridge and plunged into a cataract a mere couple of yards away. Nearby, a group of laborers under the direction of an engineer from the Department of Roads and Bridges was trying to remove the debris and save the bridge. All looked anxious and apprehensive about the task. Several gendarmes were also stationed there to oversee the work, and their mounted officer begged Kennan and his friends to tell the higher authorities of the danger of this work, and to recommend that they be relieved of their duty in that gorge. Kennan assured them that he would do so.

An hour later, as Kennan's party passed Fernand Clerc's now-deserted plantation at Vivé, a monstrous torrent of boiling water roared down the Falaise gorge into the Rivière Capot, throwing up clouds of steam along its course for a distance of several miles. Most of the workers and gendarmes at the bridge were scalded and/or drowned immediately. The few who escaped did not wait any longer for formal permission to abandon that post.

When Varian, Jaccaci, and Kennan got back to Acier, Mademoiselle Marie greeted them with some unexpected news. Professor Angelo Heilprin, from Philadelphia, and a Mr. Leadbeater, a photographer from New York, had arrived there two days earlier. They had set off that morning, by way of the Balais Arête, in an attempt to reach the main crater.

CHAPTER 17

MOUTH OF THE DRAGON

•

At 6 a.m. on May 31, Heilprin and Leadbeater had left Acier on horseback with several native boys. By 9 a.m. they had reached an elevation of 2,100 feet, where as they rested they peered down into the chasm of the Rivière Falaise. At that time, not even a wisp of vapor was rising from the gorge. A few miles beyond, however, a large region of the ocean was chocolate rather than blue—testimony to the torrent of muddy water flowing from the mouth of the Rivière Capot.

As the trail grew steeper, the ash gave way to loose rocks and scoriae. They dismounted and proceeded on foot, climbing into an eerie mist. It began to rain, and the fog grew thicker. At 11 a.m., with his altimeter reading 3,975 feet, Heilprin announced that they were probably standing on the rim of the old crater. Although they could hear the volcano rumbling, what little they could see of the basin before them was flat. Fog or not, this clearly was not the active vent. Noting that his barometer was steady, Heilprin assured Leadbeater that the rain would soon cease and permit them to explore further. The storm clouds, however, showed no regard for Heilprin's forecast, and minutes later they were engulfed in a violent downpour. There was nothing even vaguely resembling a shelter, and they huddled for forty-five minutes against some of the larger volcanic bombs while trying to shield the instruments and the camera. Lightning flashed repeatedly, and if the volcano had been detonating they would not have been able to distinguish those explosions from the crashing thunder. The magnetic compass gyrated wildly. The native boys were terror stricken, and Heilprin finally relented to their pleas. They began their descent.

Going down was considerably harder than climbing up. There was not a secure foothold anywhere. Streams of mud and water cascaded down the path, threatening to sweep them into one ravine or another. As they emerged from the clouds, they noticed that the Rivière Falaise was now seething with steam. Its whole course of several miles to the Capot and then to the sea was a long train of curling and puffing vapors, as if a series of steam locomotives was chugging toward the coast.

As they trudged toward Acier, tired, muddy, drenched, and unsuccessful, the professor had to stop and look back wistfully. High above the rain clouds ringing the mountain towered a giant steam column with its rolling puffs of yellow and brown. It was a scene of grand and unconquered magnificence, and Heilprin knew he would need to try again.

• • •

Angelo Heilprin had arrived in Fort-de-France on the *Fontabelle* on May 25, and the next day he took a boat to St. Vincent to examine the volcano there. Finding La Soufrière quiet and circumstantially less interesting than Mont Pelée, he returned on May 27 to the disappointing news that in his absence Mont Pelée had put on a major display of pyrotechnics. The next day, Heilprin happened to meet Fernand Clerc while the planter was completing his arrangements to leave the island, and he got to hear all of the fascinating details of the eruption he had missed. This was exactly the kind of phenomenon he had come to witness for himself. While others prayed that the volcano would go back to sleep, Heilprin silently hoped that Pelée's activity would continue for a while.

Fernand Clerc offered Heilprin the use of his plantation at Vivé (while counseling him on the dangers of that place) and gave him several letters of introduction, including one to Monsieur Lagarrigue de Meillac of the Acier estate. Consistent with his reputation for hospitality, Clerc even provided a carriage for the professor's journey.

The next morning, accompanied by Mr. Leadbeater, a photographer employed by Underwood & Underwood, Heilprin set off for Acier by way of Lamentin—a longer route but straighter, less hilly, and better maintained than the road Kennan had taken out of Fort-de-France a week earlier. After the two routes merged at Trinité, however, he was on the same road Kennan had followed, and he saw similar sights. Beyond Sainte Marie, the road was clogged with new refugees, almost all of them on foot and collectively carrying every imaginable kind of belonging. Everything within view was covered in ash, and most of the trees were dead. And although Heilprin's words did not always rise to the level of eloquence of Kennan's prose, he was equally conscientious about jotting all of his observations in his notebook.

Although George Kennan and Angelo Heilprin had already known each other by reputation, their first personal meeting was on that evening of May 31, 1902, at the old plantation house at Acier. Kennan at fifty-seven and Heilprin at forty-nine had both traveled extensively in an age when travel was seldom easy, and they each had a large repertoire of fascinating stories to share. After the first half hour's conversation, it was as if they had always been friends. They agreed that the next morning, they would climb the volcano together to find and explore the active vent.

• • •

Sunday, June 1. It was a marvelously clear daybreak, and the volcano was behaving itself. They started off at six o'clock, following the route Heilprin had taken the day before, and leaving their horses at the point where the trail became too rugged for the animals. After yesterday's cloudburst, the continuing footpath had turned into a quagmire of wet ash and mud, and trudging uphill through the mess was slow and physically taxing. The tropical sun rose higher, and there was not a whisper of a breeze to provide relief. One thousand feet from the top, Kennan found himself panting and dripping with perspiration and shouted to the water boy to bring him a drink. Varian was way ahead, and Heilprin and Jaccaci were bringing up the rear with the porters.

As Kennan rested, mopping his forehead and taking in the view, Heilprin caught up. Jaccaci, he said, had suffered a dizzy spell at a spot where the arête narrowed to an edge with a deep gorge on either side. The professor had sent one of the porters back to him with a bottle of Fernand

Clerc's "vin de cyclone," figuring that the effect was psychological and that a few swallows of wine would fortify his nerves.

"I doubt that it's a lack of nerve on his part," Kennan said. "Mr. Jaccaci hasn't been well for the past couple of days. But I'll be pleased to sit here awhile and wait for him. In fact," he looked toward the summit, "I'm not sure I can make it to the top myself."

"Of course you'll make it!" Heilprin retorted. "You just need to slow down a bit. We've got all day before us. If you feel you're getting over-heated, stop every ten steps and rest. One of the first things my Alpine guides taught me was to climb slowly."

As they sat, the last porter caught up to them with the message that Jaccaci was turning back. Kennan stood, looked up at the steep rocky incline, took a deep breath, and resumed the hike, very slowly. Every few minutes Heilprin would shout, "Take it easy, Kennan! Take it easy!" Kennan smiled; he felt he had already slowed to a turtle's pace.

Then, at first so gradually as to be barely noticeable, little wisps of vapor began to develop in the atmosphere. Occasionally a small patch of mist drifted across the trail, bringing a wonderful moment of cooling relief from the sun. The patches progressively grew in size and number, and soon they had combined into a general fog. When the party reached a dry lake-bed at the head of the arête, visibility was down to three hundred feet. Four diverging arêtes originated at that spot, all looking exactly alike. Recognizing that the magnetic compass was unreliable here, Kennan and Heilprin marked their return path by laying out a line of boulders pointing toward Vivé.

Aided by the drop in temperature and the disappearance of the sun, Heilprin's mountain-climbing advice worked, and Kennan made it to the top along with the others. Although the visibility was now just twenty feet, a continuous roaring sound told them the volcanic vent was not far off. They sat and waited for a sign that the cloud might lift. Kennan noted that there was no volcanic ash here; the ground was made up mostly of cinders and sharp-edged rock fragments. He looked quizzically at the professor.

"Scoriae," said Heilprin. "Lava that solidifies in the air during an eruption. When it hits the ground it often fractures into these little pieces."

This picqued Kennan's curiosity, for why should this particular type of rock be so brittle?

It was the kind of question the professor loved to answer. He began by explaining about internal thermal stresses from uneven cooling. He pointed out that this creates problems at glass factories when the molten glass is allowed to cool too quckly. You can have a lump of such glass sitting on a table, and with just a gentle brush, it can suddenly explode into a thousand shards. He went on to explain the process of annealing. If the rate of cooling is controlled, all of the internal stresses have time to equalize. Nature behaves itself when things happen slowly. It's when cooling occurs too quickly that physical materials get out of equilibrium, and we may be treated to strange and totally unexpected phenomena.

Kennan asked about the volcanic eruptions that had ejected the scoriae. What were the prospects of anticipating those events?

Heilprin shrugged. "Pretty tough to predict an eruption, let alone what will happen in one, because what's underground is so far from equilibrium with what's above the ground." Then he assured Kennan that the laws of nature will always work in a direction that gets everything back in balance.

Kennan was about to pursue the matter further by asking how things ever get out of balance in the first place, and how quick is quick when one speaks of a geologic event. But Heilprin jumped up and shouted, "Look!"

A breeze had swept away just enough of the fog to reveal the outline of the entire crater that had once held L'Etang de Palmistes. It was now perfectly dry, its bottom littered with scoriae and ragged masses of volcanic rock decorated with yellow blotches of sulfur. Fumes rose from every square yard of its surface. Heilprin scrambled into the crater and began puncturing the ground with a thermometer and taking notes. At a depth of a few inches, he got readings of 124°F to 130°F. At six inches, the mercury rose to 162°F. That was as deep as he could easily probe, and he looked around for other observations to make. The visibility was still limited.

Although the piton that once bore the cross on the Morne LaCroix had collapsed, Heilprin's altimeter showed that the rest of the mountain's height was essentially unchanged by the eruption. Meanwhile, for just a moment, Kennan and the others thought they glimpsed a vertical movement within the fog, but the sight quickly vanished as an angry wind swirled in from both sides of the mountain, bringing with it a seemingly hopeless rain. Heilprin's eyes met Kennan's with a look of profound disappointment.

The squall, however, proved to be as unpredictable as most other non-equilibrium phenomena, and it miraculously ended as suddenly as it had begun. A few hundred yards from where they stood, the scarred ground sloped upward to the edge of a precipice, and just beyond, now finally unveiled to the explorers, was the sight of the century: the furious vapor column from Pelée's main vent.

Picking their way among the boulders, they walked to a point some seventy-five feet from the column of steam, expecting that on looking over the edge they would see something like a circular bowl. Kennan would write:

I was tremendously startled, therefore, to find myself suddenly on the very brink of a frightful chasm fifty or seventy-five feet across and hundreds of feet in depth, out of which came a roar like that of a titantic forge with the bellows at work, and a curious crackling sound which suggested the splitting of rocks in intense heat. The wall of the chasm under my feet was absolutely perpendicular—even if it did not overhang—and by bending forward a little I could see down a hundred and fifty or two hundred feet. Beyond that point clear vision was lost in a sort of bright, vapory shimmer, like the shimmer at the top of a white-hot blast furnace. On the other side of the immense fissure was a huge chaotic mass of volcanic debris, piled together in the wildest confusion, and out of it, into the throat of the chasm, projected three or four long, angular, toothlike rocks, which had been so calcined as to be almost white. With a powerful glass I had seen these same white rocks from St. Pierre, and I knew, therefore, that if the ascending vapor-column south of us were removed we might look straight out through the chasm at the ruined city beyond it.

The native boys were in the same speechless awe as the explorers, and for a few minutes all stood together in meek wonder at the power of nature, oblivious to the possibility that the dragon might awake further. Heilprin finally broke the silence, saying that it was remarkable that they could stand so close without feeling the heat. Apparently, the rising column was drawing air in from the surroundings in a giant chimney effect. It did not occur to anyone, however, that the squall-cloud must have been sucked into this very chimney. Nor that the variations in visibility might be an indication that the intensity of the eruption column was fluctuating wildly.

They stood transfixed at the mouth of the inferno until the pangs of hunger sent them back to their provisions. While they ate, the sky grew denser and darker, and another thick cloud blew in and swarmed around them. It soon became apparent that they would not get another view of the source of the ash column that day. It began to drizzle as they began to descend, and when they reached the arête, the rain was hammering them in sheets. A few minutes later, a surge of floodwater burst over the trail behind them.

When they reached a near-deserted village, Heilprin, Leadbeater, and the porters took shelter in a small one-room cabin. Kennan and Varian, however, figured that they were already so drenched that they might as well ride back to Acier immediately. It was not a good decision. They got only a short distance when their progress was blocked by an impassable torrent in one of the barrancas. As Varian turned to head back to Heilprin and the others, Kennan noticed an abandoned shack by the side of the road. "I'm going to wait here," he shouted through the din of the storm.

The shack, Kennan quickly discovered, leaked terribly. He was getting cold, the rain was relentless, and the raging stream continued to swell further. He mounted his horse to follow Varian back to the cabin, but after only a short distance, he was stopped by "a chocolate-colored cataract that would have carried away a house." Trapped between two raging flooded streams, he returned to the abandoned shack and did calisthenics to counteract the chill of his wet clothing. An hour passed before the storm began to let up, and the cataract receded.

When enough of the water had run off to allow them to get through the barrancas, the group reassembled. Drenched and shivering, they rode back past Vivé to Acier.

Jaccaci, it turned out, had just returned himself, having first gotten lost and then caught in the storm. Although he'd had nothing to eat since morning and had been drenched to the skin for hours, "these physical hardships," Kennan would write, "did not trouble him so much as the attack of mountain-sickness and vertigo which had prevented him from reaching the summit of the volcano."

. . .

Fort-de-France was in chaos, both civil and economic. There were now twenty-five thousand displaced persons on the island, and fifteen thousand of these had crowded into the capital city alone—almost doubling its population. The young mayor, Victor Sévère, housed the refugees in every available public building and in temporary shelters, and begged the city's citizens to take them into their homes. For those remaining homeless, he tried to provide as many comforts as possible in the city's parks, where food rations were distributed daily.

Through the efforts of the interim governor, Georges L'Heurre, each family of refugees received a subsidy of 1.25 francs per day per person. But because the average daily wage of a cane-field worker was less than 1.50 francs, this created an incentive for some nonvictims to represent themselves as victims, and it swelled the influx into the city. Meanwhile, some of the less-scrupulous permanent citizens of Fort-de-France saw another kind of opportunity in the food distribution system, going from one center to another to claim food and other relief. Accurate record keeping had become so difficult that they often succeeded.

The normal supplies of food began to dwindle, at least in Fort-de-France. Those who had to pay for their own produce found meager pickings at the markets, while nearby relief distribution centers were burgeoning. As prices inflated, food designated for relief began to find its way onto a black market. Many citizens of Fort-de-France found themselves beginning to resent the refugees.

. . .

On the morning of June 5, having chartered the ferry *Rubis* at five hundred francs per day, Kennan, Varian, Jaccaci, Heilprin, and Leadbeater steamed up the western coast of the island from Fort-de-France. Below Pelée's main crater, volcanic rocks half hidden in a cloud of steam were tumbling from a V-shaped cleft into a gorge below. From that point to the sea stretched a broad fan-shaped region of utter devastation corrugated with chasms and ravines. Here and there, smoke rose from the desolate scene. A long curving plume of vapor drifted overhead from the summit, sifting down a shower of fine volcanic dust that irritated the men's eyes and throats and filled the air with a smoky haze.

They landed first at Precheur, which they found buried in several feet of ash. A few of the former inhabitants had returned to load their personal belongings onto a barge towed by a tug, intent on not going back to the town until the volcano was "extinct." Except for these salvagers, the town was deserted. Although the majority of the buildings on higher ground were still intact, near the Rivière Precheur the gaunt remains of dozens of foundations and piles of rubble jammed against giant boulders bore testimony to a devastating flash flood. Half of the church had collapsed some thirty feet into an excavation gouged out by the floodwaters, and other stout buildings were buried in muck. Hundreds of huge boulders packed the streambed. Heilprin, noting that many of these rocks were ten or twelve feet in diameter, scrawled some calculations in his notebook and announced that they had to weigh at least seventy-five tons each. It was astonishing that such an insignificant stream, its waters now a mere trickle, could have swept such huge boulders into the town.

When they had finished their investigations and photographs in Precheur, and Varian had folded up his sketchbook, they returned to the *Rubis* and steamed a short distance south to the mouth of the Rivière Blanche. Although the summit was smoking as usual, Pelée was making virtually no noise. Heilprin decided to go ashore in a small boat to examine the monstrous mudflow firsthand and, if possible, to take the temperature of some of the fumaroles. Jaccaci and Varian joined him. Kennan and Leadbeater, having seen enough volcanic mud to satisfy their curiosity and content to watch the fumaroles from their present vantage point, stayed on the ferry with the captain.

The shore party landed and hiked a quarter mile up the slope, then disappeared into the former streambed. A few minutes later, Kennan and Leadbeater saw a cloud of steam burst down the upper gorge, as if it were billowing from a swiftly advancing surge of boiling water. Shouting from the ferry was useless; Kennan motioned to the captain to toot the horn. Within moments, Heilprin and his companions emerged onto the mud-plain in a mad dash toward shore. The volcano began rumbling. As the trio scampered into the landing boat, clouds of dense brown smoke began churning out of the crater of L'Etang Sec and the V-shaped gorge beneath. Then, in Kennan's words:

> Two or three minutes later, before they had time to get more than a hundred feet from the dangerous coast, there was a sudden and tremendous explosion from both craters, and an enormous mass of dark yellow vapor was projected upward in rolling, expanding convolutions, not only from the craters themselves, but apparently from the entire length of the fissure that united them. Then, from the lower crater, a huge cloud seemed to roll down the slope in the direction of the boat, and the whole western face of the volcano burst into the most terrifying activity. A flood of boiling water, with a wave-front eight or ten feet high, rushed down the Rivière Blanche and precipitated itself into the sea with a great hissing and steaming; explosions in half a dozen places sent big, fountain-like jets of white vapor to heights of two or three hundred feet; geysers of liquid mud leaped into the air through the clouds of steam that suddenly began to rise from the lower slopes; and the tremendous column of mud-smoke from the crater of the Rivière Blanche boiled up to a height of more than half a mile and then began to open out in huge, cauliflower-like heads.

The captain immediately rang the bell for full speed and headed toward sea, apparently intending to abandon the landing party. Kennan shouted above the roar of the volcano, "You've got to go back for that boat!" When the captain didn't acknowledge him, he shouted again, "Go back for that boat!" The captain continued to ignore him for a few moments. Then in deference to some more noble ideal than flight, he glanced back over his shoulder at the eruption and without saying a word, he swung the vessel around. In a few minutes they reached Heilprin and Jaccaci and pulled them aboard. Both were perspiring profusely, yet somehow they appeared exhilarated. "That was one hell of a thing!" said Jaccaci. "I've never seen anything like it myself!" Heilprin laughed.

Barely waiting for the mate to tie up the landing boat, the captain again ran full speed away from the coast. Only when they were a mile offshore did he throttle back. Heilprin told him to cut the engine and let the boat drift. After all, he reminded, he and his friends were paying five hundred francs for this excursion, and it was the volcano they wanted to observe, not the sea.

They floated and watched for the next five hours, witnessing ten or twelve flash floods of steaming water surging down the Coulée Rivière Blanche and the Rivière Sèche. The prevailing opinion had been that such floods were due to rains on the upper slopes, but now there was reason to question that idea. Today it didn't seem to be raining on the mountain, or at least not much, yet still these wild floods were surging down the valleys. More curiously, the floods came at irregular intervals. If due to rain, wouldn't the runoff be more continuous?

Maybe, said Kennan, volcanic debris was piling up in the ravines and damming the streams. When the impounded water generated sufficient pressure, it would burst the temporary dam and the floodwaters would cascade into the valleys below. A few days ago, they had seen debris create such a dam at the bridge on the Rivière Falaise.

"And was the impounded water hot?" Heilprin asked.

"No," Kennan admitted, "the stream wasn't hot then. We waded through it over the breast of the bridge. But it was boiling a half hour later when the dam broke!"

"The volcano must have heated up the water after we passed," said Varian.

Heilprin shook his head. "Not likely. It takes a long time to heat up a big reservoir of water. I don't think these hot floods are due to surface water."

"You mean you think the volcano is erupting hot water?" Kennan asked incredulously. "*Liquid* water?"

"That seems to be the only possible explanation," said Heilprin.

Kennan pondered the idea. Sure, he knew of such things as hot springs and geysers of groundwater, but those small-scale phenomena were quite different from these huge sudden floods. "No, professor," he finally announced, "I think I'll stick to my dam theory."

"Before you close your mind," said Heilprin, "remember that there were boiling floods for several days before the big explosion of May 8."

"Yes, so the witnesses have told us."

"Well," said the professor, "I think these boiling floods today are telling us that there's going to be more violent activity very soon."

• • •

Around ten o'clock the next morning, June 6, Kennan heard Jaccaci shouting from the lower landing of their hotel in Fort-de-France: "Look at the volcano! There's another big eruption!"

Kennan dashed outside. Although Mont Pelée itself was hidden from view, a huge black cloud was mushrooming up and outward at a height of two or three miles above the Pitons du Carbet. Within five minutes it covered the entire northern sky to the zenith, then it eclipsed the sun and threw the city into darkness as it continued to swell toward the south. They left the hotel and pushed through the throng of frightened refugees camped in the city square, all eyes transfixed on the darkening sky. At the beach, they saw that the sea had receded a distance of one hundred feet. They wisely held their distance, and indeed the ebb was soon followed by a swell that flooded the entire beach area and the adjoining street. For the next half hour, the waters of the harbor continued to oscillate at intervals of four or five minutes.

Five miles off the mouth of the Rivière Blanche, the cable steamer *Pouyer-Quertier* had again been grappling for one of the broken cables. Those on deck saw the mountain explode with hurricane-like velocity, surge over the ruins of St. Pierre, and overwhelm four or five small boats. Despite its distance, the *Pouyer-Quertier* itself was not completely out of reach; the explosion covered its decks with ashes and pummeled it with small stones. In his log, Captain Thirion would report wild fluctuations in the barometer and lightning jumping from the sea to the sky. Had Kennan and the others decided to go up the western coast on Friday instead of Thursday, their volcano investigations would have come to an abrupt end, for they would have been smack in the path of this nuée ardente!

The eruption cloud overshadowed the whole island of Martinique and showered ashes on St. Lucia. The harbor at Castries, where the hulk of the ill-fated *Roddam* was still docked, grew so dark that the Royal Mail steamer had to use a searchlight to grope its way into the port. By all measures, the explosion of June 6 was every bit as violent as the ones that had devastated St. Pierre on May 8 and May 20. It quickly faded from memory, however, for it claimed but a handful of lives and there were no structures left in its path to destroy.

The *Dixie* did not return to Martinique. On June 9, the five men sailed for New York together on the *Fontabelle*. Varian would publish his art, Leadbeater his photography, Jaccaci his articles, and Kennan and Heilprin their books. In only one significant way would Kennan's and Heilprin's accounts differ: Kennan would continue to insist that the floods were due to the collapse of temporary dams of volcanic debris, while Heilprin would claim that the floodwaters had surged from within the Earth.

CHAPTER 18

LESSONS UNLEARNED

•

On June 23, two weeks after Angelo Heilprin and George Kennan had left the island, Professor Alfred Lacroix arrived from Paris with his scientific team. For the next six weeks, his group of French scientists would tramp through the devastation in their white tropical suits and pith helmets, interview natives whose stories had already been told dozens of times, and photograph the mountain and each other. Mont Pelée, though still emitting smoke, was not doing anything violent, and most members of the team looked forward to a safe and comfortable assignment.

Lacroix, however, viewed it as a compelling puzzle. How does a volcano kill thirty thousand people some seven kilometers distant in a matter of mere minutes? He knew that there had been no lava flow, and that molten lava doesn't flow all that fast anyway. He saw the effects of the heavy ashfall, but even if it had fallen instantaneously it was hardly deep enough to bury so many people alive. Yet the buildings, many with thick stone walls, had been reduced to rubble in a manner that trivialized the worst hurricane imaginable. A mere gust of volcanic gas could not have wreaked such devastation; clearly, there had been some sort of explosive blast of monumental violence. And the charred remains suggested that it must have been quite hot. Indeed, eyewitnesses had claimed that its front was riddled with lightning, fire, and brimstone.

It would have been helpful if he could have talked to Heilprin and Kennan, two certainly credible observers, about what they had witnessed. That, unfortunately, was not to happen. And although he might speculate on the nature and the mechanism of the explosion without their input, he well knew that no scientific theory can be developed without a firm observational foundation. Lacroix had to confront the difficult fact that he had personally observed no phenomena that remotely resembled the event that had destroyed St. Pierre. All he could do was to watch the volcano on a daily basis, hoping to see it explode once more, and to prepare himself not to miss such an event should it happen.

On Morne d'Orange, the high promontory just south of St. Pierre, Lacroix set up two cameras on sturdy tripods and aimed them toward Mont Pelée. He drilled his assistants in changing film plates as quickly as possible. Snap the shutter, slip the cover in the plate holder, unlatch the camera back, pull out the plate holder, flip it to its reverse side, reinsert it, latch the camera, snap the next picture. Oops—no, remember to pull out the plate-cover before snapping. Then repeat the process for the next picture, but this time remember to use a new plate holder. Keep track of which plates were exposed and which weren't, and on which sides. And don't jar the tripods. He timed the drills. It was clumsy at first: tripods kicked over, dropped and broken plates, double exposures, some non-exposures. But practice pays, and soon the high-speed photography drill was running smoothly. No broken glass, no double exposures. And, most importantly, the prospect of a photographic series at ten-second intervals. It was time to risk using actual sensitized film plates.

He stationed his camera crew on Morne d'Orange from daybreak until sunset each day. The glass plates were too expensive to allow idle picture taking just to pass the time. Only if the volcano launched an explosion down one of its slopes were they to take any pictures—by putting their high-speed photographic drill into practice.

It happened on July 9. The photographers were jarred from their leisure by a thunderous explosion, the sound reaching them some twenty seconds after the actual discharge. They ran to the cameras, too late to catch the beginning of the event but soon enough to record the result. A monstrous lateral blast had launched a churning cloud of steam and ash down Pelée's western flank toward the sea. Trailing behind, a giant plume blossomed high into the atmosphere. The photographers went through their drill and recorded their sequence of photographs for posterity. It was the first photographic record in history of the progressive development of a pyroclastic surge.

Lacroix himself had seen the blast, and over the next few days he witnessed additional smaller surges, similar to the one that had almost engulfed Heilprin. It was clear to him that these were not mere avalanches of hot rock and dust tumbling down the mountainside and leaving behind a smoke trail. Somehow, these great clouds rolled over the ground almost frictionlessly, grinding up and destroying everything in their path. And indeed, as many eyewitnesses had reported, they contained patches of fire. Lacroix christened the phenomenon a "nuée ardente," or "glowing cloud." And the type of eruption that gives rise to this potentially disastrous phenomenon, he named a "Peléan eruption," after Mont Pelée. Volcanologists still sometimes use the term today.

Lacroix realized that a nuée ardente can occur only in a volcano whose magma is so viscous that it does not readily release its entrapped gases. If one sees a lot of lava, therefore, there should be little danger of such an explosion. But if an eruption consists only of steam and ash and no molten lava, a nuée ardente may be on Mother Nature's agenda. To roll down a mountainside, such a cloud must obviously be denser than the surrounding air. It turns out, however, that it takes very little ash content to accomplish this: a mere few percent will do. Aided by a directed blast, as from the V-shaped cleft of Mont Pelée's L'Etang Sec, the natural motion of such a death cloud is along the ground, and only when it slows down do its particulates sift out and its lighter gaseous constituents rise. Meanwhile, anything caught in the path of such a deadly superheated avalanche is subjected to the same physical violence as if it had been placed directly in the vent of a volcanic eruption!

Alfred Lacroix would later lecture and write extensively about the phenomenon, and he would return to Martinique six months later to study Mont Pelée further. But in July of 1902, with a typhoid epidemic raging through the crowded refugee population of Fort-de-France and the volcano growing sleepy, he decided that the immediate investigation was over. He and his team sailed back to France on July 31.

• • •

Alfred Lacroix's investigations established that the ground-hugging cloud that had destroyed St. Pierre was more than an isolated onetime event. It was, rather, a natural phenomenon: one that would occur over and again, not just at Mont Pelée but probably at other volcanoes as well—even in other parts of the world. With the turn-of-the-century advances in photography, particularly the availability of more light-sensitive emulsions and the eventual substitution of celluloid for glass plates, such events began to lend themselves to objective scientific study. Not only could pyroclastic surges now be photographed in action, but their precursors could be documented, their aftereffects studied, and theories proposed to explain them. With the dissemination of even the most preliminary research along such lines, people living in the shadow of active volcanoes around the world could learn to recognize their risks and, when threatened, would know enough to evacuate in a timely manner.

It is axiomatic that one cannot build a scientific theory on a single observation. Lacroix, however, had now witnessed a number of these thundering avalanches of gas and dust, had taken time-lapse photographs of several, and had interviewed eyewitnesses to a half dozen others. With that start, and with time to reflect on the matter during his long voyage home, he was able to make a bit of sense of the otherwise confusing written accounts of some earlier eruptions. Such accounts went back as far as A.D. 79, when Pliny the Younger described the explosions that had engulfed Pompeii and Herculaneum in "a black and dreadful cloud, broken with rapid, zigzag flashes," which "began to descend and cover the sea." Pliny's story took on new meaning now that Lacroix had a set of photographs of an apparently similar event. There were also accounts of such death clouds from the Krakatau eruption of 1883, the eruption of Tarawera in New Zealand in 1886, the great eruption of Bandai-San in Japan in 1888, and other major eruptions of the past few decades. Lacroix was confident that these were not isolated incidents but clues to a more general pattern of geothermal phenomena.

A nuée ardente never seemed to burst without warning from a long-dormant volcano. There were always precursors: ground tremors, the venting of steam and ash, audible rumbling, ashfalls, electrical activity in the ash clouds, and flooding and mudflows. Perhaps, Lacroix mused, with enough scientific study, such precursors could become predictors of the precise time and place of future volcanic disasters.

Yet there was another curious puzzle. The starburst explosions and the staccato blasts in nuées ardentes had been described by numerous observers. What could possibly cause such detonations so far from a volcano's vent? Wouldn't any combustible gas streaming from the volcano burst into flame immediately on contact with the atmosphere—well before it entered an eruption cloud? Only one hypothesis seemed to work. It had to do with the common fact that water, and therefore steam, is composed of molecules of H_2O—a combination of hydrogen and oxygen atoms.

Paradoxically, hydrogen cannot burn if it's too hot. At temperatures higher than about 600°C (1,100°F), hydrogen atoms move too fast to get snagged by oxygen atoms to make water molecules. Conversely, steam that is heated above this temperature dissociates into its constituent atoms, and the resulting hot mixture of hydrogen and oxygen gases abruptly expands in volume. If a volcanic vent is glowing visibly, it is certainly much hotter than the 600°C needed to break steam molecules apart in this manner. Pockets of such dissociated hydrogen and oxygen gas, in exactly the right proportions to recombine into H_2O, are swept from the vent in eruption clouds and pyroclastic surges.

When the temperature of the mixture drops below 600°C, it becomes possible for this hydrogen and oxygen to recombine to form steam. Yet this combustion cannot take place spontaneously; just as in a car engine, where gasoline vapor and air are mixed, it takes a source of ignition to initiate the burning. Static electricity, however, is always a by-product of the turbulence of any particulate-laden gas, and lightning is a very effective spark plug for combustible gases. A discharge of lightning through a cooling eruption cloud, therefore, can be expected to set off exactly the kind of staccato explosions that Fernand Clerc heard in the initial destructive event, Kennan described in his writings, Varian drew in his pictures, and which sent hundreds of natives fleeing from their homes in terror on the evening of May 26. And this phenomenon, Lacroix realized, also adequately accounted for the "glowing" patches in the "glowing clouds" he had seen and photographed.

• • •

Although the germ theory of disease was still in its infancy in 1902, it was clear to the interim governor that there were too many refugees crowded into Fort-de-France for anyone's good health and safety. July's typhoid outbreak confirmed his concerns. Meanwhile, a dozen miles away, the killer volcano had gotten so quiet that even the scientists who had come to study it had lost interest and left the island. Which was the more serious threat—the volcano or the threat of an epidemic? The answer wasn't difficult.

On August 2, Georges L'Heurre announced to the refugees that they had until August 15 to return to their homes. If they remained in Fort-de-France after that date, they would get no more assistance from the government. Relief would be sent to the northern villages to help everyone through the recovery period and to get the farms productive again, but no more handouts would be given to displaced persons who remained in the capital.

Families began the long winding trudge northward through the mountains to dozens of abandoned hamlets and villages. They started repatriating Grand Rivière, Macouba, and Basse-Pointe on the north coast, Ajoupa-Bouillon and Morne Rouge on the south and east slopes of the volcano, and Precheur on the west coast. It was a slow process. Many homes had been destroyed—burned, collapsed, or swept away by one of the lahars. Some that survived had been looted, while others were filled with volcanic mud as much as five feet deep. The farms were in ruin, their crops and trees dead. The poor souls returning to Precheur had to shuffle down the partially cleared main street of St. Pierre. The city's devastation was not a reassuring sight, and it didn't help that the refugees' tired shuffling feet sometimes kicked up human bones.

Then on August 13, two days before the government's resettlement deadline, a series of detonations signaled a renewal of volcanic activity. By the next day, Pelée was again belching an eruption column. Beneath the newly expanding canopy of smoke and ash, long lines of weary and sad-eyed evacuees continued to hike northward to they knew not what. They had no alternative.

Although the renewed eruption gave L'Heurre second thoughts about the wisdom of his resettlement order, there was no longer anything he could do to reverse his decision. A week earlier, he had received a devastating cablegram informing him that a permanent governor had been appointed by the Ministry of Colonies: one Jean-Baptiste Lemaire. L'Heurre recognized the name. The fellow knew little if anything of

Martinique but had the important qualification of being a personal friend of Gaston Doumergue, the colonial secretary. L'Heurre would be relieved of his interim gubernatorial duties on August 21, and until then he was to make no major decisions on his own.

Mont Pelée, however, once again thumbed her nose at human political events. The volcano continued to rage through the following weeks, raining ash on all of the newly repatriated towns. On August 26, an agitated delegation from Morne Rouge arrived in Fort-de-France and insisted on an audience with the new governor. The mountain was in a dangerous state of eruption, they explained. It was behaving just as it had in May, shortly before it exploded and destroyed St. Pierre. They begged Governor Lemaire to visit Morne Rouge to see for himself, and then to evacuate the town and nearby villages.

Lemaire was taken aback by the audacity of the racially mixed delegation of semiliterate natives, and he made no attempt to hide his lack of empathy for their plight. St. Pierre was already gone, he pointed out impatiently, so what difference could it possibly make if the volcano exploded again? He didn't need to personally view the eruption up close, because he already knew that whatever he saw would not change his mind. And thus, without bothering to inspect the volcano for himself, or even to acquaint himself with the geography of the northern part of the island, Governor Lemaire arrogantly ordered the townspeople back to their homes in the danger zone. If they gave him any trouble, he threatened, he would summarily cut off Morne Rouge from all further distributions of food and other aid.

The delegation took the bitter news back to their town. The volcano continued to rumble. Father Mary began spending more time hearing confessions.

Meanwhile, Angelo Heilprin had returned to Martinique on August 23 to inspect how the volcano's geophysical features had changed during the previous two months. He was thrilled, at least from the perspective of his scientific curiosity, to find the volcano again in upheaval. On August 28 he arrived at the Habitation Leyritz on the northeastern foot of the mountain; at an elevation of five hundred feet, he figured that this would be a more convenient base of operations than either Vivé or Acier.

Over the next few days, however, Heilprin's attempts to reach the summit were repeatedly foiled by heavy ashfall and flying rocks. On August 30, he estimated that the thundering eruption column had swollen to a diameter of 1,500 feet and was rising at nearly two miles per minute (120 miles per hour)! The professor was astounded that after all of its violent explosions over the past few months, the volcano could still be discharging so much energy.

In Morne Rouge, less than three miles southeast of the raging volcano, a contingent of gendarmes distributed 2,100 rations to the people of Morne Rouge. Everything and everyone were coated with grayish white ash, and the only color in the scene was a flickering orange glow at the summit of the mountain. The effect was surrealistic, as if the Devil's workers were distributing provisions to a crowd of newly arrived ghosts outside the gates of hell.

That evening of August 30, sunset did not bring darkness. A wild display of lightning bathed the entire northern third of the island in a flickering yet continuous light. Some of the electrical discharges were rodlike, others wavy or even spiral shaped. Then began a fusillade of those weird starburst explosions and their terrifyingly loud reports.

At 8:45 p.m., it happened. A fearsome explosion rattled every loose object in Father Mary's rectory. The priest dashed outside to a horrible sight: cascading toward him, clearly on a course that would bring it straight up the main street of town, was a monstrous "whirlwind of fire." He shouted frantically, as if he might actually be heard above the thunder of the death cloud, "Into the church, everyone! Into the church!"

People spilled from their homes, including some who had barricaded themselves in for the past several days. Even if the good Father's shouts were largely lost in the din, there was no question of which way to run; everyone knew where the volcano was and where the church was. And everyone also knew that the church was the strongest building in town, having been built to withstand the onslaught of the worst imaginable Caribbean hurricane. Women stuffed their hemlines into their waistbands and scooped up small children as they scrambled down the street; men did their best to hurry along the old and infirm. Father Mary stood as a pillar of faith and courage in the midst of the chaos, facing the volcano in his cassock and pith helmet, waving everyone on, shouting that they must hurry, squeezing an arm here and a shoulder there as the flood of parishioners rushed past him toward the sanctuary. The nuée ardente churned ever closer, until it appeared to be right on the heels of scores of people still sprinting toward him. Its top billowed upward, carrying flashes of lightning and fiery explosions high overhead. Father Mary raised his outstretched hands toward the advancing harbinger of death and destruction and said a prayer. A quick one.

Miraculously, the death cloud's forward motion stalled, and its monstrous mass of smoke swept upward into the sky. It may have swallowed some of the souls fleeing it, but not all; many were still frantically running toward the priest. Although that would have been a good time for Father Mary himself to dash to the safety of the house of worship, apparently it never occurred to him to save himself until everyone else was safe. He stood steadfast in the middle of the street, waving his arms and shouting to those still approaching, "Come! Come quickly! Into the church! Hurry!"

A second violent explosion shook the air. The volcano lay hidden behind the still-dissipating smoke of the initial pyroclastic surge, and it was impossible to see what was happening. Still, the priest stood his ground. Only when he had spurred the last of his congregation past him did he turn to scamper behind them toward the sanctuary. Yet even then, he had to be sure that they were really the last, and he stopped to peer up the street one last time. Were others still coming? And only then did he realize that he was standing directly in the path of a second death cloud. It was thundering toward him through the rising dust of the first.

The priest yanked up his cassock and ran. He knew that the deadly phenomenon was fast, but at least he had a head start. Holding the heavy church door half open, a parishioner shouted, "Hurry, Father!" With the death cloud two hundred yards away, he had only another fifty yards to go, and for a moment it looked like he might make it. Then a violent blast of wind driven before the onrushing cloud threw the priest to the ground and slammed the heavy door shut. A few seconds later, the nuée ardente engulfed him.

Father Mary was burned but still able to stagger to his feet. And the church, sheltering hundreds of people, had mainly withstood the shock. Unfortunately, Pelée had launched a third nuée ardente closely on the heels of the second. Before he could stumble the last fifty feet to the church, he was struck again. When the smoke dissipated this time, the priest could barely crawl. Several horrified parishioners carried him inside. And there Father Mary spent the night in agony, his only relief coming from the holy water in the fonts.

In the morning twilight, two natives from south of town arrived by wagon to investigate what had happened. Before them they found a scene of bewildering devastation: most of the homes in the northern half of Morne Rouge had been reduced to rubble, even the stoutest masonry structures were badly damaged, and everything was blanketed in several feet of ash. Here and there, streams of smoke rose from the ruins. Even the church, which was built solid as a fort, had lost part of its roof.

But it was not a time to gawk, for Father Mary desperately needed skilled medical attention and now there was a functional wagon available. After outfitting it with a mattress and blankets to keep him as comfortable as possible, a group of the surviving parishioners escorted their beloved pastor over the hilly road to Fonds-Saint-Denis. When they found that village's small hospital in a state of terrible confusion, they continued on to Fort-de-France, arriving in midafternoon. There the nuns embraced Father Mary's care as a special mission. His treatment, however, would consist mostly of prayer, for medical science had not yet progressed to the stage of dealing effectively with such extensive burns.

Whether or not the last part of Father Mary's story is apocryphal, it is worth including here as a testimony to the man and his dedication to his faith.

At 11 a.m. on September 1, the day after his arrival at the hospital, one of his nurses heard the priest trying to speak. She went to his side and gently placed her hand on an unbandaged spot on his shoulder.

"How many died, Sister?" he questioned in a hoarse whisper.

"This isn't the time to worry yourself, Father," she said. "Let me help you drink some water."

"I really must know, Sister," he insisted. "How many died? A hundred?" She slowly shook her head.

"A thousand?"

The nurse's eyes grew glassy.

"More?"

She nodded somberly as a tear streamed down her cheek. They maintained eye contact for a moment more, then the priest rolled his head back on the pillow. His eyes suddenly seemed to be focused far, far away.

"Then you must excuse me, Sister," he whispered, "for I must tend my flock."

And with that, Father Mary died.

• • •

The three pyroclastic surges of August 30 engulfed an area roughly double that of the blast that had destroyed St. Pierre. Ajoupa-Bouillon and a dozen smaller hamlets were virtually obliterated. Most of Morne Rouge lay flattened, and no structure escaped damage. The entire region was buried deep in volcanic ash. Around 1,600 people died in and around Morne Rouge, and as many as 1,000 others succumbed elsewhere in the zone of destruction. In terms of both property and lives, Mont Pelée's August 30 explosions were more destructive than La Soufrière's terrible May 7 holocaust on the island of St. Vincent.

Jean-Baptiste Lemaire never did apologize for forcing those several thousand victims to remain in the high-risk area where they would be killed, and it is a sad commentary on his sense of responsibility as the new governor that it took a disaster of such proportions to finally gain his attention. But he and Colonial Secretary Gaston Doumergue (who would later become president of France) did succeed in deflecting most prospective criticism of their joint ineptitude by drawing positive attention to what they did next.

Shortly after the August 30 disaster (and after a frenzied exchange of cablegrams), Lemaire ordered the evacuation of the northern third of the island. To accommodate these twenty-two thousand refugees without overwhelming Fort-de-France, the government bought and leased land in the southern wilderness, where, under military authority, it built cabins, shelters, cisterns, and a dozen new schools. New roads and bridges were constructed to access the new settlements, and seeds, livestock, tools, sewing machines, and other essentials were shipped to the settlers. There would be no further deaths from the volcano.

The military rule, however, did not appeal to everyone living under it. When Pelée's eruption finally ended in 1903, people began trickling back to the northern zone, and by 1905, only ten thousand remained in the new settlements. Of those who went north, several hundred moved into the ruins of St. Pierre.

bordering on panic, their likely reaction would have been to demand to be evacuated as well. And if Andréus Hurard had reconsidered the situation and endorsed the need to evacuate in *Les Colonies,* as he might well have done under this scenario, Pelée's mighty explosion would have destroyed only brick and mortar. All of the principal players—including Louis Mouttet, Andréus Hurard, Gaston Landes, and Fernand Clerc—might have emerged as heroes. If only the volcano had waited a week or so.

Nothing in this scenario, however, would have made the evacuation any easier. With the available ships and ferries, it would have taken a week at minimum to carry all of the thirty-five thousand people from St. Pierre and Precheur to Fort-de-France. Providing security for the huge number of vacant homes and businesses would have been virtually impossible. Meanwhile, the capital, with its population of only around seventeen thousand, had nowhere near enough shelter and provisions to host an influx of thirty-five thousand. Given that external benefactors send aid only *after* a disaster, never in anticipation of one, feeding so many people would have been virtually impossible. Mouttet would have been laying his career on the line, for if he had initiated such a major human upheaval and Pelée had *not* exploded, he would never have succeeded in defending that misjudgment. Indeed, as unfolding events would demonstrate, Fort-de-France would be strained to its limit in coping with just fifteen thousand refugees even after a considerable amount of relief did arrive. And looting would still be a problem even after St. Pierre had been reduced to rubble. Certainly, Mouttet's reluctance to make a hasty decision was justifiable under the circumstances. If the man was guilty of any misjudgment, it was only in misjudging the future course of nature.

Those writers (and there have been many) who heap the blame for St. Pierre's thirty thousand deaths on the ghost of Louis Mouttet neglect to weigh the problems of evacuation and the support of the refugees against the geophysical risks as they were understood in those times. Most of these same writers also fail to credit Mouttet for his attentiveness; indeed, it was only because the governor was so concerned about his constituents that he was anywhere near the volcano when it exploded. Most curiously, however, none of the writers who are so merciless to Mouttet have much to say about the dismal performance of his successor, Governor Jean-Baptiste Lemaire, under whose stewardship more than two thousand perished in the disaster of August 30. Maybe because two thousand deaths are but a small fraction of thirty thousand, some figure that Lemaire's performance wasn't all that bad.

Lemaire, however, was in a much better position than Mouttet to take steps to avoid a disaster. The replacement governor had the advantage of knowing what devastation Pelée was capable of unleashing, and if he had any remaining questions about this, he could easily have spent an afternoon examining the prior destruction for himself. (Mouttet, on the other hand, had not known, and had no way of knowing, about pyroclastic surges and their effects.) Secondly, an evacuation order by Lemaire would have involved thirty thousand fewer people than one by Mouttet, because there were that many fewer people still alive. Thirdly, Lemaire had warehouses bulging with relief provisions that Mouttet did not have. And finally, in light of the initial disaster of May 8, Lemaire would not have looked foolish or inept if he had ordered an evacuation and he had turned out to be wrong.

Lemaire had more knowledge to guide him, more resources to draw upon, a smaller-scoped problem to deal with, and less risk exposure to his reputation than Mouttet. Yet not only did Lemaire fail to order the evacuation of Morne Rouge in the face of an escalating eruption, but he actually forced people to return to the high-risk zone where they would meet their deaths! If anyone in Martinique had blood on his hands in 1902, it was Jean-Baptiste Lemaire.

• • •

When the dead were buried and the survivors began moving to the new settlements in the south, the vicar-general deconsecrated the church of Notre Dame de la Délivrande. During the following year that Morne Rouge lay deserted, the church was looted and vandalized along with what little else had survived the disaster. As the residents began to dribble back in the fall of 1903, however, one of the first orders of business was to repair and reconsecrate the church. In 1912, the original tower clock was repaired and reinstalled. The place of worship has since eluded most of the trappings of modernization, and today it stands essentially unchanged from the way it appeared when Father Mary was struck down outside its entrance in the nuées ardentes of August 30, 1902.

Mont Pelée continued to erupt for a year after the disasters, and the last intermittent activity did not cease until early 1904. Meanwhile, both Angelo Heilprin and Alfred Lacroix returned to Martinique to conduct further studies. They each witnessed and photographed additional pyroclastic surges and documented a strange new phenomenon: the growth of a giant obelisk from the crater floor of L'Etang Sec.

This "Tower of Pelée," a huge plug of solidified lava squeezed from the volcanic vent by massive subterranean pressures, had a diameter of 350 to 500 feet and grew nearly 1,000 feet between the beginning of September and mid-October of 1902. The material was easily fractured, however, and each new tremor or detonation broke giant chunks off the top that plummeted to the ground and shattered. For over a year, this megalith monster grew faster than it collapsed, and by May 31, 1903, its main trunk towered some 980 feet above the floor of the crater with a narrower spine protruding 900 feet higher. On that date, an eruption knocked 180 feet off the top. The volcanic activity escalated again in August of that year, accompanied by giant ash clouds, and on August 31, the significantly shortened obelisk grew a remarkable 78 feet in one day. From that date on, however, the Tower of Pelée grew only in girth as it shrank in height. Another eruption in 1929 obliterated all remnants of this curious geologic feature.

Alfred Lacroix published a book about his investigations in Martinique and devoted most of the rest of his career to studying volcanoes. In 1906 he led an investigation of that year's eruption of Vesuvius in Italy, and by drawing parallels to the 1902–1903 eruptions of Pelée he interested scientists worldwide in further exploring the mechanisms of both nuées ardentes and the phenomenon of what he termed "mud torrents" (lahars). He was appointed perpetual secretary of the French Académie des Sciences in 1920. When he grew too old for the physical rigors of field investigations, he took up writing biographies of notable scientists. He survived the upheavals of World War II and died in Paris on March 12, 1948, at the age of eighty-five. A sidestreet in today's St. Pierre, one that leads to the old cemetery, is named after him: Rue Alfred Lacroix.

Angelo Heilprin wrote several articles and three books about his investigations in Martinique. In 1906, while on an expedition exploring the Orinoco River in Venezuela, he contracted an undiagnosable tropical disease. He returned to Philadelphia but never fully recovered. The following year, at the age of fifty-four, the explorer, geologist, and alpine climber died of a heart complication. His last book, a beautifully illustrated large-format volume about the Tower of Pelée, was published posthumously in 1908.

George Kennan returned to Washington, D.C., wrote a book and several articles on his Martinique adventure, then went back to his main passion of writing and lecturing about Russia. Around 1915 he became fascinated with the engineering and political challenges of bringing water from the Colorado River to the Los Angeles basin, and in 1917 he published a widely acclaimed book titled *Salton Sea: An Account of Harriman's Fight with the Colorado River*. In 1920, he and his wife, Lena, moved to her ancestral home in Medina, New York. There, on May 8, 1924, while writing an article on Japanese education, George Kennan suffered a stroke. He died two days later at the age of seventy-nine.

Despite his fame, Kennan never achieved much financial success. Lena, his dedicated wife of forty-five years, was forced to sell off his personal effects, including the various souvenirs he had gathered in a lifetime of travels and adventures around the globe. His nephew and namesake, George F. Kennan, embraced the elder Kennan's interest in Russia; he served in various diplomatic posts, including ambassador to the Soviet Union and later to Yugoslavia. As a professor at the Institute for Advanced Study in Princeton, New Jersey, he wrote numerous influential books and articles on diplomatic policy. Today, the George Kennan Institute in Washington perpetuates the intellectual legacies of George Kennan "the elder" and his nephew George F. Kennan.

For Fernand Clerc and his family, a year away from their beloved island was long enough. Considerably reduced in financial circumstances, they returned to their plantation at Vivé and began the painstaking task of returning it to full productivity. After the scare of another eruption in 1929, Clerc began a mission to ensure that future generations would never forget the lessons of the great disaster of 1902. With the help of several friends, he approached the Carnegie Institution and a number of American philanthropists for donations to establish a small museum in St. Pierre: the Musée Volcanologique, which was dedicated in 1933. Fernand Clerc died in Redoute in 1939, at the age of eighty-three. His descendants still own and operate the plantation at Vivé.

• • •

If the complete story of Augusté Ciparis (also known as Sylbaris) is ever successfully reconstructed, it is unlikely to reflect positively on the management of the Barnum and Bailey Circus. The circus's business agents seduced St. Pierre's "sole survivor" into immigrating to the United States in March of 1903, gave him a hundred-dollar bill at Ellis Island to affirm to the authorities that he was not indigent, then whisked him off to become a sideshow attraction. It may never be known exactly what he had been promised or what he expected. He was ignorant of the language, the customs, and the climate of this new land. Accustomed to working out-of-doors in a tropical paradise, he now traveled in a crowded train car from one dingy American city to another, earning his keep by displaying his scarred body to crowds of working-class Americans he couldn't communicate with. He had no friends and no way to make any. Even the few French-speaking Americans who paid to see him could not understand his Creole dialect. And to him, the American brand of racism was something new and bewildering.

His arrival was greeted with publicity in newspapers across the country. Most of the stories got various details wrong, and even his name appeared in at least a dozen forms. The *Press* of Columbus, Ohio, for instance, ran the following story on March 20, 1903:

ST. PIERRE'S SOLE SURVIVOR

Joseph Sibarace Was Buried Four Days in Prison — Was Dug Out by a Priest—Will Travel With a Circus.

NEW YORK, March 20.—A terribly scarred and health-broken mulatto, who gives his name as Joseph Sibarace, and claiming to be the sole survivor of the awful Martinique earthquake [*sic*] last May, has arrived in this city. He came from St. Pierre, the city that was laid low by the terrible eruptions of Mont Pelee. His face is streaked with deep white marks, the scars of scoriae and lava, under which he was buried on the fatal day.

Sibarace says he was a prisoner in a dungeon, having been confined there for stabbing a friend with whom he had quarreled, and it was to his imprisonment that he owes his life. He was confined in a dark cell, two terraces below ground. [This was true only if one takes the floor of the theater to define the ground level; to the north, in the direction of the volcano, the ground was, and still is, at the same level as the cell.]

He describes the disaster and his escape as follows:

"I heard the explosion and thought it was thunder. All at once my cell began to grow hot, and fine ashes began to sift between the bars and through the narrow chinks of the ceiling. The air was oppressive and the heat increased, and some of the hot ashes that came into my cell set fire to the straw on which I slept. I stamped it out. I heard the cries of the suffering and terror-stricken people above my head. I heard the hurried tramp of many feet and finally all was still. No more ashes sifted in, no more of those dreadful thunder-like noises. I knew not what happened. As time went on I grew hungry and suffered so from the heat that I became unconscious. I slept.

"The next I knew I found the father confessor of the prison bending over me. He told me what had happened. I found that I had been buried for four days and nights and never would have escaped had not the good father, who was my only friend in prison, remembered after the eruption that I must still be there, so he came and dug me out."

A representative of Barnum and Bailey's circus visited Ellis island, whither Sibarace had been removed, and to prevent his being sent back to Martinique, the show man bought him clothes and gave him a $100 bill. Sibarace was then allowed to land, inasmuch as this money would keep him from becoming a public charge. He will be exhibited with the show the coming season. He is 27 years old and was a carpenter before the disaster.

Most of this story, of course, is a concoction.

Matters quickly took a turn for the worse for Ciparis. From the *Argus*, Albany, New York, June 5, 1903, we find a preposterously dehumanizing article that says much more than its words alone:

ST. PIERRE SURVIVOR AGAIN IN PRISON

ONE OF THE ATTRACTIONS OF BARNUM & BAILEY'S BIG SHOW ARRESTED.

STABBED THE NIGHT WATCHMAN

Had Been on Toot After Receiving his Pay—
Bound by Circus Employees and Taken to Court—
Were Afraid of Him.

There was one advertised feature of the big Barnum & Bailey show which those who filled the big tent failed to see. The reason for this absence from the show was because he was in the custody of Chief Hyatt's men, and under lock and key. Ludger Morell [*sic*], the sole survivor of St. Pierre, Martinique, caused an unusual commotion among the circus employees when the early sun was struggling with the smoke charged atmosphere yesterday morning. Morell became ugly and stabbed David A. Cole, a circus attache, whose home is in Baltimore, Md. Cole was a night watchman employed by the circus management and was trying to subdue the terrible remnant of the frightful disaster of St. Pierre, when he was struck in the groin. Cole is in St. Peter's hospital seriously wounded and the only man who escaped the fire of Mt. Pelee is detained in a cell at the jail.

Morell is tall and very ugly. He was paid off on Wednesday and immediately started out to fill up with fire water. Every attache of the circus knew there was trouble ahead, and when Morell returned full to the ears, he was given a wide berth. About 4 o'clock yesterday morning the terrible remnant of the terrible blasts of lava was at his worst and he started to clean out the North End. Cole was the first man to cross his path and after a wrangle, Morell stuck a knife into his friend and ran away. Cole was so badly wounded that he could not walk and had to creep into the menagerie tent where he told his fellow workmen of the crime. Then came one grand, great chorus from among the tall man and the short lady, the human-faced horse and the snake charmer, and all others therein, who yelled in unison, "Let's kill that nigger!"

No more words were spoken. The whole bunch of freaks and canvas men, pole haulers and drivers, started after the surviving remnant. He was found, but defied the attacking party to make good its purpose. Mr. Bailey arrived on the scene at this moment and urged the indignant circus hands to let Morell live long enough to be arrested. The circus hands said they had had enough of the black animal-faced gentleman; he was as vicious as he looked, they said, and all thought it was about time that he should go to glory.

Mr. Bailey persuaded the men to be calm and simply subdue the only survivor. The animal-faced gentleman grew stubborn again and drew out a knife, but this was useless for the crowd quickly downed him and everybody, from the tall man and the fat lady, the human-faced horse and the snake charmer, sat down on the vicious black man, while some of the husky guys of the canvas brigade tied a few hundred yards of rope about his limbs. Then a call was sent for an officer and within an hour the patrol wagon went dashing along, with two policemen in it. When they saw what they were up against the policemen shivered. Morell was lifted into the wagon as powerless as a corpse, and while he growled and bit and struggled for freedom, he was taken to Police Court.

The rope tied by the circus men was still securely fastened to his legs and arms, and he was dropped squarely on the floor. The animal-faced gentleman was by this time screaming with rage. His black skin, which in many parts had been burned to a pale white, was as brilliant as a new ten-cent shine.

When Judge Brady came into court he was shocked to see the animal-faced gentleman in such a position. The court said it was not strange that a vicious man should be put in bounds, but he did not think it was necessary for the police to bring him into Police Court in that condition and throw him upon the floor. The eyes in the ugly-shaped head of the animal-faced gentleman bulged out and he

growled at the court. Judge Brady had the officers carry the only survivor down stairs to a cell in the Second precinct station house, where
he slept until 3 o'clock in the afternoon.

Captain Brennan then had a platoon of police escort the animal-
faced gentleman to court. The ropes had been removed and Morell
was sober. Louis Dube was called as an interpreter, as the animal-
faced gentleman speaks only French.

The charge was explained to the only survivor in his native tongue
and he shook his head. He denied cutting Cole; he said nobody was
cut and that he had not been in any trouble. He grew excited during
the arraignment and Captain Brennan and the court officers gathered
about in readiness for another outbreak.

Charles Andress, the legal representative of the show, and the assistant treasurer, were in court. The latter said he witnessed the cutting and would prefer the charge in the absence of the victim. The
treasurer gave Clerk Reilly the facts for the complaint and when the
warrant was drawn up, Reilly said: "I've done many things here, but
never thought I would be making out a warrant for the only survivor
of the Martinique disaster."

The circus men told Judge Brady that they were willing to prose-
cute the animal-faced gentleman. Mr. Andress told of his discovery
in a dungeon, near where the lava flowed greatest. The black man had
been sent to prison for a grave charge, probably murder, and while he
was looked upon as the most desperate native, he was the only one
to escape the terrible disaster. "We brought him to New York," said
Mr. Andress, "and there spent money on him, had physicians attend
him and saved him from dying. We clothed and took good care of
the fellow, but he has always proved an ingrate and even officials of
the show are afraid of him. We don't want to bother with him any
more. We fear he will attack a member of the show some time and all
the other hands will get at the nigger and kill him. And you know, we
don't want any such crime to lay at our doors."

Judge Brady accepted a plea of not guilty from Morell and committed him to jail. Policeman McGraw handcuffed him, while several other "brave and fearless" officers walked cautiously in the rear,
while McGraw and the animal-faced gentleman went to jail.

That same day (June 5, 1903), the *Argus*'s rival, the *Press Knickerbocker*, ran its own version of the story of Ciparis's arrest:

SURVIVOR OF MARTINIQUE

IS IN THE ALBANY JAIL CHARGED WITH STABBING A FELLOW EMPLOYEE OF THE BARNUM & BAILEY CIRCUS— IS THE GENUINE ARTICLE AND A VERY BAD MAN, ACCORDING TO REPORTS.

The sole survivor of the city [*sic*] of Martinique, which was destroyed with its 30,000 inhabitants by the eruption of Mont Pelee in the spring of 1902, is in the local jail awaiting examination before Judge Brady on the charge of assault in the second degree. He is a negro and speaks French fluently, but what his name is, is not known definitely. As far as the Barnum & Bailey circus authorities know it is Ludgar Symbaris. When Judge Brady asked his name through an interpreter he shrugged his shoulders and twisted his horrible features into a grin and refused the information. Ludgar ran amuck on the circus grounds yesterday morning and, according to several employes of the circus, drew a long knife and stabbed David H. Cole, a watchman, in the groin. The fiery negro was captured and taken to the Second Precinct station and locked up.

Is the Real Thing.

As to the identity of the negro as the survivor of the terrible disaster which wiped out the city of Martinique [*sic*] there is not the slightest question. Directly after the catastrophe the man's picture was published in about every newspaper in the country. When he was led into the police court yesterday afternoon everyone present immediately recognized his features which are of a character not soon to be forgotten. It will be remembered that the negro was found in an underground dungeon where he had been confined for some serious crime. He was badly burned, especially about the feet and hands, but the managers of Barnum & Bailey's circus got hold of him, brought him to New York and had him treated in a hospital until he was entirely well. Since that date he has been one of the drawing cards of the show.

Say He is a Bad Man.

But according to the story of W. F. Bohrer, assistant treasurer, and Chas. Andress, the legal adjuster of the circus, Ludgar has always been intractable and has given them so much trouble by his criminal outbreaks that they will have to part with him. Mr. Andress said yesterday that it was learned that he was confined in the Martinique dungeon for murder and that he has cut several people since being liberated by the disaster. He likes North American fire water and drinks all he can get hold of. When under the influence of drink he is a fiend and is liable to attack anyone.

Bound Hand and Foot.

The little unpleasantness of yesterday morning came about suddenly. After Ludgar had stabbed the watchman he was set upon by a number of employes who would have killed him but for the interference of Mr. Bailey, one of the proprietors of the circus. He told them to capture him and they did. He was bound hand and foot with about 40 yards of rope, loaded on to a wagon and taken to Judge Brady's police court. This was very early in the morning. When the judge arrived he found the negro lying on the floor of the court room with the ropes upon him. The judge sternly ordered the ropes removed, which was done. The negro was exhausted and he was taken to the Second Precinct and cared for by the officers.

Arraigned in Court.

At 4:30 o'clock in the afternoon the negro was formally arraigned before Judge Brady on the charge of assault in the second degree. Through an interpreter Ludgar declared that he was innocent of any crime. When told specifically that he was charged with stabbing Cole yesterday morning he laughed heartily, shrugged his shoulders and grinned and said that he had stabbed no one. Messrs. Bohrer and Andress were present as the complainants and said that as soon as Mr. Cole was able to leave the hospital he would appear against the accused. Ludgar exclaimed in voluble French that he would not go to jail and therefore leave the troupe, but, notwithstanding, he was led out of the court room by two officers and taken to the Maiden Lane jail where he will remain until Mr. Cole is able to appear against him.

At St. Peter's hospital last night, it was said that Cole was doing well and would be able to be out again in about ten days.

The records of what happened next have been lost. Some said that Ciparis went back to work for the circus until he died in 1929, when (according to his reconstructed birth certificate) he would have been fifty-five. The circus archives, however, do not confirm this; in fact, Barnum and Bailey seems to have stopped publicizing the "sole survivor" as an attraction after the 1903 season. It is clear that Augusté Ciparis was never respected for himself, but only for his legend. When he did not conform to the stereotype of what Americans expected of a hero, he was abandoned and the truth was left to wither.

No doubt, Ciparis himself unwittingly contributed to the incongruity. Alone in a strange land, it probably never occurred to him to correct those who got his name wrong (as almost everyone did). Nor did he have any reason to correct the escalating exaggerations and decreasing veracity of the account of his survival; after all, his circus job depended on the uniqueness of his story. Being illiterate, he did not know what was being written; lacking any knowledge of the English language, he could not even respond to what people around him were saying. Perhaps, as time went on, truth and fiction became hopelessly confused in his own mind.

Today, in the homeland to which he never returned, his name survives on the tram "Ciparis Express," which carries organized tour groups through St. Pierre on a circuit of some of the artifacts of the disaster of 1902. The cell that both saved and damned him still stands intact in the ruins of the old prison.

• • •

Approximately five hundred people were living in the ruins of St. Pierre in 1910, and by 1915 the number had swollen to two thousand. In 1923, St. Pierre again became a municipality, and in 1923–1924 the cathedral was rebuilt (although the resulting edifice bears only a distant resemblance to the original structure). By 1927, the city boasted a population of 3,250—some 12 percent of its census at the time of the disaster.

Why would so many people move into such a place? Clearly, those of financial means would not. But for the poor and indigent, the ruined city offered a number of attractions: cheap (or even free) real estate, plenty of cut building stone, foundations already in place, paved streets already laid out, plentiful sources of running water, and direct access to the sea. Most of the new buildings that were erected along St. Pierre's main thorough-fares closely resembled the stout original structures (indeed, they were constructed of the very same stones). On the outskirts of town, squatters perched less substantial homes on the old foundations. Yet even with the influx and reconstruction, ruined structures still outnumbered those that were rebuilt. As the rest of Martinique marched into the twentieth cen-tury, St. Pierre dallied behind.

Then, on September 16, 1929, Mont Pelée erupted once more. This time there were no arguments or deliberations; St. Pierre and Precheur were immediately vacated. For the next three years, eruption clouds peri-odically shadowed the northern end of the island, and numerous nuées ardentes burst down the volcano's southwestern slopes. None of these pyroclastic surges, however, were as violent as the great explosions of May 8, May 20, or August 30, 1902, and none entered the towns.

As with the previous eruption, this one also ended with the growth of a plug, or "lava dome." A collection of obelisks grew from this formation, the tallest reaching a height of 150 feet. As these lava spines crumbled in late 1932, the scientists observing the phenomenon correctly declared the activity to be over, and the residents returned.

Today's permanent population of St. Pierre stands at 4,413, down slightly from its peak of 5,007 a decade ago. Although many, if not most, of the dwellings have now been rebuilt, some of the grandest parts of old St. Pierre remain in ruin. The lighthouse is gone, and the only evidence of the commercial warehouses is their foundations and lower walls. There are virtually no overnight accommodations for travelers, and only a few restaurants. But the Place Bertin, the square on the waterfront, is now un-dergoing reconstruction, and a subscription is under way to build a replica of the once-elegant theater at its original location. And of course the most magnificent sight of all still remains, visible from virtually everywhere in town: Mont Pelée.

Meanwhile, high on a piton near Fonds St.-Denis, and commanding a majestic view of both St. Pierre and the volcano that once destroyed it, stands a modern volcanological observatory. When Mont Pelée stirs again, as it almost certainly will, the scientists there will be paying close attention.

• NOTES •

Chapter 1. Ashes from the Sky

Engineer Anderson's journal entries are from Morris (1902a, 72–75); this is also one of several books that describe the condition of the steamer *Roddam* when it made port at Castries. Miller (1902, 251–255) also includes Anderson's account.

Roosevelt's letter to Congress is in White (1902, 75–76).

The biographical information on George Kennan is from Travis (1990) and the Kennan Institute in Washington, D.C.; a grandniece, Joan Kennan, kindly supplied some additional biographical background in a personal correspondence. George Kennan relates the story of his invitation and his trip to Martinique in his 1902 book *The Tragedy of Pelée*. White (1902) and Hill (1902) give additional details about the preparations and voyage of the *Dixie*.

The information on Lacroix is from standard biographical reference sources; no comprehensive biography has been written on him. Heilprin describes his own experiences in Martinique in his 1902 article and his books (1903 and 1908). Lacroix discusses his expedition in his book (1908), and additional details of his investigation are given by Ursulet (1997).

The sponsorship of the expedition by the National Geographic Society was announced in an editorial in the society's magazine in the June 1902 issue.

Chapter 2. Islands in the Sun

I drew the background on Heilprin from the biography of his father and from Levy's 1907 memorial address before the Franklin Institute.

The "Black Sunday" passage is from Kingsley (1871). The elevations of the volcanoes of the Lesser Antilles are as given by Reclus (1873) and represent what a 1902 reader would be likely to find; present values differ slightly. The conclusion that most of the volcanoes' volumes are underwater follows from the mathematical reasoning that if a geometrically perfect cone has half its height submerged, then only one-eighth of its volume protrudes above the surface.

The geophysical information and death toll of the Krakatau disaster are from Verbeek (1884), as reported by Simkin and Fiske (1983, 219, 235).

Verbeek's detailed calculations give 18.156 cubic kilometers of ejecta. Mrs. Beyerincks's story appeared in several Javanese newspapers, then made its way into other publications; her complete first-person account is in Simkin and Fiske (1983, 81–85). Captain W. J. Watson's story is from his 1883 article.

Chapter 3. Public Servant

I drew the biographical material on Louis Mouttet mainly from Ursulet (1997), Scarth (1999), and Thomas and Witts (1969).

The history of the island is distilled from a variety of works listed in the "Sources" section; the structure of government is based on Hill (1902) and Garesché (1902), the U.S. consul to Martinique prior to Consul Thomas Prentiss, who died in the catastrophe. Incredibly, Garesché's publisher dates the preface to his book "May 14th, 1902," a mere six days after the disaster.

Census data were not consistent across all sources, and the figures I quote combine those that in my judgment seem most credible; most were taken from Hill, Garesché, and/or Morris (all 1902).

The quotation from Hearn appeared in his 1887 book and was reprinted in numerous other publications, including Morris (1902a, 40–42).

Chapter 4. Tarnished Silver

The English correspondent's comments on the egress problem are as reported by Morris (1902a, 46); to the extent that today's roads follow the same routes as those of 1902, I based some related descriptions on my own observations.

I assembled the early chronology of the eruption and the material on Gaston Landes piecemeal from Morris (1902b) and the other 1902 and 1903 works cited in the "Sources" section. Josse's letter in *Les Colonies,* April 26, 1902, is as translated in Heilprin (1903, 205–206). Romaine's ascent is from Hill (1902); Scarth (1999) describes Berté's ascent.

The election results are from Chrétien and Brousse (1988); these are essentially consistent with Hill's figures (1902) but are inconsistent with those of Thomas and Witts (1969).

Clara Prentiss's letter is from White (1902, 46–47).

Chapter 5. An Ominous Weekend

The text of Hurard's May 3 broadsheet is from Ursulet (1997); numerous other writers quote portions of it, particularly the last paragraph.

The letter from the young lady to her sister is one of several quoted in White (1902).

Mouttet's May 3 "escalation" telegram is in *Le Journal Officiel de la Martinique* (1902) and is reprinted in Chrétien and Brousse (1988, 39 and repeated on 100). The "an eruption" telegram and Philomene Gerbault's account are as given by Thomas and Witts (1969, 128–129 and 77–78, respectively).

Clara Prentiss's second letter to her sister is from Thomas and Witts (1969, 120–121). As I have not been able to corroborate this letter through other sources, it may not be entirely accurate; the reader should therefore consider it only as representative of the events and concerns of the parties on May 3 and 4. Indeed, it bears some curious similarities in wording to a letter quoted by Garesché (1902) and said to have been written by an unnamed woman to her brother in Marseilles on May 4:

> I write under the gloomiest of impressions, though I hope I exaggerate the situation. This unchaining of the forces of nature is horrible. Since last month I have wished myself far from this place. My husband laughs, but I see he is full of anxiety and is trying to show a brave face in order to raise my courage. He tells me to go. How can I go alone? Monsieur Guérin says the women and children should flee as from an epidemic, but that the men, especially those situated like my husband and himself, must stay, as otherwise it would cause a general panic. All this is very sad. The heat is suffocating. We cannot leave anything open, as the dust enters everywhere, burning our faces and eyes. I have not the fortitude to attend to the necessary household duties. Fortunately we have food, but we have no heart even to eat. All the crops are ruined. It is always thus in these accursed countries. When it is not a cyclone it is an earthquake, and when it is not a drought it is a volcanic eruption. (Garesché, 1902, 103–104)

Chapter 6. Lahar

For the early history of seismology, see Davison (1927).

Guérin's quotation is from Scarth (1999, 165–166); Du Quesne's is from Bullard (1962, 104). Father Roche's description is from Thomas and Witts (1969, 155).

There are discrepancies about Mouttet's use of the *Suchet;* Thomas and Witts claim that Commander Le Bris immediately refused the governor; others (e.g., Scarth, Ursulet) say that he cooperated the first time and feigned engine trouble only on the governor's second request. It seems most probable that Le Bris would have cooperated when he first arrived and had a full head of steam, then became less cooperative later when he had reason to believe that the situation was not so serious. In any case, Mouttet's trip to Precheur on the afternoon of May 5 seems well established, whether or not he took the *Suchet*.

Chapter 7. Kettle of Frogs

The passages from *The Voice of St. Lucia* are as given by White (1902, 38–39).

Several authors (e.g., Scarth) state that Mouttet chartered the *Topaze* for the trip to Precheur on the morning of May 6, but if the St. Lucia newspaper article is correct, that would put this particular boat in two places at one time. I have assumed that a writer on another island would not be likely to mix up two boats belonging to the same Martinique-based company, while a reporter on Martinique might easily do so; on this hypothesis, I have assumed that Mouttet was actually on the *Rubis* that morning.

The various telegrams in this chapter are as given by Thomas and Witts (1969, 178–181, 196). In the interest of clarity, I have taken the liberty of adding punctuation and some of the pronouns and prepositions that were customarily omitted from the dispatches in the interest of efficiency.

The story of the *Orsolina* and several roughly equivalent versions of that dialogue appear in Kennan (1902, 208–210), Morris (1902a, 173), and Thomas and Witts (1969, 109).

Chapter 8. La Soufrière

The May 7 disaster on St. Vincent is not as well documented as the Martinique event of May 8; most writers of the time were more interested in the circumstances that claimed more lives on the more prosperous island. Hovey (1902) and Reid (1902) are two authors who do focus on St. Vincent; they provide much of the material for this chapter. Meanwhile, virtually all contemporary books and articles on the St. Pierre catastrophe include at least some material about the St. Vincent disaster, and I have used these partial accounts to provide corroboration and in some cases additional details.

The characteristics of La Soufrière's crater lakes prior to the eruption are described by Kingsley (1871). Captain Calder's story is from Reid (1902, 635–638); because of space considerations I include only a small portion of that account and none of another interesting but lengthy eyewitness report by T. McGregor, owner of the Richmond Vale Estate, which was obliterated in the disaster. Hovey (1902) describes the volcanic bombs and lahars; Roobol and Smith (1976) give a more recent scientific analysis of the pyroclastic surge. The governor's report is from White (1902, 162). The eyewitness stories of Reverend Darrell, Mrs. Leslie, and Captain Lillienskjold are from Morris (1902a, 136–138, 132–134, and 81, respectively).

Background information on Kick 'em Jenny was drawn from Devine and Sigurdsson (1995) and the volcanic activity reports of the Smithsonian Institution's Global Volcanism Program.

Chapter 9. Final Edition

The translations of the articles from the May 7 issue of *Les Colonies* are as given by Heilprin (1902, 74–80). Portions of some of the same articles, substantially similar in translation, also appear in Morris (1902a) and Garesché (1902).

Some journalists reported that Mouttet took his children along on his last trip to St. Pierre and that the governor's entire family perished in the catastrophe. Miller (1902, 59), however, reports the text of a telegram sent from L'Heurre to the minister of colonies in Paris after the disaster, which states in part: "The three children of Governor Mouttet will sail on the mail steamer on June 1 for France. They will be accompanied by M. Miller, Governor Mouttet's chief in the Cabinet." My account reflects my judgment that Miller's sources were accurate.

Although Chrétien and Brousse (1988) state that Mouttet created his Scientific Commission in Fort-de-France at 10 a.m. on May 7, it seems unlikely that the members were first notified of their appointments on the same day they met in St. Pierre. A May 7 date of establishment is also inconsistent with the reference to a "Governor's Commission" in a letter Clara Prentiss apparently wrote on May 4, and which I have included in chapter 5. It would seem that the governor actually established his commission on or before May 4 but did not create the formal record until 10 a.m. on the seventh, when he was planning to move temporarily to St. Pierre and leave the reins of government in Fort-de-France in the hands of the secretary-general. The likely purpose of the document of 10 a.m. on the seventh was to legitimize any subsequent reports of the commission that Mouttet might telegraph to Fort-de-France, and which could later make their way to the Ministry of Colonies in Paris. There seems to be no disagreement among the sources that Mouttet indeed presided over a meeting of his Scientific Commission in St. Pierre beginning shortly after 5 p.m. on May 7. Chrétien and Brousse (1988, 58) give the full text of the commission's report, as telegraphed to Fort-de-France the following morning. I include a translation of this text in chapter 10.

It is clear that the commission members were all knowledgeable in their respective disciplines, and that each of their areas of expertise had some bearing on the evacuation issue. Yet numerous authors, including Heilprin (1902) have expressed surprise that a man of Landes's scientific background would have allowed himself to be a party to this commission's report. White (1902, 55) says that Landes indeed tried to warn the governor of the danger. My conjectured dialogue of the commission's meeting is an attempt to show how Landes's evacuation recommendation might have been rejected without malice.

Chapter 10. Whirlwind of Fire

Chrétien and Brousse (1988, 58) give the French text of Mouttet's last telegram and the times of transmission; I take responsibility for the translation I give here. The departure of the governor's boat was described by survivors of the *Gabrielle* as reported by Morris (1902b).

Fernand Clerc's observation of the fluctuating barometer and the claim that this saved his life are described by Hill (1902), Miller (1902, 246), and Morris (1902b, 94–95). Quotes attributed to Fernand and Véronique Clerc, Roger Arnoux, Captain Thirion, and Father Mary are as reported by Thomas and Witts (1969, 271–274). The account of Monsieur Albert is from White (1902, 62–63); Garesché (1902, 50–52) gives a virtually identical version. The account of Comte de Fitz-James is from Morris (1902a, 154–161). The last words of Gaston Landes are from Scarth (1999, 178).

Another statement attributed to Roger Arnoux, of the French Astronomical Society, claims that he saw the explosion travel some "eight kilometers" in "not more than three seconds." If so, its speed would have had to be some eight times the speed of sound (331 meters per second). This is physically impossible and underscores the danger of taking any single eyewitness account or its translation too literally. After such physically impossible "observations" are weeded out, however, the remaining picture of the disaster is substantially consistent. The actual speed of the pyroclastic surge was apparently around 120 miles per hour.

Chapter 11. Death in the Bay

No one seems to have compiled a definitive roster of the ships sunk in the disaster, and the literature is even inconsistent about the spellings of some of the ship's names. The seventeen vessels I have listed here were drawn from several sources, including Kennan (1902), Scarth (1999), Garesché (1902), Fine (1987), and Royce (1902). Adding the governor's steam launch brings the number of ships lost to eighteen. This figure does not include small boats and lighters that probably numbered in the hundreds.

The temperature of the nuée ardente can be established only indirectly. Bullard (1962) estimates that the cloud emerged from the volcanic vent at a temperature of 1,200°C (2,200°F) but had cooled to less than 700°C (1,300°F) when it entered St. Pierre. Branney and Zalasiewicz (1999) give a similar estimate. Because a pyroclastic surge is not in a state of thermodynamic equilibrium, however, its temperature varies considerably from place to place, and such calculations can provide no more than rough averages.

Engineer Prudent's comments are from Garesché (1902, 207). The firsthand stories of Thompson and Evans are from Morris (1902b, 55–57). The account of Mate Ellery Scott is also from Morris (1902b, 76–79); this is one of Scott's shorter versions of his story. The nurse's account appears in Bullard (1962, 107–108); her shorter earlier comments appear in Morse (1902b, 60–61). The report of Captain Freeman is from Morris (1902b, 62–66); his further account is from Thomas and Witts (1969, 281–282).

Chapter 12. Close Encounters

The excerpts from Vicar-General Parel's chronicle and the report of the *procureur* are from Heilprin (1903, 92–95 and 112–115).

The May 8 telegram from the *Suchet* is as quoted by Scarth (1999, 183); the telegram of the acting governor is from Thomas and Witts (1969, 276).

The story of Edouard Lasserre is from Scarth (1999, 172); the same author includes a second independent but similar story about a man named Lasserne and an unnamed friend (178). Morris (1902b, 96) also tells an essentially similar story about Monsieur Lasserne. Kennan (1902, 84) relates an interview with a burn victim in a hospital named Lassère, who with his friend Simonut had a very similar experience in the same area. I return to George Kennan's discovery of these men's ruined carriage in chapter 15.

The account of Léon Compère-Léandre was first published in the *Bulletin of the Société Astronomique de France* (August 1902, 352); the version I quote here is Angelo Heilprin's translation (1903, 119–120).

The brief survivals of Mademoiselles Fillotte and Madame Laurent are mentioned by Miller (1902, 164–165), Morris (1902a, 89), and Garesché (1902, 149), but no details are given other than the ones I mention. Other anecdotal survival stories have appeared in various forms in a wide variety of publications; while I can make no claims regarding the individual authenticity of the ones I have included here, taken as a whole they seem to paint an accurate picture of the capriciousness of the phenomenon with regard to human life. For other recent distillations of such survival stories, see Scarth (1999) and Ursulet (1997).

Chapter 13. Front Pages

Articles quoted are from the *Chicago Daily News* (May 9 and 10, 1902) and from the May 10, 1902, editions of the *Chicago Daily Tribune,* the *San Francisco Chronicle,* and the *New York Tribune.* These stories are substantially similar to reports that appeared in most other major dailies in the United States on those dates. The Port Royal error can be found repeated in Thomas and Witts's 1969 book.

Chapter 14. After the End

My account of Precheur's evacuation was assembled from a dozen of the listed bibliographic sources; the result is substantially the same as that of Scarth (1999). (Scarth, for instance, identifies the assisting Danish ship as the *Walkyrien;* Miller [1902, 57] gives it as the *Valkyrien.*) Miller comments that the French bank transferred its funds and books to the *Suchet* before the disaster. This is obviously not true, but the fact that it was reported is easily understood as an attempt to reassure French businessmen.

Rosenberg's account is from Miller (1902, 323–325). The excerpts from Captain Cantrell's log are from Morris (1902a, 69–70).

The Musée Volcanologique Franck-Perret in today's town of St. Pierre refers to the "sole survivor" as Augusté Cyparis. The name Sylbaris appears on a reconstructed birth certificate signed by the governor of Martinique on January 13, 1903; this spelling also appears on his U.S. immigration documents and on the Barnum and Bailey Circus posters. The birth certificate states that he was born in Precheur in 1874, son of Augusta Doreur and Eucher Sylbaris. The story of the debt-related argument is from an article in *Realm* (Boston, June 8, 1903, 11–14). The account of Ciparis's escape to the festival and his subsequent solitary confinement is from Scarth (1999, 176). Thomas and Witts (1969, 248) relate the story that Ciparis was a murderer awaiting execution but was reprieved. Miller (1902, 235–237) gives the story that the prisoner actually requested to spend the night in the "dungeon," but this is in many ways a very confused account, in which the prisoner's name is "Monat." Ciparis's apocryphal eyewitness account of the deaths of the nuns is from Garesché (1902, 48–50); the book's editor includes George Varian's charcoal portrait of Ciparis and describes it erroneously as a "photograph of Raoul Sarteret, alias Peleno" (219).

The reports of the two journalists from the *New York Herald* are as reported by Morris (1902a, 177–183). The pyroclastic surge of May 20 is described in numerous sources. I drew most of the details of the recovery of Consul Prentiss's body from Morris (1902b, 101–104).

Chapter 15. The Other Side of the Mountain

Most of this chapter is based on Kennan's 1902 book about his experiences in Martinique. I added a few details about the geography based on my own visits to the sites. Although most of the roads are now paved, today's traveler finds them just as steep and winding as Kennan described them nearly a century ago.

Chapter 16. The Cauldrons of Hell

The accounts and conversations are from Kennan (1902). Although Professor Hill wrote and lectured extensively about the eruptions, the fact that he had never actually gotten within miles of the volcano led me to bypass his descriptions in favor of Kennan's.

Chapter 17. Mouth of the Dragon

Most of this chapter is based on Kennan's 1902 book; the quoted passages are on pp. 156–157 and 179–180. The remainder was drawn from Heilprin (1902). Kennan and Heilprin give substantially consistent accounts of the same events.

Chapter 18. Lessons Unlearned

Alfred Lacroix's publications are primarily technical and say little about his personal experiences during his investigations. What I include about him is drawn from his 1908 book and from Scarth (1999), and/or is inferred from the photographs taken and documented by Lacroix's expedition team. The explanation for the starburst detonations in the gaseous emissions is suggested in several early sources, including Hill (1902).

The eruption of August 30 and the destruction of Morne Rouge are described in most books on the disaster dated 1903 or later; my main sources on this event were Heilprin (1903 and 1908) and Chrétien and Brousse (1988). There is a discrepancy about the time of the August 30 disaster; many recent sources place it in the morning; Heilprin (who was there at the time) places it in the evening. The evening version appears to be correct, as it is consistent with the rest of Heilprin's detailed account of the days surrounding the event. Scarth (1999) discusses the eventual evacuation of the northern region and its politics.

Epilogue

Many authors, including Thomas and Witts (1969), Bullard (1962), Thomas (1961), and virtually every source one finds on the Internet, either trivialize Mouttet's dilemma or else ridicule him personally for his allegedly misplaced priorities. I do not, however, claim to be the first writer to be sympathetic to Mouttet; Scarth (1999) and Ursulet (1997) are two others who suggest that he was as much a victim of circumstances as the other casualties of the disaster.

Sources differ on the maximum height of Pelée's lava dome, or "Tower of Pelée." Chrétien and Brousse give 850 meters (2,800 feet) above the crater floor, but most other sources give lower values. The figures I quote are from Scarth (1999). Information on the 1929 eruption was drawn from Bullard (1962). Other details are based on my personal observations.

Anderson, T., and J. S. Flett. (1903). "Report on the Eruption of the Soufrière in St. Vincent, in 1902, and on a Visit to Montagne Pelée in Martinique." *Philosophical Transactions of the Royal Society of London*, part 1, ser. A200, 353–553.

Aspinall, W. P., H. Sigurdsson, and J. B. Shepherd. (1973). "Eruption of Soufrière Volcano on St. Vincent Island, 1971–1972." *Science* 181 (July), 117–124.

Ball, Sir Robert. (1902). "The Eruption of Krakatoa." *National Geographic* 13 (June), 200–208.

Billings, L. G. (1915). "Some Personal Experiences with Earthquakes." *National Geographic* 27 (January), 57–71.

Branney, M., and J. Zalasiewicz. (1999). "Burning Clouds." *New Scientist* (July 17), 36–41.

Brazier, S., A. N. Davis, H. Sugurdsson, and R.S.J. Sparks. (1982). "Fall-out and Deposition of Volcanic Ash during the 1979 Explosive Eruption of the Soufrière of St. Vincent." *Journal of Volcanology and Geothermal Research* 14, 335–359.

Bullard, Fred M. (1962). *Vocanoes in History, in Theory, in Eruption*. Austin: University of Texas Press.

Carey, S., H. Sigurdsson, C. Mandeville, and S. Bronto. (1996). "Pyroclastic Flows and Surges over Water: An Example from the 1883 Krakatau Eruption." *Bulletin of Volcanology* 57, 493–511.

Chrétien, Simone, and Robert Brousse. (1988). *La Montagne Pelée se réveille*. Paris: Societé Nouvelle des Editions Boubée.

———. (1989). "Events Preceding the Great Eruption on Martinique." *Journal of Volcanology and Geothermal Research* 38, 67–75.

Clark, T. F., B. J. Korgen, and D. M. Best. (1978). "Heat Flow in the Eastern Caribbean." *Journal of Geophysical Research* 83 (December 10), 5883–5891.

Daney, C. (No date). *Catastrophe à la Martinique*. Martinique: Duquesnois Communication.

Davison, C. (1927). *The Founders of Seismology*. Cambridge: Cambridge University Press.

Devine, J. D., and H. Sigurdsson. (1995). "Petrology and Eruption Styles of Kick 'em Jenny Submarine Volcano, Lesser Antilles Arc." *Journal of Volcanology and Geothermal Research* 69, 35–58.

Editor. (1902a). "The National Geographic Society Expedition to Martinique and St. Vincent." *National Geographic* 13 (June), 183–184.

Editor. (1902b). "The National Geographic Society Expedition in the West Indies." *National Geographic* 13 (July), 209–213.

Editor. (1902c). "Sole Survivor of St. Pierre." *Realm* (Boston) (June 8), 10–13.

Fine, J. C. (1987). "Saint-Pierre Bay: Mont Pelée's Underwater Graveyard." *Sea Frontiers* (July–August), 288–295.

Fisher, R. V., and G. Heiken. (1982). "Mt. Pelée, Martinique: May 8 and 20, 1902, Pyroclastic Flows and Surges." *Journal of Volcanology and Geothermal Research* 13, 339–371.

Fisher, R. V., A. L. Smith, and M. J. Roobol. (1980). "Destruction of St. Pierre, Martinique, by Ash-Cloud Surges, May 8 and 20, 1902." *Geology* 8 (October), 472–476.

Freeman, E. W. (1902). "The Awful Doom of St. Pierre." *Pearson's Magazine* 14 (September), 313–325.

Garesché, Hon. William A. (1902). *Complete Story of the Martinique and St. Vincent Horrors*. N.p.: L. G. Stahl.

Hearn, L. (1887). *Two Years in the French West Indies*. New York: Harper and Brothers.

Heiken, G., B. Crowe, T. McGetchin, et al. (1980). "Phreatic Eruption Clouds: The Activity of La Soufrière de Guadeloupe, F.W.I., August-October, 1976." *Bulletin Volcanologique* 43, no. 2, 383–395.

Heilprin, Angelo. (1896). *The Earth and Its Story*. Boston: Silver, Burdett.

———. (1902). "Mont Pelée in Its Might: A Scientific Study of the Volcano's Activity from Data Gathered at the Crater's Mouth." *McClure's* (October), 359–368.

———. (1903). *Mont Pelée and the Tragedy of Martinique: A Study of the Great Catastrophes of 1902, with Observations and Experiences in the Field*. Philadelphia: J. B. Lippincott.

———. (1906). "The Shattered Obelisk of Mont Pelée." *National Geographic* 17 (August), 465–474.

———. (1908). *The Eruption of Pelée: A Summary and Discussion of the Phenomena and Their Sequels*. Philadelphia: Geographical Society of Philadelphia and J. B. Lippincott. [Published posthumously.]

Hill, R. T. (1902). "Report by Robert T. Hill on the Volcanic Disturbances in the West Indies." *National Geographic* 13 (July), 223–263.

Hovey, Edmund O. (1902a). "The Eruptions of La Soufrière, St. Vincent, in May, 1902." *National Geographic* 13 (December), 444–459.

———. (1902b). "Martinique and St. Vincent, a Preliminary Report upon the Eruption of 1902." *Bulletin of the American Museum of Natural History* 16, 333–373.

Jaccaci, A. F. (1902). "Pelée, the Destroyer." *McClure's* (August).

Kennan, George. (1902). *The Tragedy of Pelée: A Narrative of Personal Experience and Observation in Martinique*. New York: Outlook.

Kingsley, Charles. (1871). *At Last: A Christmas in the West Indies*. New York: Harper and Brothers.

Lacroix, Alfred. (1906). "The Eruption of Vesuvius in April, 1906." *Smithsonian Report*, 223–248. (Translation of articles in *Revue Générale des Sciences* [Paris], October 30, 1906, 881–899, and November 15, 1906, 923–936.)

———. (1908). *La Montagne Pelée après ses éruptions: Avec observations sur les éruptions du Vésuve en 79 et en 1906*. Paris: Libraries de L'Académie de Médicine.

Levy, L. E. (1907). "In Memoriam Angelo Heilprin: Memorial Address Delivered before the Franklin Institute." *Journal of the Franklin Institute* (November), 1–14.

Loomis, B. F. (1971 [1926]). *Pictorial History of the Lassen Volcano*. Reprint. Mineral, Calif.: Loomis Museum Association.

Miller, J. Martin. (1902). *The Martinique Horror and St. Vincent Calamity*. Boston: J. R. Spaulding.

Milne, J. (1902a). "The Recent Volcanic Eruptions in the West Indies." *Nature* 66 (May 29), 107–111.

———. (1902b). "Volcanic Eruptions in the West Indies." *Nature* 66 (June 12), 151–153.

Morris, Charles. (1902a). *The Destruction of St. Pierre and St. Vincent*. Philadelphia: American Book and Bible House.

———. (1902b). *The Volcano's Deadly Work: From the Fall of Pompeii to the Destruction of St. Pierre*. Philadelphia: W. E. Scull.

Pollak, Gustav. (1912). *Michael Heilprin and His Sons*. New York: Dodd, Mead.

Reclus, Elisée. (1873). *The Ocean, Atmosphere, and Life*. New York: Harper and Brothers.

Reid, S. C. (1902). "The Catastrophe in St. Vincent: Narrow Escapes from Soufrière—Observations and Narratives by Two Eyewitnesses." *Century Magazine* 64 (August), 634–642.

Roobol, M. J., and A. L. Smith. (1976a). "A Comparison of the Recent Eruptions of Mt. Pelée, Martinique, and Soufrière, St. Vincent." *Bulletin Volcanologique* 39, no. 2, 215–240.

———. (1976b). "Mount Pelée, Martinique: A Pattern of Alternating Eruptive Styles." *Geology* 4, 521–524.

Royce, F. (1902). *The Burning of St. Pierre and the Eruption of Mont Pelee.* Chicago: Continental Publishing.

Russel, Israel C. (1902a). "The Recent Volcanic Eruptions in the West Indies." *National Geographic* 13 (December), 267–285.

———. (1902b). "Volcanic Eruptions on Martinique and St. Vincent." *National Geographic* 13 (December), 262–267.

Scarth, Alwyn. (1999). *Vulcan's Fury.* Hong Kong: WorldPrint.

Scott, E. S. (1902a). "The Destruction of the Roraima." *Frank Leslie's Popular Monthly* 54 (July), 233–248.

———. (1902b). "The Eruption of Mont Pelée." *Cosmopolitan Magazine* 34 (July), 243–252.

Simkin, Tom, and Richard S. Fiske. (1983). *Krakatau 1883: The Volcanic Eruption and Its Effects.* Washington, D.C.: Smithsonian Institution Press.

Smith, A. L., and M. J. Roobol. (1990). *Mt. Pelée, Martinique; A Study of an Active Island-Arc Volcano.* Memoir 175. Boulder, Colo.: Geological Society of America.

Sparks, R.S.J., H. Sugurdsson, and S. N. Carey. (1980). "The Entrance of Pyroclastic Flows into the Sea, I. Oceanographic and Geologic Evidence from Dominica, Lesser Antilles." *Journal of Volcanology and Geothermal Research* 7, 87–96.

Staff of the *Daily News* and the *Journal-American*. (1980). *Volcano: The Eruption of Mount St. Helens.* Seattle: Madrona Publishers.

Tanguy, J. C. (1994). "The 1902–1905 Eruptions of Montagne Pelée, Martinique: Anatomy and Retrospection. *Journal of Volcanology and Geothermal Research* 60, 87–107.

Thomas, Gordon, and Max M. Witts. (1969). *The Day the World Ended.* New York: Stein and Day.

Thomas, Lately. (1961). "Prelude to Doomsday." *American Heritage* 12 (August), 4–9, 94–101.

Travis, F. F. (1990). *George Kennan and the American-Russian Relationship, 1865–1924*. Athens: Ohio University Press.

Ursulet, Léo. (1997). *Le désastre de 1902 à la Martinique et ses conséquences*. Paris: L'Harmattan.

Verbeek, R.D.M. (1884). "The Krakatoa Eruption." *Nature* 30, 10–15.

Wadge, G. (1986). "The Dykes and Structural Setting of the Volcanic Front in the Lesser Antilles Island Arc." *Bulletin of Volcanology* 48, 349–372.

Warren, William N. (1902). *Story of the Martinique Disaster*. Wheeling, W.Va.: Intelligencer Publishing.

Watson, W. J. (1883). "The Java Disaster." *Nature* 29, 140–141.

Westercamp, D., and H. Traineau. (1983). "The Past 5,000 Years of Volcanic Activity at Mt. Pelée Martinique (F.W.I.): Implications for the Assessment of Volcanic Hazards." *Journal of Volcanology and Geothermal Research* 17, 159–185.

White, Trumbull. (1902). *In the Shadow of Death: Martinique and the World's Great Disasters*. N.p.: Publishers' Association.

Wohletz, K., G. Heiken, M. Ander, F. Goff, F. Vuataz, and G. Wadge. (1986). "The Qualibou Caldera, St. Lucia, West Indies." *Journal of Volcanology and Geothermal Research* 27, 77–115.

Wright, J. V., M. J. Roobol, A. L. Smith, R.S.J. Sparks, S. A. Brazier, W. I. Rose, and H. Sugurdsson. (1984). "Late Quaternary Explosive Silicic Volcanism on St. Lucia, West Indies." *Geological Magazine* 121, 1–15.

INDEX

• ABOUT THE AUTHOR •

Ernest Zebrowski, Jr., is a university professor who has written and lectured about natural disasters for the past two decades. His books, which have been translated into five languages, include *Perils of a Restless Planet, A History of the Circle, Practical Physics,* and *Fundamentals of Physical Measurement.* He lives on St. George Island, Florida.